Called to Teach

Called to Teach

*The Vocation of
the Presbyterian Educator*

Edited by
Duncan S. Ferguson and
William J. Weston

Geneva Press
Louisville, Kentucky

Scripture quotations from the New Revised Standard Version of the Bible are copyright © 1989 by the Division of Christian Education of the National Council of the Churches of Christ in the U.S.A. and are used by permission.

Scripture quotations from *The Holy Bible, New International Version* are copyright © 1973, 1978, 1984 International Bible Society. Used by permission of Zondervan Bible Publishers.

Book design by Sharon Adams
Cover design by Eric Walljasper

First edition
Published by Geneva Press
Louisville, Kentucky

This book is printed on acid-free paper that meets the American National Standards Institute Z39.48 standard. ∞

PRINTED IN THE UNITED STATES OF AMERICA

02 03 04 05 06 07 08 09 10 11 — 10 9 8 7 6 5 4 3 2 1

Library of Congress Cataloging-in-Publication Data

Called to teach : the vocation of the Presbyterian educator / Duncan S. Ferguson and William J. Weston, editors.
    p. cm.
Includes bibliographical references and index.
ISBN 0-664-50221-0 (alk. paper)
1. Presbyterian Church—Education. 2. Presbyterian Church—Missions. 3. Education, Higher. I. Ferguson, Duncan S. (Duncan Sheldon), 1937– II. Weston, William J., 1960–

BX8917.C35 2003
371.071'5—dc21   2002029477

To our teachers at Swarthmore,
Yale, and Edinburgh

Contents

Acknowledgments

This volume draws on the Consultation on the Vocation of the Presbyterian Teacher held at the Presbyterian Center in Louisville and at Centre College in Danville, Kentucky, in 2000. The editors, who were the codirectors of the consultation, wish to gratefully acknowledge the assistance of Fritz Nelson and Ruth Daniels, of the Higher Education Office of the Presbyterian Church (U.S.A.), and Katherine Adams, now Stoner, of Centre College. John Carey and John Kuykendall acted as senior advisers to that consultation, and several other teachers whose words are not in this volume made significant contributions to our discussions. The consultation was financially underwritten by the Wabash Center for Teaching and Learning in Religion, the Presbyterian Church (U.S.A.), the Association of Presbyterian Colleges and Universities, and Centre College.

In the production of this volume, Amy Sibley of Centre College and our editor at Geneva Press, David Dobson, have been particularly helpful.

Contributors

Timothy A. Beach-Verhey is Director of the Theological Exploration Program and Adjunct Lecturer in Religion at Davidson College.

Cynthia Boyle is Assistant Director of Experiential Learning and Director of the Office of Continuation Studies at the University of Maryland School of Pharmacy.

Cynthia M. Campbell is President and Cyrus McCormick Professor of Church and Ministry at McCormick Theological Seminary.

Margaret (Peggy) Parks Cowan is the Ralph W. Beeson Associate Professor of Religion at Maryville College.

Duncan S. Ferguson is now Director of the Center for Spiritual Life at Eckerd College. He was Associate Director for Higher Education for the Presbyterian Church (U.S.A.), and President of the Association of Presbyterian Colleges and Universities.

Darwin K. Glassford is Associate Professor of Bible and Christian Ministries at Montreat College and is Visiting Professor of Ministry and Missions, Salt Lake Theological Seminary.

Stephen Haynes is Associate Professor of Religious Studies at Rhodes College.

R. Ward Holder is Assistant Professor of Theology at St. Anselm College.

Jeffrey Kisner is Associate Professor of Religion at Waynesburg College.

John Kuykendall is President Emeritus and Thatcher Professor of Religion at Davidson College.

Iain S. Maclean is Associate Professor of Western Religious Thought at James Madison University.

W. Eugene March is the A. B. Rhodes Professor of Old Testament at Louisville Presbyterian Theological Seminary.

Arlin C. Migliazzo is Professor of Politics and History at Whitworth College.

Dale Soden is Professor of Politics and History and Director of the Weyer-
haeuser Center for Christian Faith and Learning at Whitworth College.

David M. Wallace is Dean of Johnson C. Smith Theological Seminary.

William (Beau) Weston is Associate Professor of Sociology at Centre College.

Edward C. (Ted) Zaragoza is Associate Professor of Church History at United
Theological Seminary.

Introduction

1

The Dying Light and Glowing Embers of Presbyterian Higher Education

WILLIAM WESTON

Presbyterians have always been called to teach. Yet the ecumenical consensus that prevailed among church leaders for the past generation called into question the continuing relevance of denominational colleges. Today, however, a new generation is again raising the idea of the distinctive Presbyterian mission in American higher education.

For the past generation, the material resources that the church has had for all its colleges and ministries have declined. The synodical contributions that made a significant proportion of Presbyterian college budgets as late as the 1970s have all but disappeared. Today the General Assembly makes significant direct gifts only to the handful of racial ethnic colleges. The more than five hundred Presbyterian campus ministries of the 1950s had been cut in half by 1990.[1]

At the same time, the desire of both church and college to be ecumenical and inclusive undermined the belief that Presbyterian institutions had a distinctive and necessary mission in higher education. The last comprehensive report on Presbyterian higher education adopted by the General Assembly, *On Being Faithful* (1995), acknowledged that "older ecumenical models" of the church's mission in higher education are "dying like cut flowers for lack of roots in the denomination."[2] Today, many Presbyterian schools and campus ministries have declared their independence from the Presbyterian Church, usually with the church's blessing. The light of Presbyterian higher education has been dying, though it is by no means dead. Now is the time to consider whether that light should be revived, and if so, how.

Today I see the beginnings of a renewed interest in the distinct mission, approaches, and achievements of Presbyterianism in higher education. The new generation of Presbyterian teachers and scholars do want to preserve the connections and sense of openness that the ecumenical generation before them achieved. At the same time, though, they wish to conserve and renew the particular values that Presbyterian institutions brought and bring to the whole ecology of Christian higher education. The embers of the Presbyterian vocation in higher education are being fanned in many places. The aim of this volume is to consider the Presbyterian vocation in higher education—past, present, and with a renewed future.

This book grew out of a conference, the Consultation on the Vocation of the Presbyterian Teacher, organized by the editors. The support of the Wabash Center for Teaching and Learning in Theology and Religion let us invite some thirty professors from the many who applied. We gathered at the Presbyterian Center (church headquarters) in Louisville, Kentucky, and at Centre College in Danville, Kentucky, in August of 2000. Most of those invited were Presbyterians and religion professors and were from Presbyterian colleges. A few represented other denominations, other disciplines, and other kinds of institutions, including state universities and theological seminaries. Most were born after the baby boom generation that has, until recently, controlled Presbyterian higher education.

The discussions were pushed along by two background papers written by the conference "brain trust"—one on Presbyterian institutions by Dale Soden and William (Beau) Weston that forms the basis of chapter 5, and one on Presbyterian teaching by Margaret (Peggy) Parks Cowan, Jeffrey Kisner, and Stephen Haynes that forms the basis of chapter 8. From these papers, and reflections we had written about our own careers, we considered our experiences, research, and reflections on the larger enterprise of Presbyterian higher education.

In 2000 the Presbyterian Church (U.S.A.) directed the Office of Higher Education to conduct a study of the current state of Presbyterian higher education. The editors of this volume serve on the working group charged with making that study. The central objective of this working group has been to encourage and assist Presbyterian schools, colleges, and universities "to develop a strong 'dimension' of the Presbyterian and Reformed faith within the common life of the institution, especially in student learning and service."[3]

One of the stated aims of the Consultation on the Vocation of the Presbyterian Teacher, which was also cited and supported in the overture on Higher Education, is to create an ongoing Presbyterian Academy of Scholars and Teachers [PAST]. The volume in yours hands is intended to be a starting point and foundation for that academy.

There are many signs of a widespread movement to renew Christian higher education today. A spate of important books has fired this discussion—Merrimon Cuninggim's *Uneasy Partners*, Douglas Sloan's *Faith and Knowledge*, Mark Schwehn's *Exiles from Eden*, James Turner and Jon Roberts's *The Sacred and the Secular University*, and several books from George Marsden, especially *The Soul of the American University*; *The Secularization of the Academy* (with Bradley J. Longfield); and *The Outrageous Idea of Christian Scholarship*. All these books have demonstrated that academic culture is much less hospitable to a Christian mission at the beginning of the twenty-first century than it was at the beginning of the twentieth. They also make the case, in various ways, that church-related colleges were largely secularized from within, when they lost a vision of what Christian higher education is for.

The most critical, and thickest, of these studies has been James Burtchaell's *The Dying of the Light*, to which the metaphorical framework of this chapter is a response. Burtchaell demonstrates, with a relentless series of case studies, the secularization of Christian colleges when they become separated from their churches. He shows this process happening in the Presbyterian Church at least as much as in the other denominations. Burtchaell's work raises, for me, the question of how to renew the church mission in a church-founded college. One study that does explore such a turnaround is Dale Soden and Arlin Migliazzo's account of Whitworth College in Richard Hughes and William Adrian's *Models for Christian Higher Education*. Soden and Migliazzo are both contributors to this volume.

One of the largest sustained projects exploring the revitalization of Christian higher education is the Rhodes Consultation on the Future of the Church-Related College. The Rhodes Consultation is directed by Stephen Haynes, who contributed a case study of Rhodes College itself to chapter 8. In fact, the brain trust of the Presbyterian Vocation symposium met through the Rhodes Consultation.

Presbyterians have had a long and strong commitment to education. From the beginnings of the church in America, Presbyterians planted schools and colleges wherever they lived, continuing a tradition that was already well established among Reformed communities in Europe. These schools were designed for the whole community, not just the Presbyterians. They educated for the whole of citizenship, not just for church life. Over the centuries the student bodies of Presbyterian schools expanded from the core of white male Protestants to the whole range of social groups. The effect of Presbyterian education has been to produce a disproportionate share of leaders, especially in economic and political life. *The vocation to produce leaders who act as stewards of all levels of society—and not just for the Presbyterian Church—has been one of the most distinctive and valuable missions of Presbyterian education.*

Presbyterians have never had a centralized or coordinated strategy for planting or supporting their schools. Presbyterian schools have been born of the vision of local leaders, the laity more often than the clergy. Presbyterian schools have been sustained more by local, personal, and, eventually, alumni resources than by direct gifts from the church. There have never been enough Presbyterian students to fill all the church's schools even if anyone wanted that, which few did. Since the Second World War, few Presbyterian colleges have even had Presbyterian majorities in their student bodies. Moreover, the church has rarely tried to tell its schools what or how to teach. On the contrary, the church has relied on its schools to be the experts in questions of curriculum and pedagogy. These facts have meant that there has always been a strong independent and entrepreneurial streak in Presbyterian schools.

In all centuries, church colleges need broad sources of students and money to stay afloat and to be seen as legitimate in American society as a whole. This tends to pull them away from strong identification with one particular denomination. At the same time, church colleges have been pushed toward independence by the church's desire to spend its money on even needier ministries. Today, some in the church believe that Presbyterian colleges, like Presbyterian hospitals, are all grown up and can—and should—make their own way in the world.

In the twentieth century, two powerful cultural trends drove a further wedge between the Presbyterian Church and its colleges. In the academy, denominational (or even generally Christian) approaches to any academic subject were viewed increasingly as sectarian and subrational. A "Presbyterian" approach to any particular discipline came to be viewed as an oxymoron. The leading elements of the academy as a whole came to believe that a general secular rationalism was destined to comprehend all of intellectual life.[4] At the same time, the church came to regard denominational approaches to religious life as sectarian and sub-Christian. A "Presbyterian" approach to any particular ministry came to be viewed as parochial. The leading elements of the mainline churches as a whole came to believe that a general religious ecumenism was destined to comprehend all church life.

At the dawn of the twenty-first century, these cultural forces that drove a wedge between "Presbyterian" and "college" are themselves under attack, or at least are under reconsideration. The belief in one all-sufficient secular rationality that would bury all other worldviews has been undermined by postmodernism. The belief in one all-sufficient ecumenical Christianity that would bury all other church views has been undermined by evangelicalism. The older views are still powerful. The belief that there can and ought to be such a thing as "Presbyterian higher education" is still in doubt. But, as I see it, the playing field is more level now. New resources can be brought to renew the old belief that there is a distinctive Presbyterian mission in higher education, and that the world needs it.

Let the argument begin.

Section 1

The Calling to Teach: Foundations

When Jesus saw the crowds, he went up the mountain; and after he sat down, his disciples came to him. Then he began to speak, and taught them, saying . . .

—*Matt. 5:1–2*

2

The Biblical Foundations of Presbyterian Education

DARWIN K. GLASSFORD

INTRODUCTION

Throughout the Scriptures and church history the vocation of teaching has been highly valued. As a vocation, teaching is not pursued for "self-advancement nor self-fulfillment, but service of God and the neighbor," according to Gilbert C. Meilaender.[1] The vocation of teaching plays a critical role in the advancement of the kingdom of God—the central theme in Jesus' teaching.[2]

The critical role of the teaching vocation in God's program must be properly understood; to neglect it invites disaster, as Hosea reminds us: "My [Yahweh's] people are destroyed from the lack of knowledge."[3] In order to better understand the teaching vocation, I will examine the scriptural teaching on the kingdom of God, the significance of Paul's use of *katartismon* in Ephesians 4:12, and the nature of those being instructed. I will then illustrate these points from the teaching ministries of Elijah, Jeremiah, Jesus, and Paul in order to identify the relevance of this material for the twenty-first century.

TOWARD AN UNDERSTANDING OF THE KINGDOM OF GOD

Defining the kingdom of God is not a simple task. The Scriptures do not contain a formal definition or description of the kingdom of God. Yet Jesus spoke as though those who heard him understood what he meant.[4] Therefore one is faced with the challenge of constructing a definition from Scripture.[5] For our purposes, the kingdom of God will be understood as

> the purposeful reign of God over the created order that was present in the Old Testament, was announced and inaugurated by Christ in the New Testament, and is now presently being experienced in part by its citizens and is a future hope towards which all history is moving.[6]

Before examining the four key components of this definition, let me articulate why a proper understanding of the kingdom of God is essential to the intentional activity of teaching. Teaching is shaped by a vision for life, the beliefs that shape one's understanding and interpretation of life, and the desire for those being educated to be changed in some way by what is taught. A proper understanding of the kingdom of God enables one to pursue the teaching vocation with integrity, giving due attention to life as it is known and experienced, and to its spiritual dimensions in a manner consistent with the Presbyterian and Reformed heritage.

The four key components of the above definition that must be examined in order to understand the nature and challenges of the teaching vocation are: Christ's kingship, the present reality of the kingdom, the redemptive nature of the kingdom, and the future hope of the kingdom.

Christ's Kingship

Just as Yahweh is described as the one who created and rules over creation in the Old Testament, so is Christ given the title "King" in the New Testament. Both the Belgic Confession, which is favored by the Dutch Reformed churches, and the Heidelberg Catechism, which is part of the PC(USA) *Book of Confessions*, understand Christ to be an eternal king.[7] His kingship is universal and extends over all creation. The author of Hebrews states, "God left nothing that is not subject to him. Yet at present we do not see everything subject to him."[8] As the apostle Paul states, "[Christ] must reign until he has put all his enemies under his feet."[9] Anthony Hoekema captures the significance of Christ's reign for the present when he states,

> The kingdom must not be understood as merely the salvation of certain individuals or even the reign of God in the hearts of his people; it means nothing less than the reign of God over his entire created universe. . . . The Kingdom of God . . . is not a state of affairs brought about by human achievement, nor is it the culmination of strenuous human effort. The kingdom is established by God's sovereign grace, and its blessings are to be received as gifts of that grace.[10]

The biblical teaching on the kingdom of God cannot be excised from Scripture's Christology. Just as Yahweh is the one who reigns over the created order, so is Christ given the title "king," *baselia*, which refers primarily to his reign.[11] Christ's authority extends over all creation and is exercised whether it is acknowledged or not. Christ's kingship has implications for all dimensions of the created order. Hoekema captures the inseparability of the kingdom of God and Jesus:

> Jesus himself ushered in the kingdom of God whose coming had been foretold by the Old Testament prophets. We must therefore always see the kingdom of God as indissolubly connected with the person of Jesus Christ. In Jesus' words and deeds, miracles and parables, teaching and preaching, the kingdom of God was dynamically active and present among men.[12]

The Kingdom of God as a Present Reality

The kingdom of God—the reign of God—is more than a historical reality and a future hope in the Scriptures. It is seen as a present reality. This present reality is spiritual in nature. It is the reign of Christ in the hearts of his disciples. This kingdom is "within"; "it is not of this world"; it involves deliverance from "the powers of darkness, and translated us [past tense] into the kingdom of the Son of his love"; and it holds that "he made us [past tense] to be a kingdom, to be priests unto his God and Father."[13]

The kingdom in its present state, the dynamic rule of God, is the means through which God's redemptive purpose is being accomplished. The present state of the kingdom is temporary.[14]

In the New Testament a tension exists between the decisive "already-fulfilled" and the "not-yet-complete," between the present reality and future expectations.[15] This involves the mystery of the kingdom; as George Elton Ladd states, "the Kingdom which will one day change the entire external order has entered into This Age [capitalization Ladd's] in advance to bring the blessings of God's Kingdom to men and women without transforming the old order."[16] This tension results from the fact that, in Hoekema's words:

> the New Testament believer is conscious, on the one hand, of the fact that the great eschatological event predicted in the Old Testament has already happened, while on the other hand he realizes that another momentous series of events is still to come.[17]

In Christ the kingdom of God was spiritually and physically present. Christ's disciples who have subjected themselves to Christ's authority experience the benefits and blessings of the reigning Christ, though incompletely in this life.[18]

The Redemptive Nature of the Kingdom

The kingdom of God is not concerned with the status quo. For the present reality of the kingdom involves the manifestation of "God's redemptive rule, now present, in the person, deeds, and words of Jesus."[19] This redemptive role involves not only people, but also the whole of creation. The kingdom of God exists alongside the fallen world; it is not overcome by the world. Christ's disciples, who are given his Spirit, are called to live redemptively, seeking to reclaim the fallen world and place it under its proper authority.

The Kingdom of God as a Future Hope

Jesus spoke of the kingdom of God as something that will come. He sometimes describes it in the immediate future, and at other times he portrays it in the distant future. The kingdom of God as a physical, spiritual, and temporal reality will be established at the Second Advent. Hoekema describes the significance of this hope when he writes,

> *All of history is moving toward a goal: the new heavens and the new earth.* [italics Hoekema's] Though Christ has ushered in the new age, the final consummation of the new age is still future. The Bible therefore sees history as directed toward a divinely ordained goal.[20]

Summary

The art of teaching, one's understanding of the instructional process, is informed and molded by one's view of reality, including an understanding of the learner, and of the future. The scriptural teaching on the kingdom of God provides a paradigm for understanding the teaching vocation. Based on the brief understanding of the kingdom of God presented, six commitments can be identified that will shape one's understanding of the teaching vocation.

1. God is sovereign. God is the one who created the world. He ordered it into existence, fashioned it, and declared it was good. The Old and New Testaments teach that God is the one who rules over the created order. His reign is eternal.
2. God sustains the created order. The world does not nor can it exist independently of God. God's grace continues to sustain the world whether he is acknowledged or not.[21]
3. God's reign over the created order is purposeful. He has been working and continues to work to accomplish his purpose, the redemption of humankind and the created order from the consequences of the fall.
4. God is knowable. The God who created, sustains, and governs the world has chosen to reveal himself to humankind in the Scriptures.[22]

5. The Christ-event was necessary to secure the redemption of humankind. In Christ God's rule was visibly manifested in the created order so atonement for the sins of humankind could be secured through Christ's sacrificial death.
6. The world exists in a state of tension because of the dual nature of the kingdom of God. As a present reality it came in the person of Jesus Christ, who continues to rule spiritually in the lives of his disciples, the citizens of the kingdom. The kingdom is also a future hope that informs the lives of Christ's disciples, who experience tension when the obligations of the kingdom are contrary to the demands of this world.

Jesus' understanding of the teaching vocation was ultimately founded in the kingdom of God theme. In his encounter with the Samaritan woman at the well (John 4:1–42) Jesus' understanding of the kingdom of God and its pedagogical implications begin to come into view. There are five pedagogical points that can be surmised.

First, Jesus lived out what he taught. He sought out the woman at the well and engaged her in conversation. Jesus' engagement with her was intentional; it was not passive. As he claimed, "The Son of Man came to seek and to save what was lost" (Luke 19:10). Jesus' pedagogy was incarnational.

Second, Jesus respected the woman at the well because she was an image bearer of the Creator. He did not ignore her. He addressed her in light of who she was and the reality of her past. He did not condone her past, but looked beyond it to address her real needs.

Third, Jesus addressed the woman and the situation realistically. He dealt with her and the disciples in light of the reality of the situation. He showed the woman grace, which she needed, instead of justice. And he did not respond directly to the disciples' indignant questions because a response was not needed.

Fourth, Jesus moves from what is known to what is unknown, from the physical reality to spiritual truths. He begins by asking for a cup of water and then, out of concern for the woman as a person, asks her questions and offers clarifying comments and explanations until she ends up committing to him as the Messiah. Others also believe based on her testimony.

Fifth, Jesus was unwilling to compromise the message, either in form or content, in light of the disciples' questions and his Jewish heritage. In fact, Jesus knew what he needed to communicate in order to bring about the intended outcome.

According to Eugene Peterson in *The Message*, John 1:14 should be translated, "The Word became flesh and blood, and moved into the neighborhood." The scriptural teaching in light of the kingdom of God summons one to engagement with others for the sake of the kingdom. The teaching vocation is not passive in character. One should not wait for students to come and learn. It is active; it calls one to pursue students and engage them with the truth—a truth that will enhance their lives and the lives of those around them—concerning the reality of God's kingly reign.

THE TEACHING VOCATION
IN A KINGDOM CONTEXT

The kingdom of God provides a unique stained-glass window for understanding the teaching vocation. In Ephesians 4:11–13 Paul provides a multifaceted glimpse into the teaching vocation when he writes that the church should "reach unity in the faith and in the knowledge of the Son of God." This unity and knowledge is reached through the "preparation" or "equipping" of the saints for ministry,[23] which, according to R. Schippers, "refers to the preparation of the church for becoming perfect."[24] Equipping in this passage is functional, referring to a process rather than a state of perfection. It is through the equipping process that the kingdom of God is, in part, being established.[25]

The teaching vocation is concerned with the equipping of Christ's disciples. The Scriptures do not prescribe a methodology; rather, they describe four related and essential components that will be weighted differently depending on the purpose, setting, instructor, and particular needs of the student(s). These four components are: instruction, modeling, training, and discerning.

Instruction

Instruction is the formal activity of communicating information from one person to others. The various Hebrew and Greek words are used in a variety of ways, and the overview provided is intended to describe the role of instruction in the teaching-learning process.

In Deuteronomy 4:10 the Hebrew term *lamad*, translated "teach," is used to describe the passing on of Yahweh's words to one's children.[26] And in Exodus 18:20 the word *zahar*, translated "teach," refers to Moses' duty to instruct the people in the decrees and laws he had received from God.[27] The term *yara* is used in the Old Testament to describe one who is instructed. It includes everything from "getting directions" to a request to be taught (Job 6:24).[28] From the root of *yara* the word *tora* is formed. *Tora* basically means "teaching," whether it is the wise man teaching his son or God instructing Israel. The uses of these four terms demonstrate the legitimacy of didactic instruction.[29]

In the New Testament a basis for didactic instruction is found in the term *didasko*, which is generally translated "teach" or "teaching." It is used for Jesus' activity in the synagogue (Luke 4:15) and to describe one part of Timothy's ministry (1 Tim. 6:2). In 1 Timothy 6:2 Paul refers to specific material that is to be taught. Paul states in Colossians 1:28 that the purpose of instruction is that "we [Paul and Timothy] may present everyone perfect in Christ."[30]

The New Testament also uses the word *katekeo*, which refers to the things that Theophilus had been taught concerning the Lord (Luke 1:4) and is used by Paul to describe one who has been instructed by the law (Rom. 1:28b). *Katekeo* also has strong didactic overtones in Acts 18:25 and 1 Corinthians 14:19.

Two other terms are also used in the New Testament. *Paratithemi* means to instruct or set material before someone so the person might understand its significance.[31] *Ektithemi* describes instruction characterized by a deliberate logical order.[32]

The teaching vocation involves instruction: communicating information in a clear, coherent, and logical manner. Instruction is a legitimate component of the teaching vocation; it must not be neglected.

Modeling

Modeling complements instruction. Modeling provides a living example to one's student(s). In 2 Kings 14:3, King Amaziah was condemned for following the example of his father, Joash. And in 1 Corinthians 11:1, Paul writes, "Follow my example, as I follow the example of Christ." The word translated "example" is *mimetes*. According to W. Bauer, "to be an imitator of the apostle means laying hold of Christ in the consciousness of one's own imperfections and letting one's life be continually remolded by Christ in obedience to him (cf 3 John 11)."[33] To be a model does not require living a perfect life, but rather demonstrating the ongoing work of Christ in one's life.

The current interest in mentoring is a reflection of the importance of modeling within the teaching vocation. The significance of mentoring as it relates to theological education, although the implications are very far-reaching if one wishes to consider them, is captured by Robert Banks in *Reenvisioning Theological Education: Exploring a Missional Alternative to Current Models*. Banks's understanding of mentoring as it relates to congregational leadership involves "pairing more and less experienced people, whether lay or ordained, in a mentoring or apprentice style relationship. Within this whole process student excellence is redefined in terms of maturity, wisdom, and influence."[34] Modeling and mentoring are holistic in perspective. The Old and New Testaments were concerned with more than the acquisition of factual information. They were concerned with the formation of a person's character, which would serve as the basis of the person's identity individually and corporately. The definition of character and an understanding of how it is formed are rooted in the kingdom of God theme and cannot be separated from instruction. The Old

Testament account of God's dealing with the Jewish people and the New Testament account of Jesus' disciples illustrate the complexity of the challenge and the necessity of instruction that is authenticated through modeling within the context of mentored relationships.

Banks, drawing on the work of Cornel West, comments further, "He [Cornel West] rightly insists on teachers subordinating their work to the concerns of the kingdom rather than to academic or ecclesiastical goals."[35] He continues, "We do not just *present* truth, we must *represent* it to others. We do not just relate truth in the hopes that others might comprehend it, we relate to them in a way that helps them to be apprehended by it."[36] This describes, in essence, why modeling is an essential component of the teaching vocation.

Training

The third key component is training. Training is the disciplinary aspect of the instructional process. Practitioners of the teaching vocation must hold students accountable for learning. This component is dependent on both instruction and modeling for its validity.

The Hebrew words *yakah*, which is translated "reproof" or "rebuke," and *musar*, whose root is *yasar*, which is often translated "discipline," "denote correction which results in education."[37] Yakah is found in Proverbs 3:12, where it is understood that "education and discipline [are] a result of God's judicial actions."[38] Yasar also points to "God's corrective discipline [which] seeks the reformation of the people (Leviticus 26:18, 23)"[39] and also refers to the "notation of parental chastisement" in Deuteronomy 8:5.[40]

In the Old Testament one also finds the term *musar*, which is translated "discipline," and refers to God's mighty acts in history through which he has revealed himself. This "discipline" includes oral instruction (Job 5:17ff.) and/or other mighty acts (Amos 4:6–11; Hos. 5:2; 7:12; Isa. 8:11). When *yakah* and *musar* are taken together they embrace "all aspects of education from the conviction of the sinner to chastisement and punishment, from the instruction of the righteous by severe tests to his direction by teaching and admonition."[41] The role of discipline in the Old Testament is always redemptive and corrective in character; it is never merely punishment.

The New Testament also recognizes the legitimacy of training in the equipping process. Paul in 2 Timothy 3:16 uses the term *paidea* to describe the training function of Scripture in the life of a disciple. It is also used in Hebrews 12:6–16 to describe the corrective role of the Lord's discipline and the discipline of one's human father.

Paul also uses the term *nountheo* when he "warns" them to be on their guard in 1 Corinthians 4:14. In Ephesians 6:4 he links *nountheo*, "training," with the instruction a father is to provide for his children. And in Colossians 3:16 *noun-theo*, "admonishing," is used positively.

The author of Hebrews (5:8) uses *manthano* to describe what Jesus learned through his sufferings. *Manthano* describes learning from experience.[42] Learning in this passage means "recognition of the Father's will in his suffering and affirmation of that will in his acceptance of the suffering."[43]

The teaching vocation will require one to be involved in the disciplinary aspects of education. It is essential if one is going to call others to account and counsel them regarding the consistency of their beliefs.

Instruction and modeling cannot be separated from the training aspect of the teaching vocation. Training implies responsibility and accountability. Both teachers and students are accountable in the teaching-learning process. James 3:1 reminds teachers that they are held to a higher standard and accountable for what they teach. And Jesus holds the disciples accountable for their lack of understanding in Mark 8:14–21; he even seems exasperated by their lack of faith and understanding.

Responsibility and accountability are essential components in the teaching-learning process and cannot be neglected without compromising one's vocational calling as a teacher. It should be noted that Jesus' harshest words were directed at those who were self-righteous in their own sight, and he always spoke words of grace and mercy to those who knew they were sinners.

Discerning

Instructors must also be concerned with the development of discernment by the learner. The Old Testament uses the words *bin*, the ability to distinguish between right and wrong,[44] and *sakal*, "the process of thinking through a complex arrangement of thought, resulting in a wise dealing and use of good practical common sense."[45]

In the New Testament the words *suniami* and *dokimazo* contribute to the biblical teaching on discernment. *Suniami*, for example, is found in Ephesians 5:17, where the reader is challenged to "understand [or discern] . . . the Lord's will" in light of what Paul has written. *Dokimazo* means "to approve," and is translated "discern" in Philippians 1:10.[46]

Discernment in the Scriptures has four characteristics.

1. It involves the ability to distinguish between right and wrong, good and bad.
2. It involves the ability to think through a complex arrangement of thoughts in order to determine a prudent course of action.
3. It involves the art of applying what one believes to be true to life.
4. The art of discernment is closely linked to one's knowledge of the truth.

The cultivation of discernment is dependent on faithful instruction, modeling, and training. Teachers must be discerning. Jesus was discerning—note how his audience shaped his choice of parables. And in his encounter with the rich young man, Jesus both affirms him and asks penetrating questions that address the man's ultimate commitments (Luke 18:18–23). Discernment is generally not easy to cultivate. Paul challenged the Colossian church not to be taken "captive through hollow and deceptive philosophy, which depends on human tradition and the basic principles of this world rather than on Christ" (Col. 2:8). Yet, if the teaching vocation is concerned with equipping men and women to live as citizens of God's kingdom (Phil. 3:20), then the development of discernment is essential.

Summary

The teaching vocation is shaped by one's understanding of the world and responsibilities. The reality is that *the teaching vocation is a way of life*. It involves more than mere instruction. It is a way of life that seeks to shape students with the truth, equipping them for a life of discipleship. This description of the teaching vocation is applicable to all disciplines, for all disciplines are ultimately concerned with passing on a view of the world, and are thus religious in character. If these responsibilities are going to be faithfully pursued, then one must also develop a biblically consistent view of the learner to complement one's understanding of the teaching vocation.

THE NATURE OF THE LEARNER

The kingdom of God encompasses the understanding that the instructor and student, who are disciples of Christ, live in tension. This tension is due to the spiritual nature of Christ's kingdom and the physical nature of the educational context. A proper understanding of students must deal realistically with this tension if a realistic view of students is to be developed.

In the Reformed and Presbyterian tradition all people are seen as image bearers of the Creator. This image was distorted by the fall, but it was not destroyed. In order to develop a realistic understanding of the learner, original sin, depravity, and common grace must be examined.

Original Sin

Original sin is the root of all actual sin.[47] The doctrine of original sin is rooted in the belief that Adam stood as a representative of the human race. The result

of the original transgression was that the guilt of Adam's sin was and continues to be imputed to his descendants. The result is that everyone is born in a
state of willful violation of God's law. Original sin not only includes guilt, but
also moral defilement. Moral defilement is the belief that individuals are no
longer morally righteous, but have inherited a disposition toward sin. The
doctrine of original sin portrays the student as being neither naturally inclined
toward good nor morally neutral, but guilty and defiled.[48]

The teaching vocation is one means that God uses to advance his kingdom.
The consequences of original sin for the teaching vocation are many. It means
that one's instruction may not be true, that one might not model the correct
attitudes or behavior, that one might not always fulfill his or her responsibilities, that one might rebel against accountability, and that one might not properly discern between good and evil.

This understanding of sin always implies that learners might not always live
up to their responsibilities. The validity of the teaching vocation requires one
to address things as they are, not as they are envisioned to be.

Depravity

Radical or total depravity is the belief "that unaided by the Spirit of God the
sinner is unable to hear God's word, receive the Holy Spirit, submit to God's
law, understand biblical teaching, and cease from sin."[49] The implication of
this doctrine is that the student will not naturally desire to know, serve, or
honor Christ's kingly authority.[50]

One way to describe the implications of depravity is to recognize that by
nature people will construct false gods and hence faulty understandings and
explanations of the world in which they live. These constructed understandings sound promising, but are unable to deliver on their promises. This is in
essence what the philosophical meanderings of the Preacher point toward in
Ecclesiastes and the psalmist describes in Psalm 115.

Grace, Original Sin, and Depravity

The Reformed and Presbyterian tradition's understanding of the human person must be balanced by its understanding of common grace. Common grace
is that which sustains and keeps the world from degenerating into self-
destructive chaos. It is evident in God's ordination of civil governments and
the ability of the human person to distinguish between right and wrong. It
curbs the destructive power of sin.

Common grace is manifested in God's continual care for the created order.
It is a proper understanding of God's common grace that allows one to see

education as a means by which sin is curbed and individuals are taught to live redemptively as citizens of God's kingdom.

Summary

Those committed to the teaching vocation must have a realistic view of the learner. For the teaching vocation involves moving people from where they are to where one believes they ought to be. It involves a commitment to a process, and an effective teacher must be aware of the challenges and obstacles that will be encountered. A realistic view of the learner, which also means a realistic view of ourselves as teachers, allows one to grasp the immensity of the challenges that will be encountered.

One only has to look at Jesus' ministry to see the challenges that are present. Two illustrations will suffice. First, after the feeding of the five thousand Jesus delivered the "bread of life" discourse (John 6:25–29). After this discourse many left him because his teaching was too difficult to understand (John 6:60–66). In other words, Jesus spoke truth—what they needed rather than what they wanted to hear. The disciples' desertion of Jesus was not a surprise to him, though it was a surprise to the Twelve, because he had a realistic view of the learner. Second, Peter's ability to comprehend who Jesus was also illustrates this point. Peter spent approximately three years under Jesus' tutelage. He heard him teach, saw him perform miraculous signs, was present at the Mount of Transfiguration, and defended him at Gethsemane, although he denied him three times shortly after that. It was only after the resurrection that Peter began to understand. A realistic view of the learner allows those committed to the teaching vocation to understand the complexity of challenges present in moving students from where they are to where they ought to be. It also means that a teacher can take students only as far as they have gone spiritually and within the context of their discipline.

ELIJAH, JEREMIAH, JESUS, AND PAUL: RELEVANCE FOR THE TWENTY-FIRST CENTURY

Teaching is an honorable vocation. It is a way of life. It is an honorable life— the apostle Paul writes that those who teach are "worthy of double honor" (1 Tim. 5:17). Those who pursue the teaching vocation face enormous challenges, but those challenges are no greater or more demanding than those faced by Elijah, Jeremiah, Jesus, or Paul. The challenges may be different, but they are not more complex.

In light of the idea of the kingdom of God presented, Paul's use of equipping, and a realistic view of the learner, as well as the accounts of Elijah's, Jeremiah's, Jesus', and Paul's activities, Scripture provides eight commitments for the teaching vocation in the twenty-first century.

A holistic commitment to the truth is necessary. This commitment functions on two levels. At the first level it involves communicating the truth of the kingdom of God clearly to others. Truth in the Reformed and Presbyterian tradition is rooted in God's character and revealed in the Scriptures, which are God's revelation of himself and his expectations for his creation. Elijah spoke the truth to Ahab and the prophets of Baal (1 Kgs. 18:16–46). Jeremiah wrote the truth in his letter to the exiles, even though they did not want to read it (Jer. 29:1–24). Paul spoke truthfully at the Areopagus even though it did not fit "the spirit" of the assembly (Acts 17:16–34). And Jesus, who was "the truth" (John 14:6), spoke truth to all even though he knew it would not always be well received. Not only did they speak truth, but at a higher level their lives were shaped by the truth that they proclaimed.

A realistic view of the teaching vocation necessitates that one be open to correction. Because of sin one does not always reason correctly and sometimes misinterprets the data and the Scriptures. That is why the academic community is important—it provides accountability. Elijah struggled with doubt, and Yahweh reminded him that there were others who had not bowed to Baal (1 Kgs. 19:1–18). Paul struggled with his "thorn," and the Lord reminded him that God's grace was sufficient (2 Cor. 12:1–10). Jesus' teaching on the Spirit reminds one that though the Spirit illumines the text, it also corrects. Being open to correction, thoughtfully considering the objections and ideas of others, is essential to the integrity of instruction and the teaching vocation.

Pursuing the teaching vocation with integrity may cost something. If one's ultimate allegiance is to God and his kingdom, then those whose allegiance is to someone or something else will reject the truth presented. And because of sin this person will also most likely reject the purveyor of truth as well. Elijah was rejected, even though he taught and facilitated Yahweh's display of power at Mount Carmel. He was called the "troubler of Israel" and blamed for the drought that resulted from Israel's disobedience (1 Kgs. 19). Jeremiah was rejected, carried into captivity, and put in a cistern because he failed to tailor his message to fit the immediate desires of those present (Jer. 26:1–10; 38:1–11; 43:1–7). Paul was stoned and dragged before the authorities because of the message he proclaimed (Acts 16:19–20; chap. 19). And Jesus, in an act of injustice, was crucified because he spoke the truth and was a perceived threat to the political power structures (Matt. 27:11–61).

Practitioners of the teaching vocation must view and treat all people with respect. All people are worthy of respect because they are all image bearers of the Creator. This applies to students, those who disagree with the instructor, and those who oppose the truth. To treat with respect means to understand and engage a person's ideas, while valuing the student as a person. It involves bringing the truths of Scripture to bear constructively on the topic or situation at hand. Jeremiah dealt respectfully with those who opposed him. He engaged Ahab respectfully, even though Ahab blamed him for the drought (1 Kgs. 19). Jeremiah spoke about Babylon respectfully, even though Babylonians had decimated Jerusalem (Jer. 29). Paul spoke respectfully to those who opposed him in Jerusalem, both at the Jerusalem Council (Acts 15:1–21) and during his imprisonment and trial (Acts 24–28). Jesus dealt and spoke with his followers and opponents respectfully. To deal with people respectfully does not mean that one steps back from the truth; rather, it calls one to engage others with the truth out of love for them as persons. The Christian tradition's commitment to objective truth allows it to be inclusive in its view of people—out of respect, everyone is invited to speak—while at the same time being exclusive in its view of salvation.

The teaching vocation requires that one understand the context in which the art of instruction is practiced. Instructors should attempt to understand the context in which their students live and work. They must be conversant with contemporary ideas, literature, art, music, and so on. Jeremiah understood the plight of the exiles (Jer. 29). Elijah understood the reality of the people's spiritual condition (1 Kgs. 18–19). Paul adapted his message to his audience at the Areopagus (Acts 17:16–34). And Jesus' teaching, his use of parables and the Old Testament, as well as his understanding of the current political realities allowed him to communicate in a relevant manner with the various audiences.

Instructors who faithfully pursue the teaching vocation must engage the spirit of the age. The teaching vocation must engage people where they are, not where the instructor believes they ought to be. It means that one must communicate in a respectful, engaging, understandable, and relevant manner. Elijah spoke to the immediate context when he engaged the prophets of Baal (1 Kgs. 19). Jeremiah spoke to the exiles' fears and hopes when he wrote and instructed them to build houses and settle down, and to pray for the peace and prosperity of the city (Jer. 29). Paul quoted the poets, used illustrations that were appropriate, and addressed the reality of the people's context and situation (Acts 17). And Jesus engaged the people and religious leaders in ways that resounded with the audience. Mark's Gospel describes Jesus' teaching as "a new teaching—and with authority! He even gives orders to evil spirits and they obey him" (Mark 1:27).

The teaching vocation requires one to be tolerant of others. Ideas are to be engaged and perfected. And since all people are worthy of respect, engagement with the ideas of others must be respectful. Neutrality is not respectful, because it implies no one's ideas have any more value than anyone else's. It implies there is no difference between what it true and what is false, what is good and what is evil.[51] This perspective is self-defeating and contrary to God's character (Ps. 5:4) and Scripture (2 Tim. 3:16). Tolerance does not mean that everyone will agree, but it does require that everyone should be "able to give an account of the hope" (1 Pet. 3:15) that he or she possesses.

The vocation of teaching should be characterized by an attitude of hope. Hope is essential to life. The scriptural teaching on the kingdom of God and the message of the gospel is one of hope. Elijah confronted Ahab and the prophets because he was confident of God's ability to bring about what he promised (1 Kgs. 19). Jeremiah's letter to the exiles was a letter of hope—of restoration— in the midst of difficult circumstances (Jer. 29). Paul's hope was in Christ— the hope of glory (Col. 1:27)—who would accomplish his purposes in spite of appearances to the contrary (1 and 2 Thess.). And Jesus' message was one of hope, not condemnation. It was a message of redemption and reconciliation, rather than wrath and judgment. The book of Revelation ends with the new Jerusalem descending on the earth and a picture of the created order being returned to its pre-fall state, redeemed for all eternity (Rev. 21). The Scriptures end with a vision and message of hope—God's purposes will be accomplished in spite of appearances that lead one to believe otherwise. "Perfect love drives out fear" (1 John 4:18); the teaching vocation must be informed by hope in God's eternal purposes rather than fear of the present situation.

The teaching vocation is a high and honorable calling. It is a demanding vocation whose worth and importance are generally acknowledged, but rarely valued. The vocation of teaching is about shaping the hearts and minds of others. That process is shaped by the commitments of the instructor. The biblical teaching on the kingdom of God, an understanding of the role of instruction, modeling, training and discernment, and a realistic understanding of the human condition are essential to pursuing the vocation with integrity. And when the teaching vocation is pursued with integrity, then one's instruction will contribute to the advancement of God's kingdom as well as serving as a light in a dark place.

3

God, Creation, and Covenant

The Reformed Tradition and the Vocation
of the Presbyterian Teacher

TIMOTHY A. BEACH-VERHEY

Pluralism has become one of the defining characteristics of life in twenty-first century America. The formerly mainline religious communities, including the Presbyterian Church, have seen their dominance and authority dissipating as cultural, religious, and moral alternatives multiply. Previously marginalized and voiceless groups are becoming full participants in the life of society; women, people of color, and alternative religious and moral worldviews are no longer silent or invisible. In large part, pluralism is a healthy and constructive development that we should welcome, celebrate, and promote.

But it has negative consequences as well. A corollary of pluralism, in America at least, is fragmentation. Wade Clark Roof and William McKinney point out that the dissolution of the cultural and moral canopy that mainline religion provided has pressed us toward "an uneasy coexistence of splinter groups differing across race, gender, class, and, of course, religious ideology."[1] In this context, the market has become the main institutional means for cooperation and interaction. Contractual exchanges based on mutual self-interest stand in as the "moral proxy" for a common life.[2] Unfortunately, the market contributes to, rather than ameliorating, fragmentation. Robert Bellah writes, "What economic individualism destroys . . . is solidarity, a sense of being members of the same body."[3]

Pluralism and fragmentation are also apparent in our personal identities and social roles. According to Michael Walzer, we are "internally differentiated" and "divided selves," pursuing various goals in different of spheres—

24

education in school, love in the family, power in politics, and salvation in the church.[4] We are one person at work, another at home, and a third when we worship. Moreover, these identities, values, and institutional contexts often conflict with one another: we are pulled in a variety of directions, and, for many, the center threatens not to hold.

These characteristics of contemporary life are apparent in our institutions of higher education. Cultural, religious, and moral pluralism have added significantly to the diversity of perspectives on college and university campuses. Furthermore, increased specialization in academic disciplines has multiplied and differentiated the subjects of study and the methods of investigation. Certainly this diversity has enriched and broadened our educational institutions. Yet fragmentation has accompanied pluralism here as well.

> The effort to create an integrated, democratic higher education [has] degenerated into . . . the multiversity cafeteria. The research university, the cathedral of learning, rather than interpreting and integrating the larger society, came more and more to mirror it. Far from becoming a new community that would bring coherence out of chaos, it became instead a congeries of faculty and students, each pursuing their own ends, integrated by no shared vision but only by the bureaucratic procedures of the administration.[5]

In such a context, without any sense of common purpose or shared goals, colleges and universities also turn to the market as a moral proxy. Education often is treated as a product for sale on the open market—responsive to "a fixed preference in the mind of the consumer who simply shops for the best way to fulfill that preference."[6] Moreover, this fixed preference is often the personal goal of upward economic mobility. Higher education becomes, for many, a way to attain the technical skills and accreditation necessary to succeed in the market economy. The value of education is integrated into the moral worldview of economic individualism.

Professors cannot escape the fragmentation of contemporary existence in their personal lives and identities either. Within their professional lives they are teachers, researchers, faculty members; they are stretched among responsibilities to their students, their professional commitments, and their educational institution. In their lives as a whole, they are divided between family obligations, professional obligations, and perhaps religious obligations. They, like everyone else in contemporary society, are pulled in a variety of directions, and threatened by personal fragmentation.

In the contemporary educational environment, the dream of the university is being replaced by the reality of the multiversity; the collegium is being transformed into an educational marketplace. Meanwhile, students, faculty, and staff are left to negotiate the challenges and opportunities of higher education in ways that cohere with their various identities, goals, and values. The problem, it seems, concerns finding the means to embrace pluralism without falling prey to fragmentation. By returning to some of the foundational theological convictions of the Reformed tradition and applying them to the context of higher education, I hope to provide Presbyterian professors with ways to think constructively about their vocations in ways that are responsive to just this concern.

GOD, CREATION, AND COVENANT: CHRISTIAN PIETY IN THE REFORMED TRADITION

As Douglas Sloan reminds us, Christians think about the relationship between faith and knowledge in a variety of ways. One of the dominant ways to think about their relation in the American context has been the "two-realm theory of truth."

> This is the view that on the one side there are the truths of knowledge as these are given predominantly by science and discursive, empirical reason. On the other side are the truths of faith, religious experience, morality, meaning, and value. The latter are seen as grounded not in knowledge but variously in feeling, ethical action, communal convention, folk tradition, or unfathomable mystical experience.[7]

This perspective helps account for the anti-intellectualism of much of American Christianity and the secularism of much American higher education. The Reformed concept of piety, however, eschews such dualism, integrating true knowledge of God, appropriate affection (or trust) for God, and proper action in response to God.[8]

The object of these three aspects of piety, as noted, is God—the creator, sustainer, judge, and redeemer of all that is. Everything comes from, abides in, and belongs to God. So Calvin writes:

> Not only does [God] sustain this universe (as he once founded it) by his boundless might, regulate it by his wisdom, preserve it by his goodness, and especially rule mankind by his righteousness and judgment, bear with it in his mercy, watch over it by his protection; but also . . . no drop will be found either of wisdom or light, or of righteousness or power or rectitude, or of genuine truth, which does not flow from him, and of which he is not the cause.[9]

The correlate of God's universal sovereignty is the Reformed Christian's "drive toward unity, toward the integration of all of life in a religious vision."[10] The Reformed tradition emphasizes a singular unity that underlies the pluralism of the world and our personal identities and roles. The doctrine of God's sovereignty militates against fragmentation, both social and personal. There is, according to Reformed piety, a singular power, will, and order that is present under, in, and through every particular reality. Similarly, the self is unified and singular in all its roles and actions to the extent that it responds through them to the One who is creator, sustainer, judge, and redeemer of all creation. God is the God of the whole universe, and the unified self is one who lives all of life in relationship to this One. Every aspect of life is lived in relationship with God, and every part of life is an expression of piety. This holds for the life of learning as well as the life of family, church, commerce, and politics.

The concept of vocation in the Reformed tradition is an acknowledgment of a unified aim or orientation in the Christian life, namely to live all of life in relation to the one God who is sovereign over all creation. Christian piety and Christian vocation, the religious and the active aspects of life, are merely opposite sides of the same coin. As Douglas Ottati writes: "The spiritual is not a life apart, but rather, a quality of all living that both forms ordinary life and comes to expression in it. Ordinary life is not spiritually inert. Actually, our everyday converse with others in the world draws out and forms the spiritual quality of all living."[11]

At the heart of the Reformed tradition is a unifying orientation toward the one sovereign God, which is expressed in every aspect of life through the twin notions of piety and vocation. More must be said, however, about the nature of God and the human condition if we are to frame a coherent response to the conditions of life in the world, including life in an academic context. While acknowledging the unity of self and world, we must also recognize the rich pluralism and particularity of existence. We must find a way to reconcile singularity with diversity and even division in our personal and communal contexts. Otherwise we may fall prey to the tyrannical theocratic imaginations that Reformed Christianity is so often accused of embodying.

The Reformed tradition has resources for dealing with just these issues in its conceptualization of salvation history and the covenantal nature of existence. These doctrines flesh out the nature of God, the world, and humanity, building on the foundation of unity articulated by the sovereignty of God and Christian piety. In the remainder of this section, I will examine creation and covenant, fall and broken covenant, and redemption and new covenant as metaphors for understanding God and world, Christian vocation in the world, and the distinction between genuine pluralism and destructive fragmentation.

Creation and Covenant: Finitude, Diversity, and the Common Good

The doctrine of creation communicates important facets of the nature of God, the world, and ourselves. At the heart of the creation story is the fundamental conviction that God created everything that exists—creation ex nihilo. In addition, because God is good, everything that exists must be good. The constant refrain of the creation myth in Genesis 1 is the goodness of creation. Calvin reminds us that "wherever we cast our eyes, all things they meet are works of God."[12] And H. Richard Niebuhr points out, "Whatever is, is good, because it exists as one thing among the many which all have their origin and their being, in the One."[13]

All things are good, but they are also finite. They are creatures of God, and not God. They are limited and particular, having some characteristics and not others, possessing certain qualities but not others. This is also true of human beings. We are born in particular times and places, possessing specific skills and gifts. Finitude makes us particular and diverse; but it also makes us vulnerable. We have weaknesses and limitations. We are not self-sufficient; rather, we are always dependent and interdependent.

We are dependent on God, the source and sustainer of our existence and of everything around us. We are also interdependent, relying on our fellow creatures for our mutual survival and flourishing. In this sense, the sum is greater than the parts of creation. The creation story in Genesis 1 communicates this when God surveys the entire creation on the sixth day and proclaims that it is not simply good—it is "very good." The harmonious interrelatedness and mutual dependence of the whole marks God's gracious intention and orderly governance of the creation in all its variety and particularity.

Creation as a whole has a certain covenantal structure to it. While the idea of covenant grows out of human social compacts, its theological meaning can be extended to the structure of the entire cosmos. Theologically speaking, the covenant at Sinai takes center stage in the Old Testament. This covenantal relationship between God and Israel is, nevertheless, framed within a cosmic context and has cosmic consequences. God's covenantal relationship with Israel is identified as God's way of reestablishing the original harmonious structures of the universe. See, for example, Genesis 12:1–3, in which God's purpose in covenanting with Abraham is to see that "all the families of the earth shall be blessed." The covenant with Israel also becomes a metaphor that is read back into God's ways with the entire universe, including animals and plants as well as people. See, for example, the Noachian covenant (Gen. 9:8–17)—a covenant with all God's creatures. It is appropriate, consequently, to see a covenantal structure to the entire cosmos, which can be applied to the various contexts within which we find ourselves, including family, work, politics, religion, and education.

A covenant may be understood as a relationship among distinct and diverse agents built on mutual promise and obligations. Covenant, in this biblical and theological sense, differs in important ways from contract, as it is presently understood. A contract is often thought of as a limited obligation between parties based on mutual self-interest. A covenant, on the other hand, is built on unlimited responsibility to one another based on a common commitment to a good larger than either party.[14] In addition, while the negotiated agreement of the contracting parties is the substance of a legitimate contract, a covenant is "based on an enduring law, purpose, or decree established by a higher authority."[15] God creates and orders a universe of interdependent, yet distinct and separate, creatures and invites them into full participation in an order they did not create.

The concept of vocation in the Reformed tradition is closely tied to the covenantal nature of existence and the dialectic of grace and gratitude. Summarizing Calvin's assessment of the purpose and aim of human life, Brian Gerrish writes: "While the whole created order reflects God's glory, humanity is distinguished from the mute creation by its ability to reflect God's glory in a conscious response of thankfulness."[16] Gratitude is the foundation of piety and the heart of the Christian life. It involves the worship, praise, and enjoyment of God. But it also consists of a vocation—a life of gratitude lived through the practical engagement in God's creation.

The Puritan William Perkins argues that there are two parts to vocation: the general and particular. The general aspect is the calling that each Christian has to live a life of gratitude to God and service to his fellow creatures.[17] The particular aspect is the specific context and calling within which this takes place—by the particular gifts the person possesses and the particular office in which those gifts are used. Not every person has gifts for every calling; moreover, interdependence requires a variety of callings fulfilling a diversity of needs. These two aspects of vocation provide for unity in variety and distinction within commonality. Thus, following the very structure of creation, there is a variety of distinct creatures united together by the bonds of loving mutual interdependence under the gracious providence of God. Consistent with the covenantal structure of creation and the nature of Christian piety, Perkins writes:

> The particular calling and practice of the duties thereof, severed from the foresaid general calling, is nothing else than the practice of injustice and profaneness. And the general calling of Christianitie, without the practice of some particular calling, is nothing els, but the forme of godliness, without the power thereof: And therefore both callings must be joyned, as body and soul are joyned in a living man. And that we may better joyne both our callings together, wee must consider the maine end of our lives, and that is, to serve God in the serving of men in the workes of our callings.[18]

Piety and covenantal responsibility require gratitude to God through serving the common good of the whole creation. Calvin writes: "All the gifts we possess have been bestowed by God and entrusted to us on condition that they be distributed for our neighbor's benefit."[19]

Fall and Broken Covenant:
Fragmentation, Diversity, and Ingratitude

Attentive to the goodness of creation, the Reformed tradition is also mindful of its fallenness. Sin, in the Reformed tradition, is nothing but the corruption of an originally good and well-ordered nature. It is a "disease," a "contagion," as Calvin puts it, that infects, distorts, and threatens to destroy the goodness and health of the whole creation.[20] Original sin has "perverted the whole order of nature in heaven and on earth."[21]

The source of this corruption has been variously called pride, concupiscence, idolatry, disobedience, infidelity, and ingratitude. At its heart it is rebellion against God's covenantal order through ingratitude and prideful self-assertion— the desire to live for self rather than God and neighbor. Calvin writes:

> Unfaithfulness, then, was the root of the Fall. But thereafter ambition and pride, together with ungratefulness, arose, because Adam by seeking more than was granted him shamefully spurned God's great bounty, which had been lavished upon him. To have been made in the likeness of God seemed a small matter to a son of earth unless he had also attained equality with God—a monstrous wickedness.[22]

Ingratitude and pride drive fallen human beings into conflict with self, God, one another, and the whole created order.

Augustine writes, "Pride is a perverted imitation of God. For pride hates a fellowship of equality under God, and seeks to impose its own dominion on fellow men, in place of God's rule."[23] Human beings corrupted the proper order of creation by setting themselves against God's harmonious order through idolatrous pretensions of self-sufficiency and self-importance. This corruption of the heart, mind, and will bears tainted fruit in human vocations. Perkins acknowledges and condemns this corruption, writing:

> Here then we must in general know, that he abuseth his calling, whosoever he be that against the end thereof, imployes it for himselfe, seeking wholly his own, and not the common good. And that common saying, *Every man for himselfe, and God for us all*, is wicked, and is directly against the end of every calling or honest kinde of life.[24]

Under the influence of sin, human beings use their gifts for self-aggrandizement rather than service, for self-interest rather than the good of others. They thereby reject their covenantal responsibilities toward God and neighbor, turn their backs on the source and sustainer of harmonious diversity, and throw themselves and the whole creation on the path toward destructive conflict and fragmentation.

A world that was created as a harmonious interdependence of diverse and particular creatures has betrayed God's covenantal order. In this context, God is both judge and gracious preserver of the creation. God has allowed the creation to bear the consequences of its own sinfulness, as harmonious diversity turns to conflict and fragmentation, as joyful flourishing turns to self-contradiction and dis-ease. But God has also sustained the creation, even in its sinfulness and corruption. God has arrested creation's march toward destruction through "common grace," preserving the order of creation, even in its brokenness, and sustaining the gifts of creation, even in their corruption. Furthermore, through Christ, God provided for the renewal of creation and the recovery of its health and flourishing.[25]

Redemption and New Covenant: Reconciliation, Diversity, and Flourishing

In the Christian faith, the last word is not corruption, but redemption. Christian faith proclaims that the birth, life, death, and resurrection of Jesus Christ points to and empowers reconciliation, new life, and new creation. Jesus came preaching, "Repent, for the kingdom of heaven has come near" (Matt. 4:17). Moreover, he incarnated that kingdom and the new life that follows from repentance. Jesus declared God's cosmic graciousness and embodied it in his miracles and healings; he taught love for God and neighbor and practiced inclusive love for friend and foe. He died at the hands of a creation that had turned its back on God and its own true being. But his resurrection empowered repentance, reconciliation, renewal, and new creation.

Hearts contracted by self-love, minds distorted by narrowed vision, wills corrupted by idolatrous commitments are renewed through repentance and new life made possible in Christ. Jesus Christ is both priest and king; the one on whom Christians rely for salvation and the one whose way they imitate and follow. Through the transformative power of God in Jesus Christ, humans come to know God's graciousness and learn to follow God's ways.[26] Through the power of God in Christ, they are reconciled to God and to their true natures, learning once again to live as children of God.

The repentance, regeneration, and new life made possible in Jesus Christ bears fruit in a new quality of life and relationship. Mutual love and service in thankful dependence on God's graciousness characterize a renewal of the covenantal order of God's good creation, not only in the church, but also in all the relationships of created existence. God's redeeming power and presence are aimed at an eschatological renewal of the whole created order, which is already underway. Therefore, the church, as the body of believers, places its faith in God through Jesus Christ and commits itself to God's reconciling activity in every aspect of life. The Confession of 1967 professes: "The church is called to bring all men to receive and uphold one another as persons in all relationships of life: in employment, housing, education, leisure, marriage, family, church, and the exercise of political rights."[27]

There is no aspect of life that can be separated from the redemptive work of God already powerfully present in the world. Throughout the history of the Reformed tradition, the sense that God was at work transforming and renewing the creation was the source of the socially progressive (and occasionally revolutionary) aspects of the Reformed tradition—an impetus felt in ecclesial, political, educational, and other aspects of life. This accounts, at least in part, for the moniker "Reformed."

Michael Walzer traces the revolutionary consequences of the Reformed tradition in his excellent work *The Revolution of the Saints: A Study in the Origins of Radical Politics*.[28] He also notes, however, that there are conservative elements within the Reformed tradition as well. This is clearly the case. The conservative elements are related to the doctrines of creation and fall; the sense of the innate goodness of the created order and the motivation to preserve a fallen and corrupt order, despite its sinfulness, are in tension with the more radical and transformative aspects of the tradition. Walzer argues that the tension between the conservative and reformist aspects is profound, leading to deep divisions within the tradition. I am convinced that the relationship between the two aspects provides a constructive dialogic engagement with our environments that allow for a realistic assessment of the possibilities and limits of transformation in human life and society.

A Christian vocation, in the Reformed tradition, is one that contributes, by means of distinct gifts and in the context of particular offices, to a process of renewal, reconciliation, and wholesome flourishing.

Despite this energetic hopefulness, the Reformed tradition has always recognized that total reconciliation is impossible this side of God's eschatological kingdom. Calvin writes: "There remains in a regenerate man a smoldering cinder of evil."[29] The persistence of sin in the midst of sanctification calls the believer to humility before God and the rest of creation. It also motivates the believer to strive still further for truer and more genuine regeneration. The process of reconciliation is never complete in this lifetime; it is a "permanent revolution."[30] This accounts, at least in part, for the motto *ecclesia reformata, semper reformanda*. The redemption of our hearts, minds, and wills is never concluded this side of the eschaton. Humility, self-criticism, confession, and renewal are the constant companions of the Christian life.

EDUCATION, THE VOCATION OF THE PROFESSOR, AND REFORMED HABITS OF MIND

Education is a single but important aspect of human life. It is distinct and independent from political, religious, economic, familial, and natural aspects of life. Yet it is also related to and mutually interdependent with these other spheres. It studies these other spheres, criticizes them, and contributes to them. For example, it investigates the economic practices of society—practices that preceded the study of them and that continue to exist independent of it. Scholars and students seek to understand these practices: how they function, how they came to function that way, and how they fit with other aspects of human life. These scholars may help us understand our own lives better and even help us find ways to improve our practices by making them more efficient, more just, more properly integrated and distinguished from other aspects of life. Education is, as we can see from this example, a distinct aspect of life that exists in covenantal relationships of mutual interdependence with these other spheres.

In this sense, the educational sphere has a vocation within the covenantal order of existence: it is called upon to serve the common good in its own particular way and with its own distinctive gifts. The distinctive purpose of this significant but particular sphere of life is true knowledge, or the single-minded pursuit of the truth. Therefore it ought to be distinct from these other spheres. It should not let economic interest, religious tradition, political concerns, cultural heritages, or familial obligations distract it from its mission and purpose.

Certainly, education is often subordinated to these other purposes and concerns—much to the detriment of its own purpose. In totalitarian contexts like the Soviet Union or National Socialism in Germany, education was subordinated to political and cultural concerns. And this proved costly to the cause of truth and genuine knowledge. The same can be said for the religious domination of educational purposes. Take, for example, the excommunication of Galileo because his scientific discoveries did not fit within the religious orthodoxy of the day—an occasion for which the Roman Catholic Church has now repented.

In our own day there are those who say that the modern university is not free of domination, despite academic freedom and the increasing secularism of the academy. The culprit is not, however, politics or religion, but the market.[31] Higher education has come to see itself as fundamentally "vocational," in the sense of preparing students to enter the job market through offering them marketable skills and credentials. Furthermore, the sciences are increasingly dominating the curriculum because of their utility, and corporations are dominating scientific research through offering grants aimed at bringing new technologies to market. In such a context, education is placed in the service of goals other than truth and genuine knowledge, allowing these other purposes to dominate the true purpose of education.

Yet because truth, faith, and human flourishing are interrelated, it cannot be separated from any of these other spheres either. True knowledge serves faith, because it helps us better understand the God in whom we, and the whole creation, live and move and have our being. Truth contributes to genuine human flourishing because it helps us orient our lives to the conditions of existence within which we find ourselves. Faith, knowledge, and human flourishing cannot be separated; religious, political, economic, familial, and natural aspects of life are all related to one another and to the educational sphere. When the pursuit of truth becomes separated from these other aspects of life, educational institutions are rightfully accused of retreating into an ivory tower of intellectual irrelevance.

In the United States, as well as many other societies, higher education "is the institution which is trusted as the savior of society, the paradigm of perfect community, where youth are all trained to intelligent maturity and gracious living."[32] Yet, as Waldo Beach points out in his essay "Christian Ethical Community as a Norm," this is far from the case; higher education is not our messiah. It is just as fragmented and distorted by sin as any other human institution and endeavor. Educational institutions often serve themselves rather than the truth. They often use knowledge as a means to attain power rather than as a way to serve. They are often internally conflicted and divided, having no sense of common purpose or shared service to the world. Higher education is as corrupted by the distorting power of sin as any other sphere of human life.

Higher education is, however, also a good creation of God, created for flourishing in interdependent relationship with other creatures under God's sovereign rule. It cannot simply be dismissed as evil and corrupted—a threat to true religious faith and genuine human flourishing. It cannot be ignored as simply an agent of elite interests. It is a good creature of God, capable of genuine service and a participant in the interdependent existence of the whole creation.

And, finally, our educational institutions are also open—just like every other creature of God—to the vivifying and renewing power of God's redemptive presence in Jesus Christ. Under the influence of the Spirit of God, our educational institutions can embrace their true purpose and become more genuine communities of inquiry and more responsible participants in God's covenantal order of creation. When those who participate in the institutions of higher education commit themselves to the wholehearted pursuit of truth, they embrace a shared commitment and mutual responsibility that binds them together into a community of inquiry, despite genuine differences—various disciplines, conflicting schools of thought, diverse cultural and religious heritages, and different roles in the educational enterprise (students, professors, administration, support personnel). When they commit themselves to the pursuit of truth, they also serve the world by conserving the accomplishments of the past, pressing on toward better understanding of the creation in the midst of which we live, and contributing to the constant reformation of human practices, relationships, and beliefs.

This is the context, theologically understood, in which Presbyterian professors find themselves practicing their vocations. In the light of this theocentric and covenantal understanding of the enterprise of higher education, Presbyterian professors should pursue their callings with three sets of concerns in mind. First, they should be mindful of unity in the midst of diversity and plurality in the context of commonality. Second, they should respect tradition while also criticizing it and moving beyond it. Third, they should be constantly attentive to the practical and moral qualities of intellectual inquiry.

Unity and Diversity

That there is great diversity in our educational institutions cannot be denied: there are different disciplines, schools of thought, and cultural and religious foundations that orient the studies of various scholars. This is not a curse but a gift. The goodness of God is expressed in the richness and diversity of the creation. The diversity within our institutions of higher education helps us know and express the great richness of truth.

This is not to say that truth is itself plural. It is unified in the singularity of the one God who is the source, substance, and end of all things. As John Calvin writes: "If we regard the Spirit of God as the sole fountain of truth, we shall neither reject the truth itself, nor despise it wherever it shall appear, unless we wish to dishonor the spirit of God."[33] Therefore, we should be thankful for any and every discipline that casts light on the true nature of our existence and therefore gives us better knowledge of God and God's way with the world. This diversity is unified to the extent that all the disciplines are pursuing the truth—a truth that finds its source, like all things, in God.

Unity in diversity, understood in this way, is distinct from either fragmentation or artificial monism. Fragmentation arises from the sense that there is a plurality of unrelated truths or a sense that, while there is one truth, it is the exclusive possession of a singular discipline. In each case there is no sense of common purpose or reason for mutual engagement; we are each moving in our different directions with our various aims. On the other hand, we are often tempted to impose an artificial monism on our institutions of higher education—a monism of religious doctrine, political obligation, cultural standards, or economic purposes. We seek some order and common orientation short of the universal God, who is sovereign over the whole universe.

Faith in the God who transcends every particular culture, religion, nationality, and academic discipline, however, disposes the Christian professor to radical openness and inclusiveness. Faith in the God who is sovereign over every finite creature prepares the Christian professor to understand that every discipline and perspective is sanctified to the extent that it points beyond itself to God—the origin and end of truth, goodness, and existence. Richard T. Hughes, the author of *How Christian Faith Can Sustain the Life of the Mind*, writes:

> To break through the particularities of our faith means that we allow those particularities to point us to the infinite God. Conversely, it means that we refuse to view those particularities as ends in themselves, and we refuse to erect those particularities as brittle, dogmatic standards that never point beyond themselves to the God who should be the singular object of our faith. The frightening truth of the matter is simply this: if we refuse to break through those particularities but absolutize them instead, then we have engaged in a reprehensible act of idolatry.[34]

Therefore, Christianity itself can become an idol if it sets limits, based on Christian doctrine, on the questions that can be asked, how they may be investigated, or who may enter the debate concerning those questions. Christian faith should, instead, be committed to a consistent openness and inclusiveness in the academic arena due to its faith in the transcendent and sovereign God.[35]

The sort of unity described here is not one in which any particular perspective is the source of unity. Rather, the truth, which transcends every perspective, is the unifying center of the academic enterprise. Within this unity there is equality—a basic Protestant principle—among the various disciplines, perspectives, and positions. In his essay "Theology in the University," H. Richard Niebuhr writes:

> Matter and spirit, mind and body, nature and supernature proceed from the one source and are bound together in one community in which there is no high or low, no hierarchically ordered chain of being, but in which each kind of being is entitled to reverence, understanding, and service, while it in turn is servant to the rest.[36]

The professor who understands her work through the lens of Christian faith, especially Protestant Christian faith, should embrace an inclusive equalitarianism that respects all the various disciplines and modes of investigation as particular means of inquiry into the One Truth that is related to all things. Like every creature, they all stand in direct relationship to the God who is sovereign over them all.

All these disciplines and perspectives are also equal because of their common tendency toward idolatrous pretensions—another basic Protestant principle. Like all human beings and all human institutions, academic disciplines and departments often serve their own interests and imagine themselves as superior to others. "Economic interpretations of history and psychological interpretations of the self and naturalistic explanations of the way all things came into existence take their place alongside ecclesiastical orthodoxies."[37] We imagine that one approach to existence tells the whole truth about ourselves and our world, that some aspects of reality are truer than others, that a particular discipline is the only essential mode of study.

Unity in diversity requires a variety of disciplines in mutual dependence and service in the common pursuit of the One Truth. This does not mean that the college or university will always be peaceful and cooperative. Part of the service that these various disciplines offer one another is the discipline of mutual limitation. Concerning civic life, Calvin wrote: "Men's faults or failings cause it to be safer and more bearable for a number to exercise government, so that they may help one another, teach and admonish one another; and, if one asserts himself unfairly, there may be an number of censors and masters to restrain his willfulness."[38] The same should hold true of institutions of higher education. Following Calvin's conception of mutual resistance and limitation, H. Richard Niebuhr wrote:

> In a university in which the radically monotheistic idea comes to expression, the various departments, schools, and methods, are related to one another in mutual service, including the service of mutual limitation and creative conflict. . . . Creative conflict prevents such a university from becoming too beautifully ordered to be alive, since all real life involves tension and even conflict.[39]

These diverse disciplines and departments not only assist one another in the pursuit of truth, they limit one another's pretensions to ultimacy by providing alternative (and often conflicting) visions, approaches, and modes of inquiry.

Unity in diversity embodies a covenantal approach to the academic environment. All the various disciplines, departments, schools of thought, and methods are distinct and diverse, yet bound together in mutual interdependence with one another, common dependence on a singular truth that transcends them all, and shared service to that truth. This understanding of unity is radically open and inclusive, welcoming and respecting all those who share a commitment to the truth. Such an understanding of the truth does not imagine an untroubled harmony in the midst of diversity, but mutual struggle, disagreement, resistance, and limitation in service of the whole and absolute truth. A professor in this environment has a genuine vocation: pursuing the truth by using the particular gifts she has been given, and living in mutual dependence with others (both within and beyond the academic context) in common dependence on God.

Tradition and Criticism

The covenantal nature of the academic endeavor is transtemporal as well as cross-disciplinary. We are bound in relationships of mutual dependence and service under the sovereignty of God with the generations that preceded us and that will follow us. Academic disciplines, schools of thought, departments, and modes of investigation depend on the work of past generations. All teachers were first students, learning their disciplines from those who went before. Academic research in every generation relies on the discoveries of previous generations. The sciences as well as the humanities depend on legacies left to them by the past.

Brian Gerrish describes "deference" as one of the Reformed habits of mind.[40] We have inherited gifts that we did not create but with which we have been entrusted; and we are called upon to be faithful stewards of these gifts. As teachers we seek to preserve these traditions by introducing our students to them and to the wonder and gratitude we feel for having received them. Finally, we allow these inherited traditions to shape our lives and ways of thinking, and we encourage our students to do the same. As Gerrish writes: "To stand in a tradition is to hand on a sacred trust that, in the first instance, we have simply received . . . ; if we receive it and accept the duty to pass it on, then we permit our existence to be defined by the tradition: it makes us, in large measure, who we are."[41]

Faithfulness to a tradition is not, however, simply to repeat the ideas and insights of the past: it is to carry on the work of the past by critically appropriating it, even if that requires moving away from it in significant ways. The past itself must not become our deity. Rather, we should serve God in covenantal relationship with our predecessors in the academic context by pursuing the truth they sought. After all, a physicist is not faithful to Einstein by simply parroting his theories; one is faithful to Einstein by pursuing the goal he chased— the truth. A physicist teaches Einstein's theory of relativity because one cannot be a good physicist without knowing it. One cannot know how physics came to be what it is, or what problems still exist in the field, without studying, and appreciating, the work of Einstein. Yet, one cannot be a good physicist, the sort of physicist Einstein was, without pressing beyond the work of Einstein and finding innovative ways to solve some of the problems he left behind.[42]

"Criticism of tradition" is a second habit of the Reformed mind, according to Gerrish. He notes that, in response to Roman Catholics who accused him of disloyalty to the Christian tradition, Calvin wrote: "Our constant endeavor, day and night, is not just to transmit the tradition faithfully, but also to put it in the form we think will prove best."[43] The commitment to criticism in the Reformed tradition is due to its deep awareness of finitude and sin. The thought and work of any and every person is flawed and incomplete. Therefore, while it may be significant, even essential, it is neither eternal nor insurpassable. It may be challenged, revised, renewed, and even rejected—though never ignored or avoided.

By engaging critically with traditions, we serve the past by carrying on the work of those who went before. But we also serve future generations by making our own contributions to the pursuit of truth. We are the link between the past and the future, receiving and revising the traditions we have inherited from our forebears and preparing the way for those who are to come. Therefore, we should not be surprised when our students not only listen to us, but criticize us as well. In fact, we should encourage it. We should acknowledge our own finitude and fallenness and encourage our students to embrace both the gift of tradition and the responsibility of criticism. Our own work, despite its significance, is no more eternal or insurpassable than any previous generation's. Our disciplines will take new directions, the methods of research will change, and new schools of thought will be born. We are not gods: we are servants of God and our fellow creatures—past, present, and future—in our temporally particular vocations.

Morality and Practicality

The Reformed tradition has always been committed to education. Calvin considered the establishment of the Genevan Academy (1559) one of his greatest and most significant accomplishments. His followers started twelve colleges or universities in Europe. In North America, Reformed Christians were responsible for over half the colleges organized before the Revolution and a full third of those organized before the Civil War.[44] The Reformed tradition always gave high standing to the life of the mind and the quest for true knowledge.

Education was always considered a practical endeavor, however. It existed to serve the larger world, not simply to promote vain and fatuous speculation. Calvin considered such empty intellectualism prideful and slothful: it gave pretense of knowing more that it possibly could, and did no one any good.[45] The academy in Geneva was started to prepare students for civic and religious leadership: the pursuit of truth was promoted to serve the ends of piety and flourishing. These same purposes provided the motivation for the schools that Reformed Christians opened in generations that followed.[46] Education existed to serve the practical needs of life in a larger world.

Education was not, however, a simply utilitarian endeavor, aimed merely at the development of useful skills and techniques. Preparing people for religious and civic life required attention to their moral and spiritual formation as well. To participants of the Reformed tradition, education seemed the best way to accomplish these moral and practical goals, because they believed truth was essentially related to goodness and flourishing. Moreover, education as a strenuous and always incomplete pursuit of intellectual, spiritual, and moral maturity paralleled the Reformed doctrine of sanctification—the lifelong quest of the whole person for genuine humanity.

Moral issues and religious dispositions are sometimes considered the province of particular departments and courses of study in an educational institution. And, to a certain extent, this is the case. The study of religion and concern with ethical issues and approaches have become just as specialized and differentiated as all the other disciplines. Yet, the general practices of education in all disciplines, at their best, shape the spiritual and moral dispositions of the participants in ways that prepare them for life in the world and orient them toward the God who is sovereign over that world.

At its heart, the educational endeavor requires humility, dependence, and trust. Being a student requires dependence on one's teachers. One cannot begin to learn without being initiated into the traditions of thought and practice that constitute a discipline; and this does not occur without the help of a mentor who can show the way in word and deed. This relationship of dependence is built on trust—trust that the professor both has something useful to teach and will communicate it faithfully. Every educated person experiences dependence on and trust of another. Education, therefore, engenders humility because we must acknowledge our dependence. This fundamental educational experience may dispose people to carry this orientation into other aspects of their lives where it is equally relevant. We may hope they will come to understand these dispositions as essential to life in a world not of our own making, a world bound together by mutual trust and interdependence under God's trustworthy sovereignty.

The educational endeavor, at its best, also engenders openness, inclusiveness, and equal regard. Education disposes a person to be open and attentive to a world larger than oneself. It encourages people to move beyond their limited interests and visions. In all the various disciplines, people are pressed toward a larger and more complex world of interaction than they had previously imagined. Otherwise ignored aspects of existence are drawn into a person's field of vision, altering and enriching his understanding of the context within which he lives and moves and has his being. In this way, the truly educated person is encouraged to take all of reality into account in his interaction with the universe. Such a person is pointed toward a diverse yet unified reality bound together by covenantal mutual dependence and interrelationship. Such a person is oriented outwards and inclined toward an inclusiveness that tries to take all creatures into account in the search for the whole truth.

Every step forward in the education endeavor is an experience in self-criticism, engendering repentance and bringing forth conversion. A profound educational experience changes a person's way of thinking about and envisioning the world. It entails acknowledgment of the inadequacy of her previous understanding, a willingness to change her perception of reality, and a readiness to embrace a new vision of the world in which she lives and moves and has her being. Such a transformation is accompanied by the wonder and joy of knowing the world more truly—a world that constantly surpasses one's comprehension. Such experiences of transformation are the constant accompaniment of a genuine education, whether one is a student in an introductory course or a senior professor. These educational experiences prepare one to engage the world in a self-critical manner, ready to enter into a deeper, richer, and more appropriate understanding of and relationship with the world in which we live.

Finally, education depends on and engenders wonder and gratitude. A multifaceted investigation of the world in all its diversity and intricate interrelationship elicits wonder from a student—acknowledgment of the remarkable nature of the universe within which we find ourselves. Such an experience often provokes a sense of gratitude for the universe and a commitment to responsible stewardship of it. A simple sense of joy and wonder is, far from being morally or practically irrelevant, the foundation of piety and vocation. Only a person who recognizes God's goodness and generosity will live a life of gratitude that praises God and serves God's creation.

Higher education serves practical purposes, preparing people for leadership and responsible participation in religious and secular contexts. It trains students in the skills necessary to carry out their vocations. But "vocational" training alone is insufficient. Education, at its best, should also form the moral and spiritual dispositions of students, preparing them for life in covenantal relationship with God and all God's creatures. It shapes character by eliciting humility, dependence, trust, self-criticism, repentance, wonder, joy, and gratitude. Together these help prepare souls for true worship of God and genuine human society with one another.

CONCLUSION

Higher education is one of the contexts within which Christians continue to participate in God's redemptive purposes in history. This does not mean that colleges and universities are free of fragmentation, conflict, constricted vision, and narrowed interests. Like every other part of God's creation, they are infected and distorted by sin. Nevertheless, the God of the whole world is present in and through this, and every other, aspect of creation, promoting repentance and a new quality of covenantal relationship. To the extent that education expands horizons, enlarges commitments, and engenders humility, gratitude, and wonder, education points toward and participates in God's redemptive will for the world.

Higher education is simply one of the contexts within which Christians live out their vocations. Being a professor is not the same as being a minister or a politician, a parent or an industrialist. It requires particular gifts and makes a distinctive contribution to the whole. It is not responsible for the worship of God or the ordering of human life in the world; yet, its distinctive calling contributes to both of these, just as it relies on them. The special calling of higher education is the pursuit of truth and knowledge: it serves the larger society by practicing its vocation no matter what the consequences for religious faith or human society. The Christian professor is motivated by the confidence that truth, faith, and human flourishing are finally one and that genuine truth presses us toward repentance and renewal in both religious and secular affairs.

4

The Reformed Understanding
of Vocation in History

R. WARD HOLDER AND JOHN KUYKENDALL

I. CALVIN AND GENEVA

Introduction

What is the Reformed educational ideal, especially at its roots? If that is our question, then we begin with a problem. How can we set forth most profitably in considering the history of the Reformed understanding of the teaching vocation? Several possibilities crowd the horizon. One could offer thumbnail sketches of the education and vision of several of the most influential Reformed figures. Alternatively, the deep study of the institutions of learning that they founded would certainly pay a handsome intellectual dividend to the investment of curiosity. However, it seems that a mixture of the two might be most helpful to our enterprise. Thus, we begin with a consideration of John Calvin's views on education, and then proceed to examine the academy that he founded, examining the patterns of education that came from him. Then we shall trace the heritage of Presbyterian ideals of education through the British Isles[1] and to early America, noting the transformation of the models of education, and the ideals of the purpose of education in a Presbyterian setting.

John Calvin's Educational Formation

John Calvin represents for the modern Reformed mind a sort of semimagical totem—frequently noted, infrequently read. He is easily the Reformer most studied in the English-speaking world, with volumes coming forth yearly on various topics in his thought and his impact on today's world. Yet that seeming reliance on him belies the fact that of the creedal denominations that trace their heritage to Calvin, none has a creedal document that came from his pen. It seems that Calvin is important, but only at arm's length—a situation the French pastor and teacher would have preferred, given his notorious hiding of his personality in his work.

But Calvin is definitely the place to begin. His own mind stamps the Reformed tradition with the importance of schools. One of his favorite metaphors for the church was the *schola dei*—the school of God. Having been a successful student, he wished to create more students. In our delving into his thoughts on education, it will be most helpful if we first grasp the outlines of Calvin's own educational journeys. Having set that out, we then can turn to Calvin's mature mind and his orientation toward the various sciences of his own day. Finally, we have the opportunity, through the early days of the Genevan Academy, to see what Calvin felt was necessary to teach.

Calvin's Education

Calvin's education prior to his entering the University of Paris must remain largely a mystery to us. We know that he received a better education than most, due to his connection to a local family of the nobility, the de Hangest family.[2] Through the influence of the de Hangest family, Calvin received both a good early schooling and benefices to support his further education.[3]

Calvin left his home in Noyon for the University of Paris in 1523. Here, the picture becomes clearer. Though he stepped into a theological cauldron,[4] his educational influences must remain our topic. He came under the direction of one of the foremost Latinists of the day, one Mathurin Cordier. This was during his brief stay at the Collège de la Marche, from August until late in the year.[5] It was this early tutelage that gained Calvin his excellent Latin style.[6] Calvin was quickly transferred from the Collège de la Marche to the Collège de Montaigu. Erasmus had called this institution "Vinegar College."[7] Whatever the reputation of the college, its emphases in education are fairly well known. The college had been reformed by Jean Standonck on the model of piety of the *devotio moderna*.[8] Thus, if conditions from the turn of the century still applied when Calvin attended, he would have been formed in a model of piety that emphasized meditation, examination of the conscience, frequent communion, and fraternal admonitions. The required reading would have leaned on the devotional classic by Thomas à Kempis—*The Imitation of Christ*—and Scripture in general, with a particular emphasis on Paul.[9]

In the *Imitation*, Calvin would have read these words:

> All perfection in this life is accompanied by a measure of imperfection, and all our knowledge contains an element of obscurity. A humble knowledge of oneself is a surer road to God than a deep search of the sciences. Yet learning itself is not to be blamed, nor is the simple knowledge of anything whatsoever to be despised, for true learning is good in itself and ordained by God; but a good conscience and a holy life are always to be preferred.[10]

A clearer ideal for the *devotio moderna* and its relationship to academic learning can hardly be imagined. The movement was not anti-intellectual, but it was clear about the priority that piety held over pure academic learning. This would have been the kind of ethos in which Calvin would have been steeped at the impressionable age of fourteen to eighteen.[11]

But what of Calvin's curriculum? As a young candidate for the licentiate in arts, Calvin would have studied the "arts," which is to say, logic, metaphysics, ethics, the sciences, and rhetoric. Theology was reserved for higher-level students, though of course there would have been a strong religious component in the content of his courses.[12]

In 1528, Calvin's education took a new road. Calvin's father, embroiled in a financial-legal dispute with the canons of the cathedral chapter at Noyon, directed his son away from the studies for theology, and toward law.[13] Calvin went to study law at Orléans, where the famous jurist Pierre de l'Estoile taught. De l'Estoile was to have a profound impact on Calvin. His teaching was not of the new humanist variety. But his personal piety was deep, and he was characterized as a man of integrity, religious and scrupulous.[14] This choice of school had the happy coincidence of providing Calvin with the opportunity of meeting and studying with Melchior Wolmar. It was Wolmar who taught Calvin Greek, as Calvin acknowledges in his dedication to the commentary on 2 Corinthians.

Calvin did not remain long at Orleans. Though he was always fond of de l'Estoile, and would later write in his defense, Calvin and some friends left Orléans in the spring of 1529 to go to Bourges. It seems likely that Calvin would only have switched to the rival school in order to study with the brilliant Italian jurist (and rival of de l'Estoile), Andrea Alciati.[15] It is argued that it is here that Calvin becomes fully immersed in the new humanism.[16] Previously, the old methods of scholastics, and the ideals of careful categorization and ever-more-precise classification, had been his daily companions. Now, his style would betray the philological and rhetorical manner that would mark his thought to the end of his career.

From Bourges, Calvin returned to Paris in 1531. He was not to return to the Collège de Montaigu, but instead would study at the Collège Royal. Here,

Calvin would have had the nascent humanism from Alciati strengthened by constant study of the works of Erasmus and Lefèvre, and nourished by continual contact with the leading lights of the humanist movement.[17] Though there is not evidence to see him converting to Lutheranism at this time,[18] it makes sense that this would have been the period of crystallization of Calvin's conversion to humanism. He was surrounded by leading lights of the movement, and began his own literary work in a typical humanistic genre, a commentary on a classical Roman philosopher.[19]

Calvin's Humanism

We are unable to know fully where Calvin took the impression of humanism. There are gaps in his educational odyssey, and he is rather distinctively silent on some of these matters. What we can know with a great deal of certitude is that by April of 1532, Calvin had completed a commentary on Seneca's *De Clementia* that revealed all the marks of the humanist scholar he had become. François Wendel comments that

> Everything, even including the limitations of his knowledge, betrays the previous humanist in Calvin. His erudition was immense, but all within the domains that the humanists had made their own—political, ecclesiastical and literary history, philology, exegesis, law and philosophy. He seems never to have been seriously interested in physical or natural sciences nor in mathematics.[20]

Calvin had become a humanist, but of what sort?[21] To delve into that more deeply, we must consider briefly his commentary on Seneca's *De Clementia*.

Calvin published the commentary in Paris in April of 1532. As it is not our task to set out Calvin's thought, but rather his education, we shall concentrate on what this text signals to us concerning that. To begin, we see a scholar who though young (Calvin would have been twenty-three), has immersed himself in the classics. Calvin shows a firm grasp of both the Greek and Roman classics, as well as Augustine, especially *The City of God*.[22] Calvin is well versed in Scripture, especially the Pauline sources, and Ganoczy notes that it demonstrates a certain Erasmian moralism.[23]

We can conclude the consideration of Calvin's education now. We have seen that through chance or providence, Calvin moved from a traditional education toward the newer humanism. He specialized in the classical languages and could read Latin, Greek, and Hebrew. Classical politics, the law, and exegesis were his specialties. History and philology would have been strong secondary interests. What we do not see is a strong interest in theology—quite simply because it is not there to be seen.[24] Calvin prepared himself, especially after his father's excommunication, to be not a priest, but a scholar. That this education served him well is a tribute to the enormous facility of Calvin's mind, and the overall rigor of the university baccalaureate education, which, though not theological, bore the marks of preparing candidates finally to study the queen of the sciences, which was theology.

Calvin as Educator

What influences beyond his own education were important in Calvin's understanding of the task of education? What did he believe was significant in the training of the Christian mind? For this must finally be our goal—to understand not only the formation of Calvin's own education, but the mature mind's set of beliefs about the education important for students to have. This we propose to set out in three ways. First, to consider the educational models Calvin could and did know. Second, to consider what he has written about the educational enterprise in his *Institutes* and other writings. Finally, we have, as it were, a laboratory experiment—Calvin's own academy, the Academy of Geneva, established through his efforts.

Calvin's Educational Models

The first educational model Calvin would have seen, of course, was that of the University of Paris, especially the Collège de Montaigu. As noted above, this was a model that preferred piety to educational hubris, while maintaining a meditative and self-examining conscience. There was no lack of rigor, but its aim was piety.

Calvin's second model comes from his legal training. Now the pietistic emphasis would not have held pride of place; the emphasis was rather on a more academic style and accomplishment. The curriculum was exegetically based, with a strong accent on the ability to understand the classical texts and apply their lessons to present contexts.

In his second Paris sojourn, Calvin moves fully into the humanist realm. His curriculum was the Latin and Greek classics, but he also chose to immerse himself in that classic above all others, the Scripture. Calvin certainly would have been encouraged by Danès and Vatable, two of his teachers, to read the Scripture,[25] and his work on the soul, written in this period though published much later, signals an extraordinary erudition in Bible for a nontheologian.[26]

Before leaving Calvin's educational models, one more must be considered, one in which Calvin himself would not have been a student. During Calvin's stay in Strasbourg, from 1538 to 1541, he would have come in contact with perhaps the greatest educator of his day, Jean Sturm. Sturm had managed to open his school only in 1538,[27] but it was a model of the humanist's educational ideal at that time. Sturm, who placed great emphasis on languages, and the curriculum depended on knowledge of Latin and Greek, divided the schools into a preparatory school for those under age six, a gymnasium for the next nine years, and a five-year high school. The curriculum had as staples reading of the classics and training in morals and religion.[28] Many of these patterns would be emulated in the Genevan Academy.

Calvin's Writings

Calvin never wrote a treatise on education. Several of his writings, however, contain either asides or otherwise trenchant observations on the method and goal of education. The first that is worth our consideration must come from the beginning of the *Institutes* itself. Men and women must be educated in order that they not wander to and fro in the wilderness of the Scriptures.[29] This task will fall most heavily on those to whom God has given greater light,[30] but all will have the task of learning.

In the *Articles Concerning the Organization of the Church*, of 1537, Calvin gives two more fascinating asides on education for the church. The first has to do with congregational singing, where he suggests that children should practice the congregational psalms, and then sing them loudly and distinctly, so that the people may listen and then sing heartily, so that all may become accustomed to singing communally.[31] In much the same manner, he suggests that the best way to address the lack of doctrinal knowledge among the people is a program of catechism for the children, overseen by both pastors and parents.[32] Here we see the practical educator, attempting to leaven the whole lump of a society with the education of a particular (presumably moldable) class.

Finally, it is important that we understand that while Calvin preferred piety to human wisdom, he did not denigrate human knowledge completely. In the 1539 edition of the *Institutes*, Calvin included a paean to the human intellect's ability in "earthly things." While being careful to preclude the possibility of humans reaching God by the powers of unaided reason, Calvin noted the extraordinary powers of the human mind in government, household management, mechanical skills, and the liberal arts.[33] This section is not brief, but goes into detail regarding several of the human arts. Again and again, Calvin forces his reader to agree that the source of these marvelous gifts is the Lord. But just as surely, in his high praise and recognition of the human arts, Calvin sets them out as appropriate areas for study, for the preservation of the good society.

The Genevan Academy

In the Genevan Academy, we have our strongest evidence for what Calvin felt was important in education. Though it was only in 1558 that the Academy began to offer classes,[34] Calvin had certainly envisioned some kind of school in Geneva since the publication of his Ecclesiastical Ordinances in 1541. Under the second order of office for the church, Calvin wrote of the doctors that this was the "order of the schools."[35] Calvin considers the necessity of having lecturers in both Old and New Testament, at first making it seem that this order will be wholly concerned only with the teaching of pastors. But he then writes:

> But because it is only possible to profit from such lectures if first one is instructed in the languages and humanities, and also because it is necessary to raise offspring for time to come, in order not to leave the Church deserted to our children, a college should be instituted for instructing children, to prepare them for ministry as well as civil government.[36]

Clearly, Calvin had in mind a school that was broader than a seminary. Just as clearly, he felt that this was a necessary component in a godly nation. The first justification for the school is the necessity of understanding the Scriptures.[37] For our purposes, it is important to note that Calvin approaches the necessary task of understanding the Scripture with the characteristic ideals of the humanist—one cannot understand the Scriptures without languages and humanities. Calvin immediately moves beyond the reading of Scripture, however, to the instruction of children for the needs of the society.

But how was the school actually organized? The Genevan Academy consisted of two parts, following the later division of Sturm's Latin school in Strassburg. The lower-level school, which offered seven classes, was termed the *schola privata*, the upper-level school the *schola publica*. Together, they [formed] the Genevan Academy.[38] The *schola privata* offered the basic educa[tion] was education in grammar, writing, the beginnings of rhetoric, math[ematics] and Latin. Its curriculum would vary according to the talents of the [teachers] who were available to teach in it, but the classical liberal arts would [be] in its overall goal. The *schola publica*'s curriculum is clearer, as it was [set in] the statutes of the Academy. The school generally offered Hebrew, [th]eology, and philosophy.[39] After Calvin's death, courses in law and [medicine] were added.[40]

[What c]omes out of a study of the foundations of the Genevan Academy was [emphas]is on an excellent education, but not for its own sake. Instead, the [go]al [th]at of "goal-oriented training" for the formation of men who would [c]orrectly ordered society in both ministerial and civil posts.[41] Calvin, [and m]ore Beza after him, were interested in the best possible education. [But] not push this too far—education was always to be the servant of [rema]ining true to his early formation in the style of the Brethren of the [l]ife at the Collège de Montaigu, which was only bolstered by his time in Strassburg watching Jean Sturm's setting out of the Latin School, Calvin eschewed some of his own formation.[42]

Having sketched Calvin's own educational formation, and reviewed the principles that seem to have directed his own pedagogical project, what is useful to say about Calvin's views on education? First, we must grant that Calvin placed an exceptionally high value on education for the Christian. His ideal of the church as a *schola dei* was not idle prattle, but a conviction that the Christian life is one of learning, and that learning included the academic sense of training the mind. Second, it is important to register the fact that Calvin accepted the style of humanism, and its dependence on contextual examination of sources—hence his insistence on biblical languages in the Genevan Academy. Calvin envisioned broadly trained minds, formed in both the Scripture and the classics, which would serve God's kingdom in both the magistracy and the ministry. Finally, we must record Calvin's negative judgments, to avoid a too-facile picture of Calvin as supporting all educational enterprises. Calvin effectively denied legal and medical training in Geneva. These specialties, one of which he had studied and the other of which kept him alive, were not part of his image of education for the Christian society. That this may raise problems for later generations may be true, but its truth is undeniable. In this, we see Calvin's narrow circumscription of the educational enterprise to the service of God's kingdom.

II. REFORMED EDUCATION SPREADS INTO GREAT BRITAIN AND AMERICA

Calvin's special concern for education was shared by his Reformed colleagues on the Continent and in the British Isles. Other leaders of the Continental Reformation also appropriated much of the system of education that had emerged during the Renaissance, only to make application of it in a far more extensive context.[43] Their emphasis on the authority of Scripture led directly to an insistence that there be both a learned clergy to proclaim God's Word and a literate laity to read and hear it. "An almost equally patent association of early Protestantism was with renaissance humanism, so much so indeed that we may question whether the Protestant Reformation could have been accomplished without the preceding effects of the revival of learning."[44] The ideal of universal education did not become actual in most instances, but a gradual expansion of access to education, both at the elementary and higher level, was accomplished in many Protestant areas.

In virtually every setting, though, the basic medieval curriculum remained essentially unchanged. The venerable *trivium* (grammar, logic, and rhetoric) and *quadrivium* (mathematics, geometry, astronomy, and music) were the standard; additional topics of study, including professional training in theology, law, and medicine, were added in different times and manners. At Geneva for example, "The educational foundation was in the classics, and . . . theological studies came as a superstructure erected upon the classical foundation."[45] The spread of the Reformation into England and the eventual emergence of Puritanism had special significance, of course, for the eventual shape of American higher education. One of the major ways in which the Puritan movement gained its purchase on seventeenth-century English life was its accession to influence at Cambridge and Oxford. The academic and intellectual qualifications of Puritans, both clergy and lay, were notable expressions of their efforts to define themselves over against their Anglican adversaries.

In the American colonies during the Puritan era, the appeal to the academic example of old England by inhabitants of the new was direct and predictable. Harvard College was intended by its founders to replicate Emmanuel College, Cambridge; and the subsequent colonial efforts at higher education were similarly retrospective: "nine home-grown variations on a theme known in the mother country as Oxford and Cambridge."[46] The word "variations" deserves special emphasis, though, because there were other influences on the colonial colleges in addition to the two great British universities. The political failure of the Puritan experiment in England elicited a variety of educational developments within the British Isles following the 1660s, which were to have substantial impact on the colonial scene. Following the Restoration of the Stuart monarchy, restrictions placed on participation by Dissenters in public life in England and the Ulster plantations brought an efflorescence of so-called "academies," usually presided over by former university teachers who had been banished from their positions.[47] At almost the same time, the Scottish universities began to emerge from the shadows cast by Oxford and Cambridge, which had lapsed with the Restoration into a period of stagnation and resistance to change. By that time, the Scottish universities had already begun to develop some of the distinctive characteristics that would establish them in the next century as the focal points of the famous Scottish Enlightenment.[48]

Great Britain: Dissenting Academies and Scottish Universities

Dissenting academies emerged in England after 1662 with innovative approaches to the traditional enterprise of educating the young. Some of the inspiration for these innovations may have come from a predictable reaction against a university system in which the dissenting tutors could no longer participate; change may have also been caused, as Ashley Smith suggests, from a

Calvinist perception that the pervasiveness of human depravity militates against perfection in any system—especially a curriculum![49] Whatever the cause, experimentation was quite frequently the order of the day. In varying degrees in these independent academies—each typically presided over by a single scholar—the tutors explored new subjects and new ways of addressing traditional elements of the curriculum. For example, it was in the academies that the study of English language and literature, other modern languages, modern history, and modern political theory were first included as topics of instruction. The academies also pioneered in the use of the experimental approach in the teaching of the sciences, and in the expanded use of new pedagogical techniques, such as the custom of free discussion and the employment of the vernacular in virtually all instruction.[50] The academies established by Scottish émigrés in Ulster were quite similar to their British counterparts, except for the fact that they maintained strong ties to the Scottish church and Scottish universities as they conducted their schools in an alien setting.[51]

For their part, the Scottish universities were enjoying an era of success that could have been no more than a dream for John Knox and his colleagues when they wrote a plan for the national system of education into the *First Book of Discipline*. As the English universities went into relative eclipse, the Scottish universities—especially the "new colleges" at Aberdeen and Edinburgh, which exhibited remarkable similarities to the academies—gained distinction as centers of curricular change and the use of new teaching methods.[52] Both in the universities in Scotland and in the academies of England and Ulster, the incentive for adequate preparation of clergy was a primary raison d'être. In Scotland, there was a lively theological dispute between the so-called "Moderate" party, which warmly embraced both Enlightenment ideals and political patronage, and the "Popular" or "Evangelical" party, which favored a more traditional approach to religion and a more democratic approach to governmental prerogatives. The universities served as the arena in which this continuing controversy was engaged, and produced leadership for both of the contending parties.[53] In England and Ulster, the academies provided the only appropriate alternative for conscientious dissenters who were preparing for the ministry or, for that matter, for other vocations in Anglican-dominated society. In addition, there were many instances in which young men from families within the established church turned to the academies or to the Scottish universities because of the relative superiority of the educational opportunities there.[54]

In a word, there was far more diversity of academic activity in the British Isles during the time of American colonization than had been the case in recent memory, and most of it was to be found within the context of Reformed Protestantism. The relative applicability of those developments and innovations in the institutions of the New World varied with changing times and local circumstances. In addition, after the establishment of Harvard, many of those potential changes were mediated through possible contacts with institutions and personalities on the colonial side of the Atlantic. Thus, while each new "American" college derived a portion of its special identity from trans-Atlantic models, it was often influenced by colonial patterns as well. Each new school in the colonies was established under different circumstances and for different reasons. These particularities bred an early diversity, which was later amplified in the subsequent development of postcolonial institutions.

Early Efforts in Colonial America

The founding of Harvard College by Congregationalist Puritans in Massachusetts in 1636 was the first of nine successful efforts to establish institutions of higher learning in the British colonies in North America prior to the outbreak of the Revolutionary War.[55] The establishment of the College of New Jersey (first informally and later formally known as Princeton) was the first direct entry of American Presbyterians into the enterprise of college founding. If it be proper to acknowledge that "education in colonial America was the child of religion,"[56] it is equally accurate to assert that the College of New Jersey "was the institutional expression of ideas and forces that were suddenly released by the Great Awakening,"[57] at least in its Presbyterian manifestation.

The remarkable season of spiritual revival known as the Great Awakening, which touched all the American colonies in the period from the late 1720s to the early 1740s, had a profound if divisive impact on the Reformed tradition in the New World. The revival drove the clergy of the denomination into two increasingly antagonistic parties.[58] The more conservative of the two parties, which came to be called the Old Side, was averse to the revival movement and zealous for explicit and rather narrow subscription to the Westminster Standards by all clergy within the denomination. Most of the ministers on the Old Side were "Scotch-Irish" Presbyterians, who had come to the colonies from Scotland via the Ulster plantations of Ireland. The other party, the New Side (sometimes called New Light), was favorable to the revival and emphasized the importance of individual testimony to personal religious experience over rigid conformity to doctrinal standards. Some of the members of the New Side were second- and third-generation descendents of English Presbyterian Puritans who had come to New York and New Jersey; others were younger Scotch-Irish Presbyterians whose own lives had been personally touched by the Awakening.

In particular, the revival among Presbyterians had been spearheaded by a group of young pastors who had received their ministerial training under the tutelage of William Tennent, a graduate of the University of Edinburgh who had come to the colonies from Ireland and been admitted to the Presbyterian ministry in 1718. After serving pastorates among descendants of English Puritan Presbyterians in New York, he had moved to Neshaminy, Pennsylvania, where he began a small but influential academy for the training of ministers, which came to be known as the Log College. In most respects, Tennent's school was a replication of the academies of England and Ulster.[59] Despite limited facilities and resources, over the space of the few years following 1735 he trained about twenty men for ministry (including his four sons), most of whom were active in the revival efforts of the Great Awakening. Alarmed by their effectiveness in the revival (and perhaps their popularity), the ministers of the Old Side undertook to stem the tide of Log College ministers by adopting a resolution in 1738 stipulating that all candidates for ordination be required to submit credentials from a New England or European college, or complete a special examination. It was their allegation that the "graduates" of the Log College—and by implication those from other academies scattered through the middle colonies—were deficient in "physicks, ethicks, metaphysicks, and pnewmaticks"; in other words, some of the aspects of a liberal education.[60] For their part, the New Lights asserted that the ministers of the Old Side were merely "Pharisee Teachers" who had no genuine experience of the saving faith of Christianity.[61]

Eventually a breach came between the two parties, and there were two separate Presbyterian denominations in the American colonies. It was during this period of separation, which lasted from 1741 to 1758, that the New Side group undertook to obtain a colonial charter for the establishment of a college in the middle colonies, preferably in New Jersey. They took this step for some or all of the following reasons: "to discredit charges of their indifference to learning,"[62] to make a bid for "cultural respectability,"[63] and/or to provide an adequate source of trained ministers sympathetic to the revival cause.[64] The stated rationale for this "College of New Jersey," as it came to be called, was quite clear in the thinking of Jonathan Dickinson, the founding president: "The great & chief design of erecting the College is for the Education of pious and well qualified Candidates for the Ministry, that vital Peity [sic] may by that means be promoted in our Churches, and . . . Religion may be transmitted to Posterity."[65]

Although its beginnings were hardly auspicious—temporary venues in Elizabeth[town] and Newark before settling in the village of Princeton, *and* the first five presidents (including Jonathan Edwards) in their graves before the school had ended its second decade of operation—Princeton exhibited remarkable resilience, all things considered, and emerged from the Revolutionary period as one of the new nation's best-known and respected institutions. The key figure in this success was John Witherspoon, who arrived from Scotland to become the college president in 1768. Witherspoon is perhaps best known for his participation in the cause of freedom from Great Britain. The only clergyman to sign the Declaration of Independence, he had become in the space of a few years the quintessential patriot, esteemed by an admiring biographer as one possessed of "more of the quality called *presence*—a quality powerfully felt, but not to be described—than any other individual . . . Washington alone excepted."[66]

With respect to his contribution at Princeton, Witherspoon's record is complex but crucial. In the first place, his arrival elicited a measure of rapprochement between the parties of Presbyterianism, which had grudgingly reunited into a single church in 1758, but continued to murmur against each other.[67] Witherspoon, who had not been involved in the controversy surrounding the Great Awakening and had been a leader of the Conservative or Popular party in the Scottish religious conversations, soon became the most prominent leader in the American Presbyterian community. Especially as the mind of the public turned to the more urgent political matters at hand, he was viewed as a peacemaker, acceptable to all sides of the previous conflict.

This fact is all the more significant because it became quite clear during his tenure that the original mission of the college was beginning to shift. Perhaps there was already some subtle intimation of the change in the statement that had earlier been adopted by the trustees of the college: "Though our great intention was to erect a seminary for educating ministers of the Gospel, yet we hope it will be a means of raising up men that will be useful in other learned professions—ornaments of the State as well as the Church."[68] In any event, there was a change in vocational aspirations among the young men who came to the college. "If, during the first two decades of the college, religion held the dominant place in the minds and hearts of the students, in the next ten years patriotism became a strong rival."[69] John Witherspoon, lately of Scotland, was the epitome of that change; the preparation of leaders for the new nation was to be a major theme of his tenure at Princeton.

This shift of focus was not unrelated to the academic changes effected by Witherspoon during his presidency. "He gave attention to improving teaching methods and materials and to raising academic standards; he broadened and enriched the curriculum; and he brought to his students the stimulus of his own vigorous mind and personality."[70] More profoundly, though, Witherspoon's mind was the vehicle for the transmission of Scottish Common Sense Realism to Princeton. Princeton eventually conveyed these ideas to the rank and file of American higher education, and Common Sense Realism became the philosophical *leitmotiv* of the period of the nation's greatest growth. "Intellectually, culturally, and politically, Witherspoon helped to give new content

to the educational goals of the college. He provided a way for the Presbyterian college to come to terms with the Enlightenment; he transformed the ideal
images of the minister, the public servant, and the man of learning; and he
politicized the college in a new way."[71]

Witherspoon understood the Common Sense philosophy to be the basis for
all kinds of learning, and in his "capstone" course in moral philosophy, he
sought to "shape from the embryonic social sciences—anthropology, economics, psychology, sociology—an integrated system of public and private
ethics."[72] At the same time, he seemed to use both his teaching and his administrative authority quite consciously to displace the sort of idealism that had
been implicit in the intellectual patterns associated with his presidential pre-
decessor, Jonathan Edwards.[73] During much of this era of change, Witherspoon was in one way or another an "absentee landlord," absorbed in duties
of church and state in the earlier years, debilitated by blindness and other infir-
mities toward the end of his life. Indeed, Mark Noll's recent analysis argues
persuasively that much of his "achievement was personal and temporary rather
than intellectual and lasting."[74]

Noll maintains, further, that the full articulation of Witherspoon's vision
depended on his son-in-law and successor, Samuel Stanhope Smith, who had
both the time and the intellectual capacity to prosecute Witherspoon's ideas
to their logical conclusions. Smith, who was neither personally winsome nor
ultimately considered to be successful,[75] was notwithstanding "among the first
Americans to develop principles of the Scottish philosophy of common sense
into an entire educational vision and to employ them for resolving knotty
problems at the intersection of science and religion."[76] A member of the first
graduating class at Princeton during the Witherspoon era (1769), he returned
to his alma mater ten years later to abet the efforts of his mentor and father-
in-law, having already served as the founding president of Hampden-Sydney
College in Virginia. Smith remained at Princeton in a variety of positions for
the next thirty-three years, the last seventeen as president. Adopting the major
themes of Witherspoon's approach, he endeavored to bond the rationalism of
the Enlightenment to Calvinist doctrine, "under the canopy of republican
patriotism."[77]

Of particular significance to the present study is the fact that the Princeton
of the Witherspoon-Smith generation was the parent of many colleges—ten,
by the most conservative estimate[78]—and a strong if indirect influence on
many more. Despite the difficult circumstances of the latter years of his presidency, Stanhope Smith represented and embodied to a considerable degree
the ideas and structures that the first of the Presbyterian colleges conveyed to
many others, founded by representatives of the denomination in the Revolutionary and post-Revolutionary years.

The other colonial colleges also enjoyed their spheres of influence, and had significant impact on specific regional and denominational efforts to extend the scope of collegiate education in the new nation. In particular, Yale College was later to have a substantial significance in the future of Presbyterian higher education. The majority of the founders of Princeton had Yale connections, and it was only after Witherspoon's arrival that the influence of Yale—in matters of curriculum, structure, and leadership, as well as other things—slipped from centrality in Princeton's life. Then later, at the turn of the century, the establishment of a Plan of Union between the Presbyterian Church and the Congregationalist Association of Connecticut brought Yale again into connection with a number of Presbyterian efforts to found colleges, especially in the western territories of the nation. The famous "Yale Report of 1828," which is said to have been "the most influential document in American higher education in the first half of the nineteenth century," provided encouragement to most church-related schools to persist in the traditional classical college curriculum well beyond the American Civil War.[79] Indeed, there was a period leading up to the middle of the nineteenth century in which the academic ideas and structures of Yale would be more influential than those of Princeton, even in several schools that were to retain strong ties to the Presbyterian Church.[80] When the western expansion of the nation began in earnest, the "Yale Band," a group of able and dedicated young graduates who perceived their calling as the conversion of the newly settled areas of the country, worked with unparalleled diligence and skill to found colleges there. Even the eventual demise of the Plan of Union in the years following 1837 did not bring an end to some measure of denominational cooperation between Presbyterians (New School) and Congregationalists. Under joint or independent auspices, however, the generations of the Reformed tradition continued to perceive the responsibility to found colleges as a major and distinctive part of their mission.

Conclusion

After such a brief overview of Calvin and the foundational traditions of Presbyterian higher education, what conclusions can be reached? First, it is obvious that in some points the academies and universities followed Geneva and Calvin fairly closely. Just as clearly, in some aspects the later tradition transformed the foundational trajectory.

Considering continuities, we see the continuing high value on education for the Christian society. The dissenting academies, the Scottish universities, and the early American colleges all accepted as part of their raison d'être the necessity of a learned clergy and a learned laity. Academies and colleges were

founded for the training of ministers and those who would attempt to understand those ministers. The parallels with the foundation of the Genevan Academy are too obvious to be ignored in the Presbyterian educational enterprise.
Moreover, the classical humanistic education, which was the focus of the early
efforts of Calvin and his successors, seems well represented in later educational efforts, though the best methods of achieving those aims did change
with the later innovations. Presbyterians absolutely accepted the necessity of
schools, founding them wherever they went, under whatever circumstances
they discovered.

But if there is a significant sense of continuity within the early foundational
periods of Presbyterian higher education, there are significant transformations
as well. The importance of the Scottish Common Sense Realism, mediated
through Witherspoon and Smith at Princeton, gave a broadening emphasis to
Presbyterian higher education. If it had ever been wholly about the training
of men for the ministry, the winds of change opened Presbyterian centers of
learning to new visions of the ideal college, which were no longer so narrowly
circumscribed. No longer could the academies state that they were about the
preparation of minister and magistrate. Instead, a model of education that balanced the needs of the sciences and those of religion was entering into the
Presbyterian mainstream by 1800, and this new model, as it opened new possibilities for study, transformed the Presbyterian educational enterprise.

SECTION 2

The Context of Teaching: Engagement

Now every year his parents went to Jerusalem for the festival of the Passover. And when he was twelve years old, they went up as usual for the festival. When the festival was ended and they started to return, the boy Jesus stayed behind in Jerusalem, but his parents did not know it. Assuming that he was in the group of travelers, they went a day's journey. Then they started to look for him among their relatives and friends. When they did not find him, they returned to Jerusalem to search for him. After three days they found him in the temple, sitting among the teachers, listening to them and asking them questions. And all who heard him were amazed at his understanding and his answers.

—Luke 2:41–47

5

The American Presbyterian College

WILLIAM WESTON AND DALE SODEN

A BRIEF HISTORICAL BACKGROUND

The Presbyterian emphasis on education is rooted in the basic Protestant doctrine of the priesthood of all believers. Believers must be educated, first and foremost in Scripture. This requires a broad base of literacy and widespread instruction in the Bible. Preachers of the Word needed to know the original languages of Scripture, and Calvin, good humanist that he was, thought a broad knowledge of languages and classical literature was a great aid to Christian understanding for clergy and lay people. All of this required an almost unprecedented investment in education. It required common schools for the masses, of which the Scottish were the great model in Euro-American civilization. It also required colleges for the elders, lay and clerical, and further seminaries for the clergy. Thus Presbyterians created schools at all levels early and often, and wherever they were needed.

John Calvin laid out a theory for Reformed education. In the "Draft Ecclesiastical Ordinances" of 1541, he identified four divinely ordained offices for church government. In addition to the familiar pastors, elders, and deacons, he added, in second place, the order of "doctors." The doctors' job is to instruct the faithful in pure doctrine, to prevent the corruption of the gospel by ignorance or evil opinions. He called the doctors "the order of the schools." For such schools he specifically called for lecturers in theology, in Old Testament, and in New Testament. He thought that students needed to learn languages and humanities in order to profit from theological instruction. The school was not a branch of the church, but a separate order, equal in dignity to church and state, each of which were to check and balance one another. All in the school, though, were subject to ecclesiastical discipline. Schools are needed, "because it is necessary to raise offspring for time to come, in order not to leave the Church deserted to our children, [so] a college should be instituted for instructing children to prepare them for the ministry as well as for civil government."[1]

Almost two decades later, Calvin actually created schools, the only new buildings he erected in Geneva. Schooling was compulsory and free, paid for by confiscations from opponents of the Reformation.[2] The college (high school) was all classics, with Greek New Testament on Saturdays, surrounded by much praying. The academy (college) had professors of Greek, Hebrew, the arts, and theology. Everyone had to subscribe to an orthodox Calvinist creed each year, and was discouraged from impudent questioning of it. Calvin was not against science, but science and history were not included in the curriculum because humanists (though not theologians) thought them unnecessary to understanding theology and Christian life. The school's motto was *Post tenebras lux*.[3]

The *First Book of Discipline* of the reformed Church of Scotland (1560) says that schooling is necessary because the age of instructive miracles is finished. The church had previously only concerned itself with schooling for those who could not afford it. The reformed church, looking to the systematic transformation of the entire society, positively required the rich to educate their children as well. In addition to lower schools, colleges were founded as an integral part of the mission of the church. In contrast to the Lutheran stream of the Reformation, the humanism of the Calvinists also promoted classical literary education. The later Scottish Enlightenment emphasized the importance of education for the liberty of all, which made mass education an integral part of the ruling-class mission, as well as that of the church.[4]

The Scottish model did much to shape the American college ideal. Americans in the Augustinian and Reformed lines did not set head and heart in opposition to one another: as Jonathan Edwards wrote, "There can be no spiritual knowledge of that of which there is not first a rational knowledge."[5] Among Presbyterians, both the Old Side and the revivalist New Side were proeducation. The New Side promoted schooling for everyone out of educational egalitarianism, just as they preached to the uneducated masses out of religious egalitarianism. These schools offered general education for citizenship, not just for the Presbyterian ministry. In fact, only about half of the colonial Reformed academies' students headed to the ministry. Presbyterians founded many academies, which kept the Calvinist classical curriculum and Bible study, to which was added the Scottish Common Sense philosophy. While the Common Sense philosophy became associated with a very conservative Presbyterianism in the twentieth century, previously it had been a uniting element across the many competing ideological factions of the church.

American Presbyterians were zealous for an educated ministry. One fourth of the colleges founded in this country prior to the Civil War (49 out of 207) were begun by Presbyterians, more than any other denomination. William Tennent's Log College, in Neshaminy, Pennsylvania, established for Great Awakening (New Side) revivalist ministers, laid the foundation for Princeton, the "mother of colleges" for Presbyterians. Subsequent foundings followed the frontier westward. Many colleges were created as a result of schisms, with each branch wanting its own school. During the Plan of Union between the Presbyterian and Congregational churches (1801–37), no Presbyterian colleges were started in New England, and most of those planted in the upper Midwest were kept by the Congregationalists when the Plan of Union dissolved.[6]

The Presbyterian policy of requiring a highly educated ministry, and of appealing to the educated classes in general, has cost the church the masses in competition with more popular denominations, especially on the frontier. Yet, in the long run, Presbyterians have been able to effect greater stewardship of society—to take another distinctive Presbyterian emphasis—through the educated minority.[7] Even today, when just over 6 percent of the American population call themselves Presbyterians, nearly 11 percent of college graduates identify with the Presbyterian Church.[8]

These Presbyterian colleges were not, by and large, great centers of Christian learning. There was no golden age of Presbyterian higher education in the past. Nineteenth-century colleges "were small, usually elitist, racist, and sexist, with mediocre standards and strict regulation of students' lives."[9] In the fundamentalist/modernist controversy of the 1920s, the northern Presbyterian church (PCUSA) tried to raise the Christian educational standards for its colleges. The denomination wanted the faculty to be professing Christians and members of some evangelical church, with Bible taught in the regular curriculum by a full faculty member. Regular worship services were expected, and a "positive Christian point of view in the teaching of all subjects" should be laid down in the curriculum. The supreme end of this education was the "development and culture of Christian character."[10] No specific doctrinal requirements were laid down, relying on "evangelical" church membership and general evangelical culture to keep the college's Christianity substantive.

Northern Presbyterian colleges drifted leftward in the 1920s, liberalizing the interpretation of all these standards. In the southern Presbyterian church (PCUS) the colleges were more traditionally orthodox, but they, like the northern colleges, followed a liberalizing pattern, with a small time lag. This

led to an identity crisis in the 1940s, and the movement against racial restrictions in the 1950s contributed to a rejection of all restrictions and religious
distinctives in the 1960s. In 1963, the northern church dropped most specifically Christian standards for its colleges, and had ceded almost all control by
the late '60s. The southern church, in effect, did the same, though it did not
formally complete that movement until the 1980s.[11]

In the twentieth century, half of the Presbyterian Church's colleges would
greatly attenuate their church ties, or lose them altogether. This was not
mainly the result of a deliberate secular conspiracy, but mostly the unintended
result of other cultural changes.[12] At the beginning of the century the old curriculum, which aimed at cultivating classical and biblical learning, was dis-
placed by a new curriculum. This new curriculum based on specialized
disciplines, aimed to *create* knowledge. The new curriculum was not a deliberate move to drive out Christianity, but rather was an attempt to profession-
alize the new "disciplines." The American colleges, starting with the Johns
Hopkins University, were here following the model of the German research
universities. The unintended, but real, consequence was that the curriculum
had less and less place for Christian teaching.[13] Likewise, the movement in the
1960s to reduce religious requirements came from liberal church people who
believed that accommodating secular society was truly Christian. Today, any
religious requirements in faculty hiring stigmatize a college in the academic
market. The consequence is that once hiring is religion-blind, "then it seems
only a matter of time until the majority of the faculty will be more loyal to their
profession than to the institution and will vote to drop any residual loyalties
to the institution's religious heritage."[14]

The official statements of the church on higher education show this atten-
uation of a distinctive vision for Presbyterian colleges over the twentieth century. In 1899, the southern church's General Assembly took this forthrightly
Presbyterian and competitive position:

> The General Assembly does not consider it safe for any Church to
> turn over to any other parties, either religious or civil, the entire edu-
> cation of her sons and daughters. The history and traditions of the
> Presbyterian Church in this and other countries amply prove that
> denominational fidelity in this and other matters has not only secured
> the best results for our Church, but has accomplished great good by
> its influence on all others. . . . We believe that very much may be done
> along denominational lines without antagonizing any good work done
> by others.[15]

By 1981, the Presbyterian Church had a more ecumenical, less denominational vision of higher education. It proclaimed the more general educational
aim to transmit past revelation and human achievement, inculcate moral values,

and prepare students for productive and responsible involvement in social, political, and economic spheres of life. The church college must do this, though, while being, "sensitive to the needs and realities within the Academy today."[16]

PRESBYTERIAN COLLEGES TODAY

Today, nearly 70 colleges and universities have, or seek, a covenant relationship with the Presbyterian Church (U.S.A.). The Presbyterian Church (U.S.A.) categorizes their relation to the church as "historical," "dimensional," or "pervasive." Table 1 defines these categories, and shows the percentage of the Presbyterian colleges falling within each category.

Beyond the schools still in covenant with the church, there are perhaps three times that many other colleges and universities that have followed Princeton into independence and, to a greater or lesser degree, secularity. The path from pervasively Christian to secular independence is normal for Presbyterian colleges—"normal" in the sense that that is what most colleges do.

Let us consider some of the features of these three kinds of still-Presbyterian colleges. The PC(USA) Higher Education Office study included a rating of a number of features of each school, usually assessed by the chaplain. These include a measure of spiritual life, spiritual nurture, chapel, religious programming opportunities, community service, and the degree to which these religious and service programs are student led. Table 2 gives the average rates for each of these items for each category of school.

These numbers show that all forms of relation to the Presbyterian Church show some religious vitality, and the stronger the Presbyterian dimension, the greater the religious vitality.

The colleges and universities created by Presbyterians fall along a spectrum in their religious identities. At one end of the spectrum are evangelical

TABLE 1 Relation of Presbyterian Colleges and Universities to the Church

Historical	Has a written covenant with the church and speaks of its heritage, but endeavors to be nonsectarian and diverse.	45%
Dimensional	Intentionally cultivates church-relatedness, with the church being an important dimension in the life of the institution. While endeavoring to be nonsectarian and diverse, purposely sustains a vital Christian community.	45%
Pervasive	The educational mission is viewed as an extension of the Christian gospel. All areas of the institution are developed in reference to the Christian faith.	10%[17]

TABLE 2   Religious Service Programs at Presbyterian Colleges

	Spiritual Life (max. = 10)	Spiritual Nurture (max. = 10)	Attend Chapel	Take Part in Religious Program	Take Part in Community Service	Student Leader rate (max. = 5)	% of Students Presbyterian
Historical	3.8	5.4	11%	19%	24%	3.1	10%
Dimensional	6.4	6.6	10%	22%	28%	3.4	13%
Pervasive	7.3	8.0	39%	54%	33%	3.5	19%

Christian colleges; at the other are secular enlightenment universities. At all points along this spectrum, some institutions are strong and some weak, some academically oriented and some more practically inclined. The schools with the strongest Presbyterian identities are in the middle of this spectrum. They assert a distinctive Presbyterian strand against the pull of a general evangelicalism on the one side and against the pull of secular academic and commercial culture on the other side.

On what might be thought of as the left end of the spectrum are the many colleges and universities founded by Presbyterians that have, for a variety of reasons, cut all ties with the church. The best known of these is Princeton University, the mother college of Presbyterianism, now a national private and largely secular university. More common are a number of liberal arts colleges across the country. Lewis and Clark College, the most recent institution to leave the official Presbyterian fold, may stand as typical. Like Lewis and Clark in several respects, but maintaining their covenant with the Presbyterian Church, are such liberal arts colleges as Lafayette, Macalester, and Centre. They honor their Presbyterian founders, but prefer to be independent of current church obligations or religious commitments. This is an honorable position, as long as it is honestly maintained. Some of the twenty-some institutions in this historical category are likely to cut their ties with the church in the next decade, and church and college may bid one another Godspeed.

On the other side of the "dimensional" divide are such colleges as Maryville, Waynesburg, and, in a more contested way, Rhodes, which are all profiled in this volume. They all, in quite different ways, are trying to keep alive their Presbyterian and explicitly Christian tradition. They might even turn around the normal pattern of drift toward secularity. Some of the dimensional Presbyterian colleges will, no doubt, cross the line to a merely historical relation with the church in the next decade. Others, though, seek sincerely and urgently to find ways to keep a Presbyterian dimension alive within a college that accepts all kinds of students. Some of the colleges currently in the historical category will reverse the trend as well, and redevelop a distinctively Presbyterian dimension.

The Presbyterian dimension in such colleges is a real service to those students who want that kind of religious learning. The older pattern of Westminster Fellowships still serves in some places as a Christian fellowship for Presbyterian students. Some students are connected to the national church through the Presbyterian Student Strategy Team or the National Network of Presbyterian College Women. A few new programs, such as Celtic Cross at Presbyterian College and Activators at Austin College, are vital Christian organizations rooted in the specific mission of their founding colleges and partner congregations. Beyond service to a subgroup of students, the Presbyterian dimension shapes the whole ethos of the institution, in subtle as well as obvious ways. Moreover, a strong Presbyterian dimension within some of the church's colleges is a way for the college to develop leaders for the church, and thus partly repay the many sacrifices that church people have made to make the Presbyterian colleges possible.

A few Presbyterian colleges have, like Whitworth, made the step to become "Christian colleges"—that is, they require specific Christian faith and, usually, practice commitments from students and faculty. Among the pervasively Presbyterian institutions, we might lift up King College as an example: in addition to its high levels of Christian activity and participation in both the curriculum and extracurricular activities, King has the highest proportion of Presbyterians in its student body of any Presbyterian-related institution, at 45 percent.

There is one anomaly in the list that turns out to be instructive about the forces pulling on Presbyterian colleges from, as it were, the right end of the spectrum. Grove City College is an explicitly Christian college with the high levels of religious commitment and practice that that entails. Yet it is classified as only historically related to the Presbyterian Church. This classification is subjective, and not too much should be made of it, but it makes sense. Grove City, like all the formally Christian colleges in covenant with the denomination, is constantly pulled toward the broad culture of evangelical Protestantism and away from the mainline and relatively liberal Presbyterian Church (U.S.A.). To be an evangelical Protestant college without specific denominational flavor is also an honorable position, if it is honestly maintained. Few Presbyterian colleges are likely to leave the Presbyterian fold to go in that direction, but the sheer existence of that possibility shows that renewing the Presbyterian dimension cuts both ways.

The General Assembly in 1998 asked what the Presbyterian colleges were doing to promote Christian scholarship. A study of the colleges' mission statements, their course requirements, and a survey of deans about faculty hiring and research support found that nearly all the Presbyterian colleges and universities are teaching institutions first and foremost. This means that none of them emphasize scholarship—Christian or otherwise—very strongly. Most of the Presbyterian schools do support faculty scholarship in some way, but how much they support it has more to do with their financial resources than with their Christian commitment. The subject of scholarship is left up to the individual faculty members, and whatever they choose to study is supported to the limits of the college's ability. While most are glad to report whatever Christian scholarship their faculty (and sometimes their student collaborators) happened to do, few specifically promoted scholarship on Christian topics or "Christian scholarship" as a pervasive aspect of all research subjects.

The Christian intellectual commitment of the college appeared more in the curriculum required of students. All the schools in the Pervasive or Dimensional categories had clear Bible and/or Christianity course requirements as part of general education. Many of the schools in the Historical category did too, but some had no such requirements. Even among the Historical institutions with a religion requirement in the curriculum, however, there was a clear drift away from teaching Christianity and the Bible toward teaching about the Judeo-Christian heritage and general "values."

The most important factor in determining a college's promotion of Christian scholarship seems to be the institution's commitment to hiring Christian faculty. The Historical colleges, almost without exception, make it a point of pride that the religious commitment of the faculty plays no role in hiring or promotion. They view this as a commitment to academic freedom and the true spirit of critical inquiry. This view, that academic freedom opposes any required Christian commitment for the faculty, is almost universal among our highest-ranked, most selective, academically superior schools. Indeed, in many ranking systems such a view is a requirement for getting a high evaluation as a truly academic institution. This norm exerts a magnetic attraction for all colleges, including Presbyterian ones, which wish to be highly esteemed by the world.[18]

We want to highlight two further points about the historical pattern of American Presbyterian colleges. First, Presbyterians created colleges in a highly decentralized, uncoordinated, scattershot way. This was often lamented by denominational officials, but to no avail. As a result, the church never had enough resources to support all the schools it had, never had a sustained commitment from the whole church to sufficiently nurture specific institutions, and never had much will to tell the schools how to be Presbyterian colleges. Instead, the church has expected the colleges to depend on their alumni, local Presbyterians, and each college's other resources to sustain them. The Presbyterian Church has expected the colleges to tell the church what a Presbyterian college is supposed to be like more than the reverse. Second, Presbyterian colleges, like most church colleges, changed their basic mission, from the nineteenth century to the twentieth, from shaping Christian character to teaching skills and passing on useful knowledge. To be sure, shaping character is something that all colleges do, but the professionalization of the academy, and the redefinition of the pedagogical aim of colleges to teaching "critical thinking," has changed the entire environment in which Presbyterian colleges operate.

This changing environment in higher education has created several challenges that every Presbyterian college faces. These include the tension between a focus on teaching and on research, the crucial role of faculty hiring, the changing curriculum, and the issue of supporting faith in student life.

INSTITUTIONAL ELEMENTS OF EVERY PRESBYTERIAN COLLEGE

We believe the core mission of all the kinds of colleges and universities is teaching students, especially undergraduate students. The distinctive function of research universities and their professional schools—discovering knowledge through disciplinary research and applying it in professional training—is a valuable part of the entire ecology of higher education. That mission, though, is not the same as the distinctive mission of colleges to educate students to be culturally literate, useful, and faithful citizens. Almost all Presbyterian institutions, including the universities, put undergraduate teaching at the heart of their mission. Even Princeton, which today is thoroughly a university and far from its Presbyterian roots, is unusual among universities for insisting that its professors, and not their graduate students, teach the undergraduates. Therefore, while universities are a very important part of higher education as a whole, and there can in principle be Christian universities,[19] our focus will be on the Presbyterian college.

Faculty

The colleagues are the college. Faculty hiring and faculty culture are the single most important determinants of what the college is at any given moment. It is in faculty hiring and promotion that the college's vision matters the most. If it does not consistently reward faculty members for advancing the college's vision, then they will start to pursue some other vision. The usual alternatives that fill such a vacuum are the professional research standards of the separate academic disciplines. These are valuable standards in their place, but they are not enough to guide teaching. Moreover, if faculty members owe more to the professional research culture of their disciplines than to the common mission of the college, the institution will start to dissolve or be pulled apart.

The presidents, backed by the boards of trustees, can play a crucial role in shaping a college through the faculty they hire. Colleges that have deliberately retained their church heritage, and especially those colleges which have turned around a secular drift, did so because the administration hired faculty committed to the school's religious mission. Without such a sustained administrative commitment in faculty selection and retention, the normal workings of the academic market will soon fill a college with a critical mass of professors indifferent to the school's religious mission and hostile to any attempts to tell them what to do.

Hiring only Presbyterians would be bad for a college, even a pervasively Presbyterian college. Students and professors alike benefit from the critical rubbing together of different ways of understanding. This is perhaps most valuable when students are trying to learn *why* they are committed to a specific worldview, how to defend it, and what characteristic excesses they should be on guard against and humble about. On the other hand, hiring without reference to religion is certain to kill the faith and erode the founding vision of a college.

Presbyterian colleges often used to require all faculty members to submit to a creed of the church, usually the Westminster Confession. This had the advantage of providing a clear theological standard for everyone, and of keeping the college in line with the church. The disadvantages, though, were several. First, confessions of the church were not designed to guide college teaching, and most of what is in them is not directly relevant to the great bulk of the work of a college. Second, submitting to the creed tended to become either an empty ritual, or too legalistic. Third, even when creedal submission worked as intended, it limited the faculty in a way that was not good for the breadth of students' learning. Moreover, in the past generation the church has had not one confession but a whole book of them, making it difficult to use submission to the church's creeds as a standard for faculty, even with the best of intentions.

It is, though, necessary for the faculty to accept the stated mission of the college. The more substantive that mission statement, the richer the faculty's shared understanding can be. Each way of being a Presbyterian college has a core tradition from which it comes, and a broader mission derived from that tradition. Some members of the faculty will be of that core tradition, even at the most pluralistic school. Others will not be of that core tradition, but can find a valuable place as honored guests from another identifiable tradition, even at the most pervasively Christian school. No one is second class, because the mission is above all.

To be sure, there will always be nuances in how professors (of all people) understand a text. To deal with this question, the Presbyterian tradition has developed a useful mechanism. The Presbyterian Church has a common constitution to which all its officers submit, but each presbytery examines candidates and judges whether their nuances of interpretation of that constitution are suitable for that presbytery. Adapting this same notion, each faculty, or some commission of the faculty, could examine prospective professors and judge whether their nuances of interpretation of the college's mission were suitable for that college. Such a task, in these postmodern "nonjudgmental" times might seem distasteful. However, assuring that your prospective colleagues share the college's values is as important as assuring that your prospective spouse shares your values.

Curriculum

In the nineteenth century the classical curriculum at most church colleges assumed a basic knowledge of the Bible. The central "religious" course concerned moral philosophy, often taught by the president as the capstone of a Christian scholar's college career. In the twentieth century, however, the classical curriculum has given way to a more scientific, technical, and discipline-driven plan of instruction. Declining student knowledge of the Bible and even of their own church's tradition has made new religion courses necessary. Since about World War II, the heart of the Presbyterian college religion curriculum has been the Bible course. From this normally has sprung a course in Christian thought, of which church history is often a subordinate element. Recently, the world religions course has joined the normal core. These subjects can be expanded into any number of different courses.

These names, though, hide two quite different approaches to their subjects. The traditional approach was to teach the Bible and Christian thought as knowledge necessary to be a good Christian. Knowledge of other faiths was useful in getting along with them, to be sure, but was especially important when evangelizing non-Christians. The approach increasingly common in recent decades, though, has been to teach all these subjects—the Bible, Christian thought and history, and the other world religions—as an important kind of cultural literacy. All of them are taught as history, and none of them, to put it bluntly, are taught as true. This approach is especially common in the schools with a Historical relation to the church. Indeed, it is this approach that, more than anything, separates the Historical category from the Dimensional and the Pervasive church colleges.

Teaching about Christianity as the product of historical forces often liberalizes students' faith.[20] Indeed, for many students it undermines their faith altogether, convincing them that all beliefs are equally valid relative to one another. Teaching students to be modest and civil about their faith, and to resist dogmatic triumphalism, is a good Reformed educational goal, based on an understanding of how pride can render even the best understanding sinful. Still, an education that leaves students with no faith but relativism seems a poor conclusion for a church college to reach.

It is possible, though, to "relativize the relativizers," to show that relativism is, itself, a faith, an "ism" among other isms. A curriculum that taught all the principal worldviews as worldviews could do justice to the historical approach to Christianity, without leaving it at that. An education that aimed at teaching the worldviews would bring students to see that any way they live requires a choice of worldviews. The college need not try to make the choice for students, but it can ask them to choose this day whom they will serve.

Student Life

The student bodies of Presbyterian colleges have long been religiously diverse, and are growing more so. None of the Presbyterian-related colleges now has a Presbyterian majority in the student body, so they couldn't impose a Presbyterian ethos by sheer weight of numbers even if they wanted to, which they do not. Presbyterians have long seen the education of society, not just of Presbyterians, as part of our mission, and therefore mixed student bodies have usually been seen as a good thing. What is different now is that much of American higher education has embraced diversity, and even pluralism or "multiculturalism," as an end in itself, rather than as a means for broadening students' understanding and faith.

The college's usual vehicle for supporting student religious life has been the student fellowship. For Presbyterians, this is normally the Westminster Fellowship. It has counterparts in other denominations, notably the Baptist Student Union and the Newman Society for Catholics, as well as in partly overlapping parachurch agencies such as Inter-Varsity, Campus Crusade for Christ, and the Fellowship of Christian Athletes. The college can be an honest broker among all the religious groups, supporting them all and giving some kind of credit to the grownups who advise them. Colleges can also cooperate with local churches in serving students, which may provide additional adult help for student denominational fellowships.

Most Presbyterian colleges have a chaplain. The chaplain is increasingly caught in a dilemma between serving all students and caring particularly for the Presbyterian students. Seeing the college's role as that of honest broker among student religious organizations gives the chaplain a role that is less torn by internal conflict, and partially solves the problem of a chaplain who is increasingly driven to the lowest common denominator. The chaplain's office can also promote service projects that bring together the different religious fellowships.

Promoting worldview discussion among students is an important extracurricular objective too—that is what bull sessions are for.

Why Would a College Stay Presbyterian?

Finally, we want to highlight an important change in the larger institutional environment in which all Presbyterian colleges operate. A century ago, all of American higher education, even at the state schools, was pervaded by a generalized Christian ethos, and often by a specifically Reformed Protestant ethos. A seriously Presbyterian college was not that different from any other college. Since that time, however, there has been a sea change in the whole culture of American higher education. The level of religious life that would have been normal in 1900 would mark a college as distinctly countercultural in 2000. It requires greater effort and imagination for a college to be meaningfully Presbyterian now than it did then.

Finally, let us consider the general question of why a college founded by Presbyterians would want to remain a "Presbyterian College."

1. Gratitude. Generations of pious church people sacrificed to make each Presbyterian college possible. Simple gratitude, and a desire to keep trust with those past—and current—generations should make us want to find a way to carry on some version of that legacy with integrity.
2. Stewardship. One of the most distinctive Presbyterian doctrines has been that we are stewards of the talents God has given us. The Presbyterian educational mission has been driven, in large part, by this sense of a special calling to serve all of society through schooling. Keeping the Presbyterian heritage vital helps renew a college's commitment to that basic educational mission.
3. The Search for Truth. One of the six "great ends" of the church listed at the beginning of the *Book of Order* of the Presbyterian Church (U.S.A.) is "the preservation of truth." There is no more contested issue in all of academic life in postmodern times than what the nature of truth is. Any Presbyterian college, though, must preserve enough of a belief in the existence of truth to permit the "search for truth."

6

Teaching in the Collegiate Institutions of the Church

DUNCAN S. FERGUSON

A CHALLENGING ASSIGNMENT

It is not an easy calling to teach in the church-related, and more specifically in the Presbyterian-related, colleges and universities, although there are those who would characterize the assignment as relatively easy, and in some cases even idyllic. After all, goes the argument, the professor can set the schedule for the week and semester, good students abound, the course content is interesting, even compelling, and there are the endless holidays. There is some truth to this line of reasoning, and for those who truly do have a keen sense of being called to this mission it can be a very fulfilling vocation. But in reality it is hard work, and for those who find it hard to live with the gap between the ideal and real, it can be very frustrating and stressful.

There are all of the usual "headaches" of any work assignment in a somewhat bureaucratic system. There are deadlines, some of which are unrealistic. There are forms to fill out, committees on which to serve, and colleagues who in varying degrees are less than compatible.[1] There are administrators who view the institution from a different perspective, perhaps in terms of balancing budgets, pleasing trustees, or projecting an image for the annual fund, or who suggest that you should really not introduce such controversial topics into your syllabus. There are unmotivated students who do not complete assignments and some who do not have basic writing and mathematical skills. There are faculty meetings in which hours are spent on parking rather than the curriculum or the fundamental mission of the institution.

But even if one adjusts to these inevitable characteristics of academic life, there can be even more troubling dimensions of working in the church-affiliated college or university. For example, there is the reality that the institution in which one teaches has likely changed dramatically over the past several decades. The changes are many, and often reflect the changes that have occurred in our society and world. Fundamental to these changes is that the institution has probably become more *secular* in character.[2] Further, there is the reality of *globalization*, apparent in the economy but present in nearly all dimensions of life. We now must educate our students to face the emerging world and to be equipped to understand and pursue careers in a "global village." In addition, there is increasing *cultural diversity and social pluralism*, and it is present on campus as students and faculty members come from every corner of the world. There is also the dramatic expansion of *knowledge and information*, challenging the way in which we build a curriculum for higher education. There are five thousand books per week added to the Library of Congress, and print media carry just a fraction of the knowledge that is now available through *information technology*. There continues to be a *questioning of the assumptions of modernity* with the *counter force of growing conservatism, even fundamentalism*. There appears to be a clash of civilizations.[3] Finally, let me mention the profound changes that are taking place in the *two institutions that exist in an "uneasy" relationship*, the church and its related colleges and universities.[4] Institutions of higher education, by nature conservative, are being challenged to maintain their relevance and being asked to make changes faster than their infrastructure can facilitate. The major church bodies also seem unable to respond quickly enough to the rapidity of change in the contemporary world, and young people in particular find the church's program and message less than compelling.

So the reality is, except in a few cases, that students do not necessarily come to our church-related institutions with a church background, and few come with membership and formation in the Presbyterian Church. Only a handful of faculty colleagues share the vision of teaching as a true calling from God and maintain a vital and growing faith with roots in the Reformed tradition. Even the trustees and the senior leadership of the institution tend to be more concerned about fiscal integrity and becoming "the best liberal arts college in the region" than about being true to the founding principles of the institution.

The fact is that the nearly 70 institutions that are formally linked to the Presbyterian Church (U.S.A.) are filled with ambiguity, are quite diverse, have a variety of self-defined missions, and have varying degrees of institutional

health. Although it is not a view universally held within the church and by dedicated Christian faculty, an argument can be made that this diversity is one of
the great strengths of the family of institutions. It is not just the diversity, however, but more frequently the lack of clear Christian identity that troubles
many.[5] Both faculty members within and church leaders without view the
institutions as not necessarily Presbyterian in character and generally quite
expensive, and in some cases even elitist. So faculty members within struggle
with what some have called institutional hypocrisy, and the external church
community asks why it should send its children to these institutions and support the colleges with its financial resources. The General Assembly Council's
listing of this mission as a relatively low priority may have reflected some of
this feeling.[6]

The case can be made, even when acknowledging the partial truth in these
perceptions, that the institutions have retained many of the essential principles
of the church-related college or university. Some of the institutions openly
claim a clear church affiliation, although they run the risk of being too easily
identified with the more conservative wing of the church and of being absorbed
by one cultural expression on the Christian faith. Other institutions say little
about their Presbyterian identity and do not give their church linkage a high
priority. But in spite of these risks and tendencies, the vast majority of these
institutions have common values that find expression in their common life.
They are committed to the holistic formation of students, not just to the students' cognitive development. The institutions, although profoundly engaged
in serious research and scholarship, remain primarily teaching/learning centers
devoted to the finest possible education for *the students*. Issues of peace and justice are central to the curricular and extracurricular programs of the institutions, and there is intentional instruction in responsible citizenship. The vast
majority have programs for worship, spiritual nurture, and service.

CALLED TO BE A TEACHER/SCHOLAR

It is into these "mixed" institutions that dedicated and faithful people are called
to teach and empower students to learn and become all that God intends for
them to become. No setting is ideal, and not one of the colleges and universities formally related to the Presbyterian Church (U.S.A.) has every quality
often listed as essential to the perfect church-affiliated institution. They are
human institutions, as are the churches that support them.

The vocation of the Presbyterian teacher is lived out in diverse settings
and less than ideal circumstances. And so it has always been, as it was with Jesus,
who taught people in synagogues who misunderstood his message, followers

who missed the point, and those who betrayed him. The challenge is to be faithful to the calling—the vocation to be a teacher/scholar undergirded by the theological principles and ethical teachings of the Reformed tradition. What are these foundational principles and teachings? There are many, but three seem essential for the teacher/scholar who is endeavoring to remain faithful to this vocation as a Presbyterian and informed by the Reformed tradition.

The Sovereign Love of God Created the World

The Brief Statement of Faith, whose final adoption by the Presbyterian Church (U.S.A.) was at the 203rd General Assembly (1991), reads, "In sovereign love God created the world good." From this theological affirmation comes the primary mandate for the church's educational mission and profound guidance to those of us who understand our vocation as teacher/scholar. As Presbyterians, we believe in the God of creation, stand in awe before the majesty and mystery of the cosmos, and see in the world around us the hand of the One who is the creator of all. "The heavens are telling the glory of God; and the firmament proclaims [God's] handiwork" (Ps. 19:1). Teaching and learning begin in wonder.

Traditionally, the college and university have said that the world is here for us. The world and all that dwells therein are ours to study, and as Presbyterian Christians we celebrate this great truth. It is fundamentally good to know, and our institutions of higher education have pursued knowledge and met humankind's insatiable hunger to know. Science has set out to uncover the secrets of the created universe and has learned how to marshal the forces of nature. The social sciences trace the strange and jerky rhythms of human behavior and how it is that humans go about living together. The humanities and fine arts probe the creative energies and value-making qualities of the human spirit and how it is that goodness, truth, and beauty fill our lives.

It is an integral part of the vocation of the Presbyterian teacher/scholar to enjoy the exploration of the world and engage in the quest to learn. But nearly all the teachers/scholars, regardless of heritage and tradition, might affirm this point of view. This perspective does not go far enough for the Presbyterian teacher/scholar, for one who is informed by the Reformed tradition also affirms that she or he is there for the world. The phrases "knowledge for knowledge's sake" and "truth for truth's sake" have a certain appeal, but they should not carry the day. All knowledge should be directed by values. "If I . . . understand all mysteries and all knowledge, . . . but do not have love, I am nothing" (1 Cor. 13:2).

A fundamental principle guiding the vocation of the Presbyterian teacher is that "truth is in order to goodness."[7] The Presbyterian teacher/scholar serves God's purpose by pursuing a positive social purpose, by improving the condition of humankind and, indeed, of the whole earth. It is not enough to titillate, to provoke and stimulate the brain cells, although there are few human activities as gratifying as learning. Thomas Wolfe, American author of a previous generation, as a freshman at Harvard began at the first shelf with the goal of reading every book in the library.

But ultimately knowledge for its own sake does not satisfy and, in fact, as the preacher of Ecclesiastes remarks, "And I applied my mind to know wisdom. . . . I perceived that this also is but a chasing after wind. For in much wisdom is much vexation, and those who increase knowledge increase sorrow" (Eccl. 1:17–18). The critical question is, knowledge for what? and the answer is knowledge for a more just and humane world. Knowledge has a social context and needs to be guided by the values that affirm the well-being of the human family and of the earth.

A corollary principle guiding the Presbyterian teacher/scholar, following from the affirmation that "in sovereign love God created the world" is that we should resist with all of our energy any attempt to censor and limit the pursuit of knowledge. The Presbyterian tradition at its best maintains that *faith and knowledge are a unity*, not fundamentally at odds, although it may not always be possible to see the unity. "And the Word became flesh and lived among us, . . . full of grace and truth" (John 1:14). Jesus is viewed as embodying both dimensions in his life, the dimension of the religious (grace, faith, love, value) and the dimension of truth (knowledge, integrity, light). In the first epistle of John, God is described as love and light. We pursue the vocation of the Presbyterian teacher with the conviction that all truth is God's truth, and that as we study, learn, and teach, our subject matter is God and the divine creation. As we study, learn, and teach, we engage in holy endeavors and love God with our minds.

The Sovereign Love of God Redeemed the World

It is from the church's understanding of creation that Presbyterian teachers/scholars get one set of marching orders for the pursuit of their vocation. It is from the church's understanding of redemption that another set of principles emerges to guide our calling. Not only is the world here for us to study, enjoy, use, appreciate, and tend, but we are here for the world, to assist in its healing and care and to give ourselves to the task of setting its creatures free. The calling is to serve God's design for redemption, to have a part in healing and emancipating individual students, corporate structures, warring nations, a threatened world, and an exploited planet.

The Bible records that Jesus spoke about redemption in terms of the kingdom of God, the entrance of God into the world to heal it and set it free. The purpose of God's sovereign reign, as Jesus proclaimed it, is the liberation of people and to bring all in accord with God's will and way. The calling of the Presbyterian educator is to participate in this mission in the classroom, in scholarship, and in the common life of one's institution. It is to incarnate the forgiveness of God, challenge all forms of oppression, and help to relieve human suffering in all of its diabolical manifestations. God is not indifferent to sick and sinful, the plight of the poor, the hungry, the illiterate, and the victims of war and prejudice. An essential part of the vocation of the Presbyterian teacher is to dive in and help those whose worldly address lies within the many suburbs of hell.

Presbyterian teachers and scholars take seriously the Reformed understanding of human sin and frailty. It is to acknowledge that we consistently "[ignore] God's commandments, we violate the image of God in others and ourselves, accept lies as truth, exploit neighbor and nature, and threaten death to the planet entrusted to our care."[8] Presbyterian teachers and scholars know that what they teach and the knowledge they generate should be a part of the liberation not only of their students, but of all those who might benefit from the knowledge and the resources of the institutions in which they serve. It is to use one's gifts and education for the stewardship of the earth.

The Gospel of John records the saying of Jesus, "And you will know the truth, and the truth will make you free" (John 8:32). This insightful aphorism is another way of articulating the calling of the Presbyterian teacher and scholar. To enable those whom we teach and serve to learn the truth about God's marvelous world sets them free from ignorance and opens them up to the rich treasures of creation. To be introduced to the finest that has been thought, said, and done in the history of the human enterprise is liberating. Ignorance is not bliss, but is often slavery. Knowledge and truth enable us to flourish.

To be educated is to have the capacity to see the beauty and complexity of all that surrounds us and all that is inside of us. To be educated is to have scales drop away from our eyes so that, all of a sudden, a starry night, a crashing ocean wave, a dazzling red sunset, and a glistening snowy peak are there for us in a way they have never been before. So too is the complex world of human thought and activity. To be an educated person is to stand on a high hill on a clear day and be able to see forever. Pierre Teilhard de Chardin, the French scientist and theologian, said that the essence of life is wrapped up in the verb "to see."[9] To be fully human, to become all that God wants us to become, is to have the capacity to see clearly.

To be educated is to see new vistas and perspectives, to see new relationships and connections, to see the depth and subtlety of meaning. It is the capacity to see the many in one and the one in many.

More specifically, it is to have a sense of self, to know who we are and where we are going. It is to have a sense of place, to know one's roots, one's cultural identity, one's personal history, and to discover how we fit into the flow of time through space. It is to have a sense of judgment, to be clear about one's values, what is right and wrong, and the basis for making good decisions. It is to have a sense of confidence and competence, knowing that we can earn a living and contribute to our society and world. To see the truth is to be set free.

To seek and find the truth not only frees us from ignorance and opens our eyes to the beautiful world we inhabit, but empowers us to become a mature, congruent, and fully actualized person. It gives a center and the deep and abiding peace of knowing who we are and what we value. A mature person is one who has woven the various pieces of his or her life into an artistic pattern of color and strength.

It is to become a person of integrity, to live truthfully and authentically, not to be a slave to our own interests and concerns, being exclusively preoccupied with sensual pleasures, pride in one's own achievement, the praise of others, and our power over them. How easy it is for all of us, as teachers and scholars and as students, to fall victim to the slavery of self-deception and self-centeredness, with the result that we find no real fulfillment and suffer from constant anxiety about "how we are doing." Worse yet, caught in fear and desperation, we often hide the truth, deny reality, and live defensive and distorted lives.

Our calling as Presbyterian teachers is to empower those whom we teach and serve to be redeemed from their sickness and self-centeredness. It is to invite them, as it is appropriate in our setting, to trust their lives into God's care and to devote their lives to God's intentions for the world. This orientation means abandoning all false quests for security and giving up attempts to carve out a secure place that we can control. It means giving up our preoccupation with our little worlds and the desire to impress others or have power over them, for when we do this, we lose sight of our possibilities of realizing our full potential. When everyday life takes over, we calculate our every move, we understand ourselves primarily by what others say about us, and we live only with a trite curiosity about the beautiful and complex world we inhabit; we engage in chatter about mundane things. We get lost.

But by putting our lives in the hands of God who liberates, we are set free from petty preoccupation. Without denying the reality of our ordinary concerns, we discover a deeper concern that calls into question our daily routines. We perceive that we have forgotten something about the true nature of our being, and we marvel at the possibility of becoming what God intends for us to be. We cease calculating and making attempts to understand ourselves in terms of the approval of others. We are "taken over" by an ultimate concern, one that goes far beyond our own selfish drive for security and pleasure. Our chains fall off, and we are no longer driven by fear, no longer controlled by compulsive need, but liberated and "saved."

As those committed to the vocation of the Presbyterian teacher, we teach, do research, and serve in order to participate in the mission of redemption. We help people to see so that they might flourish, and we help them to an ultimate concern. So, too, do we empower people to commit their lives to service. To know the truth is to be set free to serve the cause of God. For each, it is a different call, but for all it is a call to an unjust world, filled with suffering people. It is an invitation from the God of love, truth, and justice to be a partner in the creation of a better world. It was the call that Jesus heard and followed. He was fearless in attacking the hypocrisy of the religious and social systems of his time. His words were a direct challenge to the oppressive political and economic structures that were characteristic of the governments of his time.

We should not be surprised that Jesus acted the way he did. His education, built on the Hebrew Bible, would create in his sensitive and keen mind an uneasiness about empty religion and social injustice. He had read over and over again about Moses, the great champion of social protest, who challenged Pharaoh and said, "Let my people go." He had read about Isaiah and Jeremiah, who lashed out against a religion that had no soul and government that kept people in poverty. He had immersed himself in the great prophets of the exile, who were murdered for protests against Babylon. Jesus, set free by the truth, turned the course of his life toward the welfare of the human family, challenged all forms of oppression, and helped to relieve the suffering of all those whom he met. To encounter the truth of God is to learn that God cares about the suffering of people and calls all who are followers to help relieve that suffering in ways unique to each of us.

The Sovereign Love of God Is Sanctifying the World

It is from the Reformed understanding of creation that the Presbyterian teacher finds the affirmation that the pursuit of knowledge is fundamentally good, that to share this knowledge through teaching and scholarship is a true vocation, and that the love of truth and the love of God are harmonious and synergetic. It is from the Reformed understanding of redemption that the Presbyterian teacher is guided to act, teach, and study in a way that heals, forgives, and sets free. It is from the Reformed understanding of sanctification that the Presbyterian teacher is encouraged to nurture, provide community, and empower others to find their vocation.

The Brief Statement of Faith affirms that "The Spirit . . . sets us free to accept ourselves and to love God and neighbor, and binds us together with all believers in the one body of Christ, the church." We generally think of the church as the primary support community and its ministry of education as one means of this support and sustenance. It is also true the church-related educational institutions and those who serve in them provide ministries of nurture and sustaining Christian communities.

The faculty member in the church-related calling has the primary responsibility of being a teacher and scholar, but he or she is also in a position to relate to students in life-giving ways. Not every faculty member is naturally gifted to serve in the role usually designated for the chaplain or campus minister, but there are many ways that the faculty member can minister to students (and to colleagues). A faculty member is often held in great respect and as a role model by students. To be open to informal conversations, to be in settings that enable students to ask questions and seek guidance, and even to engage in limited personal counseling and career direction are important ways for the vocation of the Presbyterian teacher to take tangible form. The questions from students are often quite personal, having to do with family, girlfriends and boyfriends, human sexuality, and finances. Then there are the usual questions about majors, courses, classwork and exams, the usual topics under discussion between a student and an adviser. Many students are vitally interested in the "big" questions as well, such as the existence of God, the nature of ultimate truth, the meaning of life, and defining and finding what is good and beautiful. They are also concerned about the course of human events, how government policy is encouraging racial justice, how foreign policy might lead to war or peace, and how the environment might be affected by recent oil explorations on the Alaskan North Slope. The morning paper or the evening news may be the stuff of an important conversation, and the faculty member should never underestimate how even the most innocent conversation can have an influence or be remembered by a student.

Central to these conversations and the work with students in the classroom is assisting the students to discover and develop their vocation and ways that their gifts and talents can be used in the actualization of the vocation. "For this reason I remind you to rekindle the gift of God that is within you"(2 Tim. 1:6). The Reformed and Presbyterian faith has always maintained that every person has a vocation and that all of us are called by God to serve an important function in society for the good of all. There has been great care not to teach that one vocation is more important or more spiritual than another, although there are times when we apply the concept of vocation almost exclusively to being called into Christian ministry. But this tendency is a slight distortion of the Reformed teaching. All people have a vocation; but it is somtimes difficult to discern it and live it.

It is during the "critical years" that students really find themselves, discern their interests, gifts, and talents, internalize values, and take their first steps toward family life and careers.[10] The entire college community should provide the resources for students to engage in these crucial developmental tasks, but it is often a faculty member who can assist in this growth and development. The college community, often represented by a faculty member, will be the catalyst for the steps toward maturity. The student, during these years, must develop several characteristics.

One characteristic of development during these years is the management of the stresses and strains of life. Students learn how to manage pressures, not to be toppled or "blown away" by life's demands. They gain a certain measure of self-awareness, insight into their needs, wants, and personal style that enables them to cope. They discover their own strengths and weaknesses, which allows them to act constructively under pressure rather than defensively and compulsively. They learn how to manage their emotions, rather than being managed by them. They cease to be driven people, tyrannized by wild extremes of feeling. Anxiety, insecurity, loneliness, and fear may be present, but the maturing student learns to channel these feelings into a constructive pattern.

The student also develops a measure of autonomy. Mature people are somewhat self-contained, enjoying the company of others but not desperate for approval and acceptance. Students begin to enjoy time alone, feel good about themselves, and delight in their own mental and emotional lives. They learn how to be at peace with themselves, relaxed and confident.

Still another characteristic of the maturity learned by students is integrity. Most students, and indeed all people, have many selves, all in competition with one another. Often students feel torn apart by conflicting drives and desires. Not infrequently, they violate their deepest core and truest self. But during these important years the student becomes more congruous, acts in harmony with her or his values, and has emotions that match judgments and reason. The students learn how to be honest with themselves and with others. Each must discover the truth of Søren Kierkegaard's small classic, that *Purity of Heart Is to Will One Thing*, to become undivided, a person who is one, an integrated person.[11]

Closely related to integrity is identity. Students begin to get in touch with their deepest feelings, talents, skills, style, heritage, and roots. They discover that to be true to oneself is to be content and that to follow one's destiny is to be happy. "Blessed are the pure in heart, for they will see God" (Matt. 5:8).

In addition, students gradually learn how to be free in interpersonal relationships, free from self-preoccupation and able to reach out and make contact with others. They learn how to overcome feelings of shyness and insecurity and take steps toward genuinely touching another person. They learn how to be real, reaching out to others in transparency, openness, and directness. They discover the joy of being relaxed and genuine in the company of others, learn how to be spontaneous with laughter, crying, and play.

Finally, students learn how to be responsible, appropriately managing the tasks that come along. They begin to see life as a calling and know that they have been tapped on the shoulder with a divine hand and have been given an assignment. They begin to view life as a gift and become good stewards of their talents and gifts. They learn that all persons have a responsible task out in front of them, perhaps in the next hour, day, or week, and to be responsible in the performance of this task is to become a part of the solution to the world's problems rather than to be a part of these problems.

It is not just an individual faculty member who is in a unique position to enable students to move toward maturity, to discern their calling, and to find ways to gain the knowledge and skills to express this calling; it is a supportive community. Part of the mission of the church in education is the building of nurturing communities for those whose vocation is being discovered and is being expressed in an educational setting. We educate in the church, but we also create educational settings outside the church that are inclusive and supportive, enabling and empowering, ones that respect the dignity of all. These communities provide the human resources and behavioral norms that facilitate growth toward maturity and incarnate justice in policy and practice. Faculty members can play an important role in the formation of these communities, whether it be in the form of worship, Bible study and prayer, a service project, or an international study seminar. As faculty members become more human in the eyes of students, less of an ideal or an intimidating presence, then true community becomes possible. When there is honest exchange about life and learning, when roles disappear and authentic human beings interact, then communities that nurture growth and maturation take shape.

Fundamental to these ministries of sanctification (set apart for sacred use) is the stewardship of human life. My wife, as one who works with children in the public school system, has often remarked that "there are no throwaway kids." Presbyterian faculty members, true to their vocation, understand the value of every student. Each one, created in the image of God, needs the best we have to give. As frustrating and irresponsible as students can sometimes be, we nevertheless, using our knowledge and skills, our roles as teacher and scholar, do what we can to help these students become all that God wants for them to be.

THE PRACTICE OF TEACHING

The Presbyterian teacher, with a clear sense of vocation and guided by a Reformed theological understanding, approaches the classroom in a particular way. There is an attitude, an outlook, and a "spirit" about the teaching task, even in those subjects that would not be viewed as related to a theology or those that have skill building as their goal.[12] Not infrequently, the argument is made that the teacher of mathematics or computer science does not teach from a "Reformed or Presbyterian perspective," because the subject is a matter of fact or skill and does not intersect with beliefs and values. This point of view is true as far as it goes, but it does not account for the "spirit" of the teacher or soul of the institution, and it is this spirit and soul that are the heart of the matter.[13] There are many dimensions to this spirit of the teacher and the soul of the institution.

The first is that the Presbyterian teacher is integrally *engaged* with the subject and the students. Parker Palmer, in *The Courage to Teach*, argues that truly great teaching emerges from the inner landscape of the teacher's life. If the teacher is passionate about the subject and authentic and congruous in the classroom, then it is likely that learning will occur. He writes that "good teaching cannot be reduced to technique; good teaching comes from the identity and integrity of the teacher."[14]

The argument is not that technique is unimportant or that tips are not of value to the beginning teacher.[15] It is rather that techniques and practices are not the essence of great teaching. Great teaching occurs when faculty member and student connect and explore together the subject of the course.

One of my responsibilities during my several years of serving as a vice president for academic affairs was the assessment of teaching effectiveness. I often reflected on what quality a teacher possessed who was consistently given high evaluations. Yes, there were references to being scholarly, well organized, having clear assignments, being fair and timely in grading, and assigning interesting reading. But hidden behind these comments, and often only alluded to, was the student's sense that the professor was engaged with the subject and made true human contact with the students. Year after year, the "professor of the year" was the one who "taught with heart." Of course, there were those who were cynical and referred to these awards as rewarding teaching as a popularity or best-personality contest rather than the imparting of knowledge. My observation was that knowledge was imparted and received or discovered so that learning took place.

Presbyterians have no claim on this kind of teaching, but when they teach this way they fulfill their calling. They are teachers with a center, who genuinely care for students despite the difficulty of overcoming the fears and cultural norms that might prevent them from being open and caring.[16]

A second dimension of the practice of teaching in a "Presbyterian way" is that it is done *in community*. Again, there is no special claim to the value of community by Presbyterians; in fact, it is fundamental to the academy. But it is a deeply rooted and abiding value in the Reformed family as well. From the beginning, the Reformed tradition has affirmed that faith is nurtured in community, that theological beliefs are formed and checked in community, and that decisions for the ongoing life of the church are made in community— Presbyterian governance is grounded in the conviction that God's will is known in and through community life.

So it is in the vocation of teaching.[17] Learning may occur in a more isolated way, as in reading, doing research, and experimentation in the laboratory, but the learning is expanded, nuanced, given context, and enhanced in the natural exchange of ideas that occurs in community life. In addition, learning must be subject to the checks and balance of colleagues. A fundamental value of the community is that it keeps us honest, ensures that we have done our "homework" and faced down our biases, that we have fully studied the subject, probed its depth and breadth, clarified our thinking and findings in both oral and written forms, and have the capacity to place our learning in a larger frame of reference.

It is in community that we begin to discover our vocation, and create a context for our students to own values and convictions, form their identity, better understand their gifts, and discern their calling in life. It is in community that we begin to grasp who we are, where we are going, and how we might get there. It is not surprising that the vast majority of Presbyterian-related colleges and universities are relatively small and personal, committed to exchange in the classroom and dedicated not only to providing the knowledge, information, and skill development that are expected in any university, but to emphasizing and encouraging the discernment of vocation and the formation of the person.

A third dimension is that, with only the predictable number of exceptions, Presbyterians are also committed to *academic freedom or freedom of inquiry*. In part because of the Reformed understanding of human sin and frailty, there has been a reluctance to settle on absolute and final positions—not that there are not many Presbyterians and Presbyterian movements that believe that they have arrived at "the truth, the whole truth, and nothing but the truth."[18] But at its best, there is in the Reformed faith a commitment to "being reformed and always reforming." There are deep convictions and passionate beliefs, and we affirm as one of our "great ends of the church" "the preservation of truth." But our knowledge and understanding are viewed as standing under God and Scripture, not limiting and prescribing for God and Scripture. We approximate our faith formations, and our theology is in constant revision.

So free inquiry is necessary to protect against idolatry and dogmatic absolutism. There is a need for continuing study, dialogue, and exchange as we seek the ever-elusive truth.

A fourth dimension (mentioned earlier in the chapter) of this spirit of the Presbyterian teacher and the soul of the Presbyterian college or university is that of *stewardship*. There is the conviction, again shared with many other traditions, that we are responsible stewards of the world and partners with God in the ongoing processes of creation. This is to affirm that every human being is the creation of God, made in the image of God, and needing the liberating and life-giving power of education. All the students, and indeed all the members of the college community, are viewed in this way, and treated by the dictates of the Golden Rule.

Frustrated and angry as we may be at times, we nevertheless treat our students and colleagues with respect, honoring their need to learn and grow into the persons God intends for them to be. My wife, a public school educator for many years, has told me endless stories of children with problems and behavior that would test the patience of a saint, but as we stated before, again and again she says there are no "throwaway" children—or we would say, no throwaway students—only those needing discipline and our best attention.

A fifth dimension of spirit and soul is the commitment to *service*, that we educate to enable, equip, and empower persons to fulfill their vocation for the well-being of the world. Education is a means of enhancing the talents and gifts given to all people by God, gifts and talents that are to be used in the service of God. In the Reformed faith, as we have underlined again and again in this volume, there is a strong sense that all human beings have a calling, not just those who serve the church in a professional way.

The Presbyterian teacher (and college or university) has the responsibility to assist students to understand their careers as more than a way "to make a living," or to be rich and powerful, but as a way of contributing to a better society and world, that is, to serve a larger purpose regardless of the career path. Of course, some choices must be made; there are some career paths that do not serve the public good. But neither is there a hierarchy, with God "blessing" only those careers that are directly linked to the church or that have prestige in the culture. We do the will of God by contributing to the public good in our own way. The Presbyterian approach to education is "worldly," in the sense of seeing full participation in building a better world as fundamental to our vocation.

A closely related dimension of the spirit of the Presbyterian teacher and the soul of the Presbyterian-related college or university is that we *nurture ethical responsibility*. In "just such a time as these," it is especially important that ethical issues be addressed. Attention must be given to the understanding of those from different cultures and religious traditions. There must be study and discussion of the causes of violence and the ways of building a more peaceful world. Let me provide two specific examples, chosen from among many, that will illustrate the nurturing of ethical responsibility.

One is, regardless of the class subject, and central to many subjects, the need to cultivate an ecological perspective. We are all citizens of the good earth and must care for it, to tend its delicate gardens. But it is so easy to live with the assumptions and view of reality that come from a time that is past, an assumption that viewed nature as that which needed to be conquered and exploited. What is needed now, however, is a more holistic view of reality, in which we see ourselves as interdependent and belonging to the intricate, constantly changing cosmos, an ecosystem. So the Presbyterian teacher assists students to develop a global consciousness and conscience in relation to the earth and all that dwells on the earth. This perspective suggests an ethic toward others that is characterized by justice and care. No longer can the universe's unruly and unrivaled child, the human being, live out of control and without thought for the rest of life. The heartbeat of the world is relationship and interdependence, not dominance and hierarchy.[19]

A similar argument might be made in reference to world hunger. Again, regardless of the class subject, and in some cases central to the class subject, the Presbyterian teacher should enable students to understand how it is possible to do justice to the hungry. For example, the college or university has the resources to help students understand the causes of world hunger, going beyond the immediate impulse of merely providing relief. Students need to understand the issues of food production and distribution and how the present system may be problematic. They need to understand the problems of an expanding population, and the increasing numbers who live at starvation levels. They need to understand the problems of developing countries, and how their priorities may differ from those of developed countries. In short, the Presbyterian teacher may give the student the eyes to see how all these issues are connected to world hunger and how solutions may be found.

Finally I mention, as a concluding dimension of the spirit of the Presbyterian teacher and the soul of the Presbyterian-related college or university, the need for *high quality and academic excellence*. Again, Presbyterians make no unique claim on quality and excellence, and in fact may often be assisted by others in the quest for quality and academic excellence. But Presbyterians, sensing a calling from God, can do no less than pursue quality in all aspects of institutional life and academic excellence in every dimension of the educational endeavor, in teaching, research, and service. The students, society, and the world deserve nothing less.

Time and space do not permit a full development of the way quality and excellence should be pursued, and there are many publications on these subjects.[20] But as our world changes, as knowledge expands exponentially, and the human situation becomes increasingly complex and problematic, we must carefully define and plan for what is emerging as quality education. For Presbyterians, the particular task of connecting learning and faith is one critical item on the quality agenda, and for all institutions the building of the curriculum around a more integrated model may be another.

These dimensions and the many others are integral to the spirit of the Presbyterian teacher and the soul of the Presbyterian-related college and university.

7

Teaching in the Theological
Schools of the Church

W. Eugene March

There are numerous ways that one might begin to reflect upon education for Christian ministry. There have been a number of studies in the past decade concerning theological education.[1]

These studies have been useful in describing where we have come from and some of the current challenges. They have offered helpful suggestions for the future of theological education in North America. This particular contribution to the subject is far more personal in character and reflects my own involvement in seminary education for the past four decades.

Since 1964, I have taught biblical studies in two of the Presbyterian Church (U.S.A) theological institutions: Austin Presbyterian Theological Seminary and Louisville Presbyterian Theological Seminary. My own theological training began at Austin Presbyterian Seminary and then was completed formally at Union Theological Seminary in New York in conjunction with studies at Columbia University. As a student I experienced what I consider to be the best of two worlds. On the one hand, I received a foundational, confessionally based theological education in a very fine denominational, freestanding seminary. Austin Seminary is located at the edge of the University of Texas campus, and as a student I was able to participate in some educational events on the university campus as well. On the other hand, my graduate study (for a doctor of philosophy degree in Old Testament) was done in a setting that was quite interdenominational and, in fact, interfaith. There were Jewish students in some of my classes as well as Christians from a number of different denom-

90

inations. Union Seminary in the early 1960s had an outstanding faculty of world-famous scholars and a library that was unsurpassed. The same can be said of Columbia University, Jewish Theological Seminary, and Hebrew Union College, each of which I also attended.

The two seminaries of the Presbyterian Church (U.S.A) in which I have taught are similar in size and expressed purpose. In comparison of size with other seminaries in North America, both Austin Seminary and Louisville Seminary are in the large category. They are not large in comparison with a few of the very large seminaries (Princeton being one such in the Presbyterian family), but in comparison with most of the theological schools that belong to the Association of Theological Schools, Austin and Louisville are relatively large. Each has a student population (considering all degree programs) of between 275 and 325 students. Each has a library that has in excess of 135,000 volumes, and relationships with other libraries that expand the resources even more. Each seminary belongs to several consortia of other schools, which provide students opportunity to study at other seminaries as well as in various universities and colleges in the region and elsewhere in North America.

The faculties of Louisville and Austin Seminaries are roughly the same size. Each is composed of persons from varied backgrounds in terms of race, sex, age, and denominational affiliation. Most faculty members have Ph.D.'s, and approximately two-thirds are ordained in their particular denominations. Many of the faculty members of both institutions have had some pastoral experience at some point in their careers, and most have current and ongoing involvement in local congregations. Both institutions are accredited by regional accreditation organizations and by the one national theological accreditation agency especially concerned with theological education, namely, the Association of Theological Schools. Involvement in those organizations requires the participation of some of the faculty (and I have been one) in peer evaluations of other schools. This has enabled me to visit a number of different campuses in various parts of the United States to consider and compare programs of different theological schools, very large (2,000+ students) and very small (fewer than 35 students), with my own institution as we go about the task of theological education. Further, many of the faculty at both Austin Seminary and Louisville Seminary belong to and participate in various professional organizations such as the Society of Biblical Literature and the American Academy of Religion.

All of the above is to give some indication of where I begin my reflection. I have contributed to and am a product of my educational environment, both before I became a professor and since having become a professor. My perception of what is important and what we should do is clearly shaped by my years of teaching in these two theological institutions.

THE PRIMARY TASK

In the seminaries where I have taught the primary task was the education of women and men for ministry in the local congregation. Certainly there were students who came to seminary with other goals in mind. Some came to prepare for careers in higher education. Others came out of a quest for basic theological education so that they could better understand their own faith and participate in the life of congregations as educated laypeople. Nonetheless, from the institution's point of view, the main task remained education for Christian ministry in the context of the congregation.

Let us consider for a moment each part of the statement of that purpose. First of all, these institutions are dedicated to education. Education is not the same as training. Certainly, there is training that is done in a variety of ways in a basic program of theological education in denominational seminaries. People are trained how to conduct services of baptism or develop a stewardship program or use computer programs for organizing and carrying out various programs in the life of the congregation. And such training is valuable! But more important is the task of education, the careful introduction of students to a body of knowledge and the development of the faculties of rational analysis and synthesis important for articulating the faith and guiding others in learning and appropriating the faith.

Education at a seminary level assumes previous education and experience. The work done at a seminary, in the Presbyterian tradition at least, is graduate education. While some students with special circumstances may be allowed to begin a program without a prior formal education, the vast majority of students bring with them undergraduate programs of study. The variety of these programs is amazing, and we will consider some of the implications of that below. The point here is that this education is conducted at the graduate level and is assessed accordingly.

The fact that institutional purpose is aimed at education also requires that adequate resources be provided (e.g., a good library and adequate classroom space). A well-trained faculty representing a spectrum of theological disciplines is required. There was a time in the history of Presbyterian theological schools when well-seasoned pastors were called to teach at the seminary. Many of these professors had not done doctoral-level graduate study. What they provided was certainly solid and appropriate at the time. Now, however, graduate study on the part of faculty is considered necessary in most instances. We will return to this issue below.

One further implication of the fact that education is the primary intention of Presbyterian seminaries is that curriculum and pedagogy are very important. Much attention is given to each.

Solid teaching is held at a high level in terms of institutional value. Carefully planned curricula are equally important. Students are not allowed to take any and every course that they would like. There are required courses that build one on the other and guide the student toward the educational goals adopted by the institution. This may seem obvious, but for some it comes as a surprise. Seminary education is not merely an extended stay at church camp!

The fact that this is education for ministry introduces the second important element, ministry. In the seminaries where I have taught, ministry was primarily understood as pastoral ministry, leadership of local congregations. But in each institution it was understood that ministry had wider dimensions. Certainly there are ministries of counseling, of teaching, of social service. But most of the basic master of divinity curriculum is aimed at educating women and men for work in particular congregations. Thus, there is a concern that students reflect on ministry as a vocation. What does it mean to be involved in education aimed at equipping a person for ministry? What is ministry?

A denominational seminary may provide good preparation for people going on to do doctoral theological study or to pursue work in law or social work, but its first responsibility is to introduce students to ministry in and through local congregations. This means that the curriculum has to enable students to explore and learn about educational ministry in a congregation, pastoral counseling, appropriate methods of evangelism, different forms of private and public worship. It means that a network of cooperating congregations in the region around the seminary must be developed where the education of students can be extended to actual ministry settings under competent supervision. Competent education for ministry relies heavily on the involvement of adjunct faculty who are themselves engaged in ministry.

Finally, the purpose of the seminary for education for ministry in the church again makes what may seem to be a self-evident statement. This education is directed at persons who will serve within the institution of the church. There are some types of theological reflection done in other educational settings that may be very valuable, but the aim may not be service in the church as such. The fact that the education of which I speak is so directed means several things. First of all, unlike colleges and universities, denominational seminaries are purposely Christian. In the school where I currently serve we occasionally have Jewish students. They are welcome and benefit from our program quite well. Nonetheless, when they enter our setting, they know that this is a self-consciously Christian setting. Their education will be done in a place that aims to educate for service in the church, and not in the synagogue. We can and should be welcoming to strangers in our midst, but nonetheless our purpose is clearly defined by our goal to train people for ministry in the church.

In Presbyterian seminaries there is another dimension of the fact that this is service for the church, namely, a confessional implication. As an institution related to the Presbyterian Church (U.S.A.), my seminary is obligated to introduce students to the basic theology and tradition of the Presbyterian Church. Being Presbyterian, of course, means that at our confessional base is an openness to persons of other denominations. Presbyterians have historically been ecumenical. That makes it easier to welcome students of other backgrounds into the seminary. And insofar as we are able, we owe students from non-Presbyterian denominations our deepest respect and educational attention to their own historical and creedal foundations. Nonetheless, the overall requirements are still shaped by our allegiance to the Reformed tradition. One of the most striking consequences of our denominational heritage is the requirement in most Presbyterian seminaries that each student have some introduction to biblical Hebrew or Greek or both. The aim is to enable a more thorough study and understanding of the Bible.

The fact that this education is directed toward those who will participate in the ministry of the church also means that as an institution we are concerned with enabling students to be qualified for ordination. Not everyone who graduates from a Presbyterian seminary will be ordained. Some may choose not to pursue ordination, and others may not be able to meet the requirements of a particular ordaining body. One of the true burdens of teaching in a theological institution is realizing that some students may be able to squeak by and garner enough course credits to meet graduation requirements, even though they are clearly unsuited for and unprepared for ministry in the church! Thankfully this is not the case in most instances. But the very fact that, as faculty in Presbyterian seminaries, we see ourselves as obligated to prepare students for the possibility of ordination means that we do not have time in the curriculum for every possible subject of interest. A fair amount of work in the curriculum is directed toward both the fact that we are preparing students for ministry and that this ministry will be in the Christian church.

THE CHALLENGE OF DIVERSITY

When I began my own theological education, the average age of the all-male and practically all-white student body was somewhere in the mid-twenties. Many of us had decided to go to seminary during the time of our college education, and thus we took courses that would help us in pursuing a theological education. Undergraduate concentrations in English, history, and philosophy were common. Some of us had had two or more years of biblical Greek. Some had Latin and German. Many of us came from church-related colleges, where we had been required to take courses in Bible and religion. At least two-thirds of us were single and lived together in dormitory settings. Most of us intended to be pastors in Presbyterian congregations. There were a few people, very few, from other Christian denominations. There were one or two women, who were training to be directors of Christian education.

Such a context for theological education in the present-day Presbyterian seminaries that I know has almost totally vanished. Most of our institutions now have an average age of thirty-five or older. Most of our students are married or have been married. There are an almost equal number of women and men. The denominational representation is widely diverse. Most of our schools have at least 30 percent of the students from non-Presbyterian denominations. Persons of color are becoming more numerous in our institutions, though most of us still need to do much work in recruiting larger numbers of such students.

Very few of our students made a decision to come to seminary while they were still in college. Most have been pursuing careers as electrical engineers, teachers, accountants, social workers, lawyers, doctors, members of the military, and so forth. In their previous educational work, they built no foundation for doing theological education. In their lives as members of local churches, and out of their own particular interests, they may have done some background reading, but it has not usually been done in an organized way or with any sense of critical analysis. Many students come because they have had disastrous marriages or have otherwise been hurt in abusive situations in their lives and have found healing in the church. Thus they come wanting to participate in the continuation of ministries of healing.

These students are often not certain whether service in a local congregation is what they are really pursuing. While they have often come because of the influence of a Presbyterian, a Disciples, or a Methodist congregation, they are not necessarily committed to those denominations in any profound sense. Being older, these students are often impatient to get on with the practice of ministry and are willing to take shortcuts through the educational programs the seminaries offer. Though circumstances seem to be changing somewhat, we have gone through at least a decade when students were not terribly exercised over social issues that confront North American society. For the most part they are highly individualistic in their religious perception and pursuits. They are often quite willing to experiment with new forms of worship without ever having actually known the old forms of worship. They are a very diverse group of people, by and large, who bring with them a great variety of experiences, interests, commitments, and abilities.

From the standpoint of a denominational seminary dedicated to the purpose of educating women and men for ministry in the church, the diversity of our current student bodies presents quite a challenge. There are a number of students who need remedial work in primary subjects if they are to be able to participate in the educational program that Presbyterian seminaries consider minimal. The different backgrounds require seminary professors to spend a larger percentage of their time just getting to know the students so that they can help the students cross the communication barriers that their different backgrounds present. There is a greater need to make certain that students have a grounding in the basic traditions of the Christian church as a whole as well as the particular backgrounds of their own denominations. The fact that there is such a wide variety of denominations represented requires faculty to be more sensitive in the use of examples and the choice of bibliographies representing writers of different denominational backgrounds as well as different genders, races, national backgrounds, and so forth. It has never been the case, in my forty years of involvement in theological education, that one cookie cutter fit all. But it is the case now that we are no longer faced with merely cutting cookies. We have a whole variety of people who are from different backgrounds, who see themselves preparing for a wide variety of different ministries, some of which are directly related to congregational ministry, but many of which are not.

There is another type of student that some of our institutions are encountering ever more frequently. Students are no longer assumed to be residents on our campuses; many are commuters. Some of them can come to school only in the evenings or on the weekends. They cannot participate in the vocation formation that goes on in common campus experiences. It is challenge enough providing vocational formation for students you see on a regular daily basis, students with whom you have opportunity to work in common chapel and retreat experiences, and so forth. Part-time students, so-called nontraditional students, present a new challenge. A few seminaries have done more in meeting this challenge than others. The number of people who find they must participate in theological education in this mode is growing. How Presbyterian seminaries will respond yet waits to be determined.

THE NECESSARY COMMITMENTS
AND SKILLS OF FACULTY

Teaching in a Presbyterian seminary involves several levels of commitment and the necessary development of a number of skills. In terms of commitments, there are at least four levels that faculty must acknowledge. In my particular institution, the first commitment is a commitment to the church. By that we mean that faculty members will demonstrate a mature Christian faith that includes a concern for and dedication to the work of the institutional church. When faculty are employed, one of the main categories of exploration has to do with involvement in the church, particularly at the local level. We believe that it is very important for a faculty member to have an ongoing relationship with a congregation and to be involved in congregational life.

There has been occasional debate about whether faculty of theological institutions should be required to have experience as pastors in local churches before they can join a faculty. We think it is far more important that individuals have an ongoing engagement with local congregations. Even if one has been a pastor, that experience soon becomes past history. Certainly pastoral experience provides numerous examples and illustrations by which to assist students in learning what pastoral ministry is all about, but being employed as pastor by a local congregation is not the only way such experience can be achieved. Teaching in adult Sunday school classes on a regular basis, assisting in pastoral visitation, participating in worship as a leader of liturgy and an occasional preacher, being involved in the work of presbytery or whatever the denominational equivalent, all are ways to maintain a sense of the reality of the local congregation. That is what is important to be able to share with students. Thus, we are very concerned to know how a faculty member views such work in the local church and in the denomination at various levels.

This commitment to the church is one factor that often separates faculty in theological institutions from faculty in other institutions of higher learning. Christians who serve as faculty in universities may well be involved in the local church in many significant ways, but it is not viewed as something necessary for their work in the classroom. They seldom are asked to reflect on the significance of the topic they are teaching for life in the local congregation or to do the reverse—reflecting on how something that goes on in the local church should be considered from a theological point of view. Further, commitment to the local church and the larger church brings with it additional requests for time and talent. Professors of theological seminaries are constantly being asked to teach or preach in churches other than the ones they normally attend. They are asked to lead denominational workshops, regional and national. They are often invited to serve on special committees at the regional and national levels of their denominations. They are asked to contribute articles to educational curriculum resources and to review materials produced for their denominations. Faculty members find themselves being asked to participate in ordination and installation services far more often than average lay or ordained members of the church. Most faculty members are eager and pleased to have such opportunities, but nevertheless they require of faculty a commitment of energy and time beyond what is called for in one's normal day-by-day responsibilities.

A second level of commitment is to academic integrity. This means that the faculty member has all the commitments that any faculty person would have to ongoing scholarship at the personal level and contribution to scholarship at the communal level. Seminary faculty have an obligation to ongoing research in their disciplines. They are expected to be well informed with respect to the literature that is constantly coming forth in every area of scholarship. They are expected to contribute in writing and in presentation before scholarly groups to that stream of ongoing work. That is no easy task.

It is often difficult for faculty in theological seminaries to have a wide circle of people with whom they can talk and share ideas at the technical level of particular disciplines. Frequently a faculty member will be alone as representative of a particular discipline. Thus, to find a community of learning centering around one's special interests, it is often necessary to find conversation partners beyond one's immediate faculty colleagues. Improvements in communication across the years have made this more feasible, but it still takes initiative and resolve beyond what it would take if that conversation partner was officed next door. Involvement in professional societies is another way this is accomplished, but it too has its difficulties in that it requires travel and time away from institution and family.

Then, of course, this commitment to intellectual and scholarly integrity involves one's commitment to the colleagues in the institution where one serves. How do you help junior colleagues to develop their skills and knowledge? How do you assist someone in a discipline that is not yours to sharpen ideas and to better articulate arguments? How can the general intellectual climate of the particular institution be kept vigorous and interesting? All these questions are ones that faculty in theological seminaries ask and seek to answer.

To some who do not share in the vocation of professor it may seem unnecessary to have a life of ongoing study. But, of course, for those of us who are professors, we know how important in fact it is. This means that individual faculty members have to take responsibility for devising and maintaining an ongoing continuing education program for themselves. They have to stay involved not only for their own careers, but for the sake of their students. This is again an added commitment that must be made.

Another level of commitment apart from commitment to church and scholarly integrity involves the area of pedagogy. Most faculty in theological seminaries did not train to be teachers. They may have determined at some point that they wanted to have greater depth of knowledge and understanding, but few stopped to take courses in instruction, the science of evaluation, instructional technology, and all the rest. Some doctoral programs now require candidates to do some teaching, and many doctoral students are involved as tutors and instructors while they are pursuing their studies. But there are only a few programs where pedagogy is considered of great importance. When these recently graduated persons arrive on the faculty of a seminary, however, their teaching skills become crucial. This same concern does not seem as important in some other settings of higher education that I have observed. Perhaps this emphasis on developing one's pedagogical skills is peculiar to Louisville Seminary, but at this seminary it involves an added level of commitment that faculty members are expected to make. Evaluation of classroom performance is regular and taken seriously. Part of the consideration for tenure centers on teaching ability. With the changes that have been taking place for the last fifteen years involving computers, for instance, there is no end to ongoing learning in the use of instructional technology. Such technology improves one's teaching, but it also takes a great deal of time. Time becomes more and more important to the seminary professor!

A fourth level of commitment involves the students. Seminary faculty are viewed not only as gurus in terms of their scholarship but also in terms of their spirituality. Students come for advising on their course work, as would be expected, but they also come seeking guidance in terms of their spiritual lives. Faculty members are expected to know their students and be concerned for the lives of their students both in and outside the classroom. Obviously, some professors do this more willingly than others, but in most of our institutions, which are certainly small in comparison to university settings, students expect a degree of personal attention, and faculty generally desire to have that kind of relationship as well.

When I began life as a seminary faculty member, most of my students were of approximately the same age and from the same general background. Most of them were Presbyterian. While there were wide differences between individuals, I could nonetheless assume certain things about their background. Now I do have my share of Presbyterian students, but they may vary in age from twenty-two to sixty-two. They have widely different backgrounds of formal education and life experience. Further, there is an increasing number who are A.M.E. Zion or United Methodist. I have had several Unitarians among my list of advisees. All these factors add up to making a commitment to students at the individual level more difficult. And yet, it is an ongoing desire on the part of the faculty and an expectation on the part of students that such involvement will be there.

Finally, faculty members, believe it or not, are human beings. Surprise! Faculty members have families, friends, personal hobbies, and interests. Faculty have to eat and sleep like everyone else. Faculty members have a relationship with God that is as important and difficult to maintain as that of anyone else. Thus it is extraordinarily important for faculty to have a commitment to themselves as well as all those commitments already mentioned. They must structure their lives in such a way that they take care of themselves, because no one else will. That is a common plight of pastors as well.

As faculty members are able to manage their own lives appropriately, at the same time they model something very important for students who are seeking to be pastors. Most faculty that I have known, including myself, are relatively reluctant to admit that this is a difficult task. We like to think of ourselves as able to do it all. In fact, most of us can't. We need the support of one another, as well as the support of our families, in being able to keep a proper perspective on our various commitments.

HOW ABOUT THE FUTURE?

It is very difficult to determine what the future holds for theological education in North America. Most of the research that has been done indicates that there will be a consolidation of schools. A number of weaker institutions will fail, and ones that survive will find it necessary to join forces with others. This is likely because expenses keep rising in terms of maintaining a well-educated faculty, providing sufficient student aid, and keeping campuses in good repair. When I began my teaching career, the synods (in the south) and the General Assembly (in the north) provided a large percentage of the funds allocated by the budgets of the seminaries, well over 60 percent! Today my seminary receives only 2.3 percent of its annual budget through the governing bodies of the Presbyterian Church (U.S.A.). To be sure, there are a number of congregations and many generous individual Presbyterians who contribute support, but theological education is not a serious budget commitment of the General Assembly, under whose oversight the theological institutions are lodged. It is only by the careful building and investment of endowment funds that the seminary can keep pace with rising costs. The larger church needs to make a much more serious commitment to the education of its future ministers than is currently the case.

The other major reason for this trend toward elimination and/or consolidation of seminaries is the declining numbers of candidates. As the membership numbers of some denominations decrease, so do the number of candidates. It seems quite possible that it will be prudent and beneficial to organize seminaries as multidenominational institutions, rather than as institutions with a single, primary denominational allegiance. The Presbyterian theological institutions, for the most part, are less likely to face the trauma of institutional failure, but we could be prime candidates to become ecumenical centers engaging the support and commitment of other denominations. In my own particular institution, along with a long-standing relationship with the United Methodist Church, we have forged ties with several historic African American denominations such as the Christian Methodist Episcopal, the African Methodist Episcopal, and the African Methodist Episcopal Zion churches. Such accommodation to new sociological realities is important.

One of the biggest challenges, already alluded to above, is the expanding number of nontraditional students. A number of people want to go to seminary but cannot afford to do so full time. More and more, people want to serve as part-time ministers. This has to do with family commitments, denominational requirements, educational background, and many other factors. Further, seminaries are joining, in partnership with presbyteries, in the preparation of commissioned lay pastors. Certificate programs in specialized skills are emerging. Distance learning involving the use of technology, already well underway at the college and university level, is being developed by some seminaries. But most of the Presbyterian seminaries, so far as I am aware, are only beginning to explore these opportunities. This is an area of challenge and potential that we will need to examine far more carefully.

In the Presbyterian Church (U.S.A.), the theological institutions remain among the most healthy of the institutions of the church. This means that seminaries are providing more and more services that once were channeled through synods and presbyteries. General Assembly agencies have been reduced considerably in the past fifteen years, requiring that many activities formerly centered there have been shifted to other places in the church, often the seminaries. What this means for the future is a greater drain on seminary personnel and financial resources. There is a greater need on the part of the seminaries to plan carefully and strategically so as to assist the wider church in meeting its needs in ways that complement the work of the seminary rather than fracturing it. Seminaries will probably need to coordinate some of this work among themselves so that each seminary is not trying to respond to all the legitimate requests for assistance. It has been difficult in the past for institutions to cooperate in this way because of institutional rivalry and the desire to protect one's own turf. But declining numbers in the denomination may in fact provide the necessary challenge to enable seminaries to make better use of their resources for the work for the larger church.

The decline in the denomination also brings with it a new challenge of developing proper leadership. It is important that we find strategies of cooperation in locating and challenging new people to consider the ministry as a viable vocation. Identifying possible ministerial candidates as early as possible is important. Providing sufficient monetary and human support in preparation for a difficult vocation is critical. Of course, we also will need to find better ways to care for the ministers we already have and to eliminate the high level of burnout that has been occurring among ministers during this past couple of decades. More realistic expectations of ministers by congregations are important to foster. Important also is the development of more aggressive denominational requirements and financial assistance to encourage and enable significant continuing education for our ministers. Such continuing education seems to be one of the most effective ways for ministers to avoid burnout. The seminaries need to cooperate actively with the larger church in this whole endeavor to develop new ways of identifying new leaders and supporting people already serving as ministers.

Another challenge that stands before seminaries in the immediate future is the replacement of a large number of faculty who will soon retire. The growing shortage of ministers in our various denominations is part of the same problem. A great number of faculty began teaching in the seminaries in the '60s and early '70s and have been teaching there since. Now they are reaching retirement age, and a number of shortages are expected in terms of filling faculty slots as currently defined by discipline. Many people doing doctoral study now assume that they will teach in universities or colleges rather than in the seminary context. Certainly there have been relatively few openings in seminary faculties! Thus, students have chosen doctoral programs that would enable them to teach in nonseminary settings, such as the sociology of religion, comparative religion, psychology of religion, and so forth. A number of these people are certainly bright enough to make the transition required to join a seminary faculty, but they may not have the willingness. Further, seminaries will need to look at whether they are going to rearrange their curricula or are going to require additional training on the part of their new faculty.

To meet the challenge of preparing ministers for the increasingly diverse conditions of the church in North America, seminaries are also going to have to do serious work in attracting and keeping persons of color on our faculties. This is not an easy task, since there are relatively few persons of color even pursuing doctoral study at the present. We further need to consider how to educate the next generation of ministers with regard to other major religious traditions. The challenge of diversity is not going to lessen. How seminaries, and the church for that matter, will respond is not at all clear.

CONCLUSION

Education for Christian ministry has been, and promises to continue to be, a challenging and fulfilling pursuit. The best of pedagogy, combined with intellectual zeal, integrity, and faith commitment, is what is asked of the faculty. How seminaries should be organized is open to consideration, but a commitment on the part of the church to the highest standards for an educated clergy must continue. Unless and until something better emerges, the seminaries remain the best hope of the church for educating and maintaining clergy capable of meeting the challenges of the twenty-first century.

Section 3

Case Studies of Teaching: Application

While Paul was waiting for them in Athens, he was deeply distressed to see that the city was full of idols. So he argued in the synagogue with the Jews and the devout persons, and also in the marketplace every day with those who happened to be there. Also some Epicurean and Stoic philosophers debated with him. . . . So they took him and brought him to the Areopagus and asked him, "May we know what this new teaching is that you are presenting? It sounds rather strange to us, so we would like to know what it means." . . .

Then Paul stood in front of the Areopagus and said, "Athenians, I see how extremely religious you are in every way. For as I went through the city and looked carefully at the objects of your worship, I found among them an altar with the inscription, 'To an unknown god.' What therefore you worship as unknown, this I proclaim to you. The God who made the world and everything in it, he who is Lord of heaven and earth, does not live in shrines made by human hands, nor is he served by human hands, as though he needed anything, since he himself gives to all mortals life and breath and all things. . . . For 'In him we live and move and have our being.'"

—Acts 17:16–28

8

The Vocation of Teaching
in the Church-Related College

INTRODUCTION

Margaret (Peggy) Parks Cowan

While theological and historical reflection are essential for defining a distinctive Presbyterian/Reformed approach to the vocation of teaching, it is in the dedicated service of teachers that such vocation finds life. This chapter explores the lived experience of teachers and students at three very different Presbyterian colleges in order to illustrate ways in which the vocation of the Presbyterian teacher is currently being expressed and to stimulate further reflection on the role of church-related higher education in the twenty-first century.

Maryville College in Maryville, Tennessee, Rhodes College in Memphis, Tennessee, and Waynesburg College in Waynesburg, Pennsylvania, represent some of the great diversity that exists in Presbyterian higher education. The Presbyterian Church (U.S.A.) has developed a set of categories (see chapter 5 for definitions) as one way of describing the differences among church-related colleges. According to the church's definitions, Maryville represents a "dimensional" college, Rhodes is "historical," and Waynesburg is "pervasive." As Stephen Haynes's description of Rhodes illustrates, these categories are not perfect matches for complex and living institutions. They provide a useful device, however, for thinking about Presbyterian colleges and church-related higher education.

The oldest of the three colleges, Maryville, clearly defines its mission in terms of its Presbyterian/Reformed heritage and nurtures an understanding of teaching as vocation consistent with its theological roots. From its infancy, the college was guided by an affirmation of the sovereignty of God, which encourages viewing all areas of knowledge as legitimate subject matter, which recognizes the limitations of human knowledge and thus the need for critical

evaluation and revision of that knowledge, and which views knowledge as unitary, that is, interconnected rather than isolated in distinct disciplines. Thus it
seeks to combine strong emphasis on academic study and critical thinking with
an innovative interdisciplinary core curriculum. Recognition of the limitations
of any one human perspective has meant an emphasis on diversity of perspectives among faculty, students, and staff. The college has sought to empower
students to become literate about the Christian tradition and, whether or not
they are Christian, to grow spiritually as well as intellectually. While faculty
bring diverse perspectives, all are expected to support the mission of the college and are encouraged to reflect on their teaching vocation as part of the hiring and tenure and review processes.

Like Maryville, Waynesburg has sought to express its church-relatedness
through an innovative General Education program. The first learning objective of that program is that students will "relate the Judeo-Christian tradition
to contemporary issues, personal identity and the academic disciplines." Thus,
the integration of the Christian faith and learning is an essential component
of the academic program at Waynesburg. The second section of this chapter
describes ways in which such integration takes place in five academic departments at Waynesburg: Communication, Computer Science, Political Science,
Nursing, and Religion. In communication, students reflect on the ethics of
media management and production and evaluate the potential contributions
of the media to the kingdom of God. In computer science, the integration
takes place primarily through ethical reflection. In political science, students
explore the contributions of a variety of religious perspectives to their discipline. Nursing students explore religious beliefs related to health and their
impact on the expressions of illness, on the use of rituals and other spiritual
interventions, and on relationships between patients and health-care providers.
In the study of religion, students connect biblical materials to personal concerns, participate in service learning assignments, and relate some aspect of
their major discipline to content of biblical studies courses. At Waynesburg,
the careful and intentional integration of faith and learning exemplifies the
institution's commitment to being a Christian college that defines its mission
in terms of service to Christ.

In contrast to this clear curricular expression of church-relatedness, Rhodes
College most visibly embodies its denominational connection in cocurricular
programs and the effects of engagement in Presbyterian history on its institutional identity. It is the potential for Rhodes's "usable history" to continue to
shape its identity that suggests the college may not fit neatly into the "historical" category. While the college grew out of a southern Presbyterian church
that justified slavery as a biblically ordained institution, its students, faculty,
and administration made strong stands for integration and civil rights during

the 1960s, when such positions were unpopular in the region and in the southern church. Even the threat by major donors to withdraw financial support did not deter a courageous administration from supporting its students in their efforts to call the Presbyterian Church U.S. to stand for justice. Retelling these stories offers the possibility of correcting the misconceptions of some faculty members who assume that religious affiliation necessarily results in narrow sectarianism, restrictions on academic freedom, and interference by donors with whom they disagree. More positively, reclaiming this history can provide a shared tradition for faculty, students, and administrators at Rhodes and other similar colleges to use as starting point for discussion and debate about the issues that shape the institution in the present and future.

The stories of these three Presbyterian institutions offer some examples of church-related colleges where the vocation of teaching is lived out in the concrete realities of higher education in the twenty-first century.

THE VOCATION OF TEACHING AT MARYVILLE COLLEGE

Margaret (Peggy) Parks Cowan

Maryville College was founded in 1819 as the Southern and Western Seminary, at the instigation of Isaac Anderson, pastor of New Providence Presbyterian Church in Maryville. Anderson had been frustrated in his attempts to recruit pastors for Tennessee. He decided that the solution was to establish a seminary to serve the area. When the Synod of Tennessee approved an overture from Union Presbytery to establish the seminary, Isaac Anderson was appointed to the lone professorship as well as the presidency.[1] By 1821 the liberal arts college department had been formed, and the college was born.[2]

According to a college historian, "It was as a teacher . . . that Dr. Anderson was most influential and revered."[3] He combined catechetical and Socratic approaches that involved giving each student a set of questions to explore from different perspectives. When they had progressed as far as they could on their own, he delivered lectures in the form of questions and answers on the topic.[4] While one account of his teaching suggests that if students reached a position that did not conform to his, Anderson had the students read further, consider related texts from the Bible, and pray until they reached the appropriate conclusion,[5] one of his faculty colleagues suggests something quite different. According to Dr. John Robinson, professor of sacred literature, Anderson "possessed the rare faculty of impressing himself on his pupils, while at the same time requiring no servile assent to his mere dictation. . . . His constant aim was to make his students think and understand for themselves."[6] Anderson seems to have combined a very traditional approach that required students to learn the fundamental questions and seminal answers from the past with an emphasis on teaching them to think for themselves.

Pedagogical approaches used by Isaac Anderson were consistent with Reformed theological principles. The affirmation that God is sovereign over all creation suggests that all genuine efforts to seek truth, that is, all academic disciplines, are to be valued and pursued. This principle also implies that human knowledge is limited and can never contain the fullness of truth, and must, therefore, be subject to revision as new knowledge is attained. Finally, even though all human knowledge is limited, secular as well as Christian writers have been gifted by God's grace, and therefore should be studied for the knowledge they may impart. Thus, Anderson's students encountered the classics and a variety of writers on different topics and were expected to evaluate the materials critically and draw their own conclusions.

A century after Isaac Anderson founded the college, Dr. Horace Eugene Orr, a Maryville alumnus, returned to his alma mater to teach. Realizing that his religious views diverged significantly from those of the president, Samuel Tyndale Wilson, he offered to tender his resignation. According to Dr. Orr, President Wilson declined, saying that he hoped "that I would stay at Maryville until my hair turned as white as his."[7] Thus, Dr. Wilson affirmed diversity of thinking on the faculty. As a result, Dr. Orr taught for thirty-nine years. He was noted for challenging students and, as President Wilson had done with him, encouraging them to become independent thinkers, even when that meant disagreeing with their beloved teacher. He was held in the highest esteem by students, except for "a fundamentalist minority who regarded him as a heretic."[8] Both Dr. Wilson, as mentor to faculty, and Dr. Orr, as classroom professor, illustrate an approach to teaching that empowers students to think for themselves rather than imposing on them a body of knowledge to be accepted as authoritative. This was done, however, in a setting where students were expected to learn the tradition and understand basic Christian principles as foundational knowledge for their thinking.

The emphasis on empowering students to think critically while gaining literacy about the Christian tradition and exploring a broad range of academic disciplines continues to shape the vocation of teaching at Maryville College. In defining its relationship to the Presbyterian Church, the college has sought both to maintain a relationship to the church that is truly meaningful and central to the life of the institution and to be a genuine liberal arts college that challenges students to think critically about all areas of knowledge, including faith perspectives. According to a report of the Faith and Learning Committee to the president in December 2000:

> For the many students who come to campus with Christian convictions, our goal is to help them become spiritually reflective and to provide them an opportunity to [grow as] thinking Christians. In seeking this goal, we recognize that this educational experience may . . . call into question previously unquestioned or unexamined issues of faith and practice. . . . Only by engaging and challenging them in a serious way can we offer them the tools to build a credible faith for an increasingly complex world. Likewise, for those students who are not Christian, our goal is to provide them with an opportunity to become spiritually reflective and to see what a thinking Christian is or looks like.[9]

Thus, teaching at Maryville does not involve evangelizing, but empowering students by providing them with literacy in the Christian tradition, teaching them to use a wide variety of academic tools to reflect on questions regarding the nature of God and of human life, exposing them to a broad range of knowledge, and encouraging them to think deeply about issues of faith and practice.

For this vision of being a church-related college to become a reality, faculty must share a common commitment to the mission of the college. During the hiring process each prospective faculty member is asked to respond to the college's "Statement of Purpose," which says in part:

> In an atmosphere of freedom and sensitivity, Maryville College bears witness to God's revelation in Jesus Christ who challenges all human beings to search for truth, to work for justice, to develop wisdom, and to become loving persons. Continuing in this vital faith, the College believes that it must listen attentively and humbly to all human voices so that it may hear the call of God no matter how God may speak.[10]

Affirming this mission does not mean that every faculty member must be Presbyterian or even Christian, but that each professor seek to contribute to the mission of the institution. In fact, the college has taken the position that diversity of perspectives is essential if students are to be truly challenged to think critically about faith perspectives as well as other academic disciplines. The diversity of thinking among the faculty that President Wilson affirmed nearly a century ago continues to shape teaching at Maryville College. Openness to diverse perspectives reflects the Reformed understanding that all human knowledge is limited and, therefore, subject to revision as new insights are gained.

Beyond the hiring process, the sense of teaching as vocation has been expressed through the college's emphasis on teaching as the primary criterion for faculty evaluation. Annual reviews for nontenure track and probationary faculty, reviews for tenure and promotions, and posttenure five-year reviews focus first and foremost on teaching. The *Faculty Handbook* lists "Excellence as a Teacher" as the most important category of evaluation.[11] As part of the review process, the faculty member writes a reflection on his or her teaching philosophy, perceived strengths and weaknesses, and proposed directions for growth. Faculty peers visit the classroom, interview students, review course materials and evaluation forms, and submit narratives commenting on strengths and suggested areas for improvement. The faculty member's division chair or the academic dean and a representative of the Faculty Personnel Standards Committee meet with the faculty member to discuss his or her strengths, problems when they exist, and plans for continuing development. In general, the peer review process is experienced as a positive opportunity for reflection on vocation and directions for future growth.

Supporting this approach to faculty evaluation are the use of faculty development funds to provide workshops on teaching and to send faculty to teaching conferences; use of faculty retreats and weekly forums for discussion of pedagogy; and the presentation at commencement of two awards for outstanding teaching. Thus, the college is a community of learning in which, as an alumnus who became a high school teacher told one of his former students, "Although [the faculty] remain scholars who write books and give papers and do scholarly research, they are dedicated first to the art of teaching."[12]

The sense of teaching as vocation at Maryville College is expressed not only in the criteria for faculty evaluation, but also in the nature of the curriculum. Maryville has developed a carefully designed General Education curriculum as its signature academic program. While recognizing the importance of majors in preparing students for some career tracks or graduate programs, the college has focused a major portion of its instructional resources on providing students with an integrated curriculum in the liberal arts. Faculty members are expected to teach in both discipline-specific and interdisciplinary core courses. The college believes that the curriculum reflects the theological conviction that all of reality is interrelated as part of the creation of one sovereign God.

If all areas of life are to be included in the search for truth, academic inquiry must examine faith perspectives along with other dimensions of human life and the world. To meet core curriculum requirements, students take a course in biblical studies, either Old Testament or New Testament. These courses are a key point at which the college seeks to educate students about the Christian tradition. They are also critical points at which tension arises between students from conservative, southern Bible Belt churches and the demands of academic inquiry. Faculty teaching these courses challenge students to gain a basic knowledge of the content and diverse genres of biblical writings, to recognize the historical, social, and cultural realities that have shaped biblical texts, to identify the major theological ideas developed in the Bible and the diversity of those ideas, to grow in their ability to read ancient texts critically, and to examine their own religious positions. They are encouraged to ask questions and challenge assumptions. Teaching in this context does not mean fitting students into a model provided by the church, college, or professor, but empowering them to wrestle with difficult issues of faith, culture, and knowledge, so that all students, Christian and non-Christian, are encouraged to grow spiritually and to become more critically reflective in their faith stances.

As faculty members teach General Education courses, they are encouraged to make connections with other courses in the core. For example, an instructor in Western Civilization can make use of the concept of justice introduced in the Old Testament course or make connections to Western World Literature, since both courses examine social, ethical, and aesthetic ideals and realities, questions of religious belief, and questions of the relationship between the individual and the community.

As faculty members teach in interdisciplinary courses, they use a variety of approaches to enable students to learn about a complex world that cannot always be neatly divided into disciplinary categories. For example, the entire freshman class is involved in a January term course titled "Perspectives on the Environment." The students are exposed to a nearly pristine segment of the Appalachian environment as part of their fall orientation course. During the January term course, they learn about the Cherokee interaction with the natural world, and about the impact of early European settlers on the region's environment, through readings, videos, discussion, and museum visits. Then they explore the impact of current lifestyles on the local environment through trips to water treatment plants, national forests, garbage dumps, and power plants, and through hands-on projects that use data analysis. Such projects include determining the value of logging the College Woods, analyzing one family's garbage for a week, and studying water use on campus. Finally, they write their own environmental ethic, outlining the impact of the course on the way they live their lives. While the pedagogical approach used in this class could not apply to every course, it does model the emphasis on holistic teaching and learning that enables students to make connections among disciplines, to see the interrelatedness of the natural world and human society, and to grow intellectually, spiritually, and ethically.

Teaching at Maryville College is designed not only to encourage students to view the world holistically, but also to encourage education of the student as a whole person. In the spring of 2000, an alumna who is a world-renowned opera mezzo-soprano gave a concert on the college campus. During the concert she stopped singing and spoke briefly. The concert, she said, was her gift to the college where faculty, staff, and peers nourished her. Expressing deep appreciation for the teachers she had encountered, she explained some of the important lessons she had learned. A professor of biology taught her that the physical world is important. A professor of religion and philosophy encouraged her to read a book that was too difficult at the time with the expectation that she would read it again later with a different level of understanding. A voice teacher awakened her talent and made her realize that she had a voice. A theory teacher taught her that opera was great and that her life journey could go in that direction. She concluded with the statement that the college must continue to provide this kind of nourishment to all students, regardless of their talents and interests.[13] Her comments illustrate two points. First, the teaching she experienced encouraged her to grow as a whole person, not just as a musician, and second, learning took place in the context of relationships that empowered her through nurturing, encouraging, planting seeds, opening doors, offering opportunities, and drawing out her potential rather than shaping her in the image of her professors. Thus her experience illustrates the effects of pedagogy that is holistic and empowering.

The interdisciplinary freshman seminar on the environment and the opera singer's experience also illustrate teaching that is designed to go beyond intellectual development to engagement in the world. In recent years, service learning has increased dramatically as a teaching strategy among Maryville College faculty. For example, a sociology professor has worked with students doing community-based research projects as part of their academic work. These projects focus on issues raised by a local community in order to empower members of that community to design solutions for themselves. Another example is the Student Literacy Corps. After academic training in causes and effects of illiteracy and in methods for teaching adults to read, students work in the Blount County jail, teaching inmates to read. A basic Business and Organizational Management course has been redesigned to include management of nonprofit organizations, and another course, which focuses specifically on nonprofit management, was added to the curriculum. When taken in conjunction with internships in nonprofit organizations and other curricular and cocurricular experiences, these courses permit students to acquire the competencies necessary for completion of a nationally recognized nonprofit management certification program. Such strategies are consistent with the Reformed conviction that Christians are to participate in the transformation of the world by engaging in service to the world.

CONCLUSION

The vocation of teaching is central to the mission of Maryville College as it strives to be both a genuine liberal arts college that challenges students to think critically and carefully about all subjects and a college with a relationship to the Presbyterian Church (U.S.A.) that is central to the life of the institution. Faculty, whether or not they are Presbyterian or even Christian, contribute to the mission of the institution by teaching students in ways that empower them to think for themselves and to grow spiritually as well as intellectually. Even instruction in Bible or other religion courses is designed not to provide a single model to which students should conform, but to engage them in examining questions of faith and ethics as they learn about the Christian and other traditions. Such a view of teaching recognizes the Reformed principles of the sovereignty of God as ultimate source of all truth, the limitedness of human constructions of truth and knowledge, the contributions of diverse perspectives to the store of human knowledge, the interrelatedness of all of reality, the importance of educating students as whole persons, and the call of God to participate in the transformation of the world.

The mission of Maryville College and its particular understanding of what it means to be a church-related institution have enabled me to live out my vocation teaching biblical studies and interdisciplinary core courses. In General Education biblical studies courses, I seek to give students the kind of liberating experience that I had when first introduced to the academic study of the Bible. These courses are designed to challenge students to move beyond a nonreflective reading of ancient texts to a critical engagement that recognizes the impact of historical, social, and cultural realities on the biblical writings. Teaching students to recognize that biblical texts are shaped by historical forces need not result in a relativism that undermines their faith. Providing a supportive context for wrestling with the difficult questions raised by this study allows them to reappropriate—or to approach for the first time—the texts with deeper appreciation for their meaning.

Another important component of my work at Maryville College is teaching in and coordinating our core curriculum. That curriculum is a carefully designed general education program that seeks to enable students to approach the world through the methods and perspectives of a range of academic disciplines and to integrate knowledge gained through these approaches. It includes interdisciplinary study in all four years, and seeks to instill a global perspective with a strong sense of personal values, commitment to the common good, and enhanced capacity for making responsible ethical decisions. With its holistic approach to knowledge as more than isolated disciplines and to students as whole persons, this curriculum is a meaningful expression of the Reformed conviction that all knowledge is God's and that knowledge is unitary. Thus, teaching and directing implementation of the core curriculum is an ideal expression of my sense of vocation as a Presbyterian teacher.

Empowering students to engage in critical reflection about faith issues and to recognize the power of the liberal arts for shaping their lives far beyond job or career is a calling that is both challenging and extremely rewarding. It is exciting to participate in the mission of an institution that seeks to challenge "all human beings to search for truth, to work for justice, to develop wisdom, and to become loving persons."

⋘⋙⋘⋙

While Maryville College expresses its commitment to church-relatedness through an understanding of the vocation of teaching that empowers critically reflective approaches to all areas of life, including faith, Waynesburg seeks to relate the Christian tradition explicitly to all academic disciplines.

FAITH AND LEARNING
AT WAYNESBURG COLLEGE

Jeffrey Kisner

Under the leadership of a visionary administration engaged in careful strategic planning, Waynesburg College has recently witnessed a "decade of transformation." Major campus improvements and the development of innovative academic programs highlight this era of rapid institutional change as Waynesburg translates the original mission of its Cumberland Presbyterian founders into a Christian college for the twenty-first century. At the forefront of this shift is the move toward the integration of faith and learning in the classroom. First among the learning objectives in the recently redesigned General Education curriculum is that Waynesburg College students will "relate the Judeo-Christian tradition to contemporary issues, personal identity and the academic disciplines." This portion of the chapter will cite five different academic departments and show how courses in those departments relate Christian faith to academic disciplines through both course content and student learning activities.[14]

William Hasker has defined the integration of faith and learning as "a scholarly project whose goal is to ascertain and to develop integral relationships between the Christian faith and human knowledge, particularly as expressed in the various academic disciplines." Such integration, according to Hasker, includes "the cognitive content of faith, without excluding or minimizing the all-important dimensions of trust and commitment." The endeavor ascertains and develops the "integral connections between faith and knowledge, the relationships which inherently exist between the content of the faith and the subject matter of this or that discipline."[15]

Various ways this integration might take place include: identifying the *worldview foundations*, the "fundamental . . . convictions, derivable from the

Christian world-view, [that are] relevant to the discipline"; analyzing *disciplinary foundations*, "the foundational assumptions of a discipline to determine its relationship to the Christian world-view"; determining what aspects of *disciplinary practice* are of interest to Christians and whether or not others have adequately treated them; recognizing *worldview contributions*, that is, contributions a particular discipline makes to the understanding of God and human nature; identifying the practical implications of *applying academic theory to practice*; engaging in *ethical reflection*; and identifying *contributions to the kingdom of God*, that is, to "what God intends and desires for human creatures." Each of these practices applies to the integration of faith and learning in theoretical and applied disciplines at Waynesburg College.

Communication

One of the many new major programs given birth during the "decade of transformation" is the Department of Communication. The program features four "tracks," all of which share a core curriculum. One of the courses in the core is a upper-level practicum required of all students in the Communication major. Students are placed at a variety of worksites during the course (newspapers or magazine publishers, radio or television stations, or a number of other types of businesses in the communication field). Course instruction emphasizes the management of media outlets and techniques for producing mass-mediated messages.

The integration of faith and learning in this course involves both ethical reflection on media management and production and assessment of the contribution of the discipline to the kingdom of God. Students read three books in preparation for classroom discussion and brief writing assignments: Nicholas Negroponte's *Being Digital*, which expresses optimism about the use of technology; Neil Postman's *Amusing Ourselves to Death*, which, in contrast, is rather pessimistic about the use of technology; and Quentin Schultze's *Communicating for Life*, which utilizes a stewardship approach to technology. Schultze asserts that persons are cocreators of culture with God and that professional communicators are called to create shalom. In classroom discussion, students question whether the ethical ideals posed by Schultze demand commitment to the Christian worldview he professes. Students assess in writing the problem each author addresses, the relevant data cited by each author, and the solution suggested by the author, and give their own informed evaluation of the book. At the end of the semester, students in the Communication practicum write a comprehensive paper that describes their philosophy of communication based on the practicum experience, the readings, and experiential educational activities.

Computer Science

As in the Communication program, study in Computer Science at Waynesburg College provides multiple tracks. Two of these options are applied programs in business information, and in graphics and technology science. The
other track, simply called computer science, concentrates more on mathematics and, hence, is more preparatory for graduate study in the discipline.
One of the goals of the entire department is "to provide an environment in
which students are exposed to the ethical and societal issues that are associated
with the computing field."

Students in all three tracks are required to complete a course entitled
Computers and Ethics in Society. Readings include *Gift of Fire* by Sara Baase,
who raises ethical questions about the use of technology. Early in the semester, students write a substantive paper that relates the Association for Computing Machinery Code of Ethics to a variety of biblical materials.[16] Since it
might be possible to live up to the professional ethical standards without
being Christian, students discuss ways a person with Christian commitments
might use the technology differently from a person without such commitments. The course also includes an on-line investigation of e-ministry Web
sites and consideration of whether e-ministry is a viable way to facilitate relation with God or whether the technology necessarily alienates people from
God. Classroom discussion investigates the possible future of computerization and the impact of its technologies on human nature. Lecture and discussion also deal with the moral and social implications of free speech,
wiretapping, censorship of on-line materials, and other concerns. Students
compose short papers in which they investigate ways technology has altered
human nature by changing the ways people relate to one another, per-
petuating anonymity and technology dependency, and encouraging the
investment of time that might be spent in what has been traditionally conceived as "more intimate ways," and reflect on what human nature and society gain and/or lose as a result of the technology. Hence, the integration
utilized here is primarily ethical reflection, but also disciplinary practice and
theory applied to practice.

Political Science

The integration of faith and learning in the Political Science discipline at
Waynesburg has a very heavy emphasis in Political Theory, American Politi-

cal Thought, and Introduction to Politics, and receives somewhat less empha-sis in courses on International Relations, Comparative Governments, Ameri-can Foreign Policy, and American National Government.

In Political Theory, Augustine's *City of God* serves as a primary source for the study of the influence of Christian thought and teachings on medieval gov-ernment and politics. Additionally, Augustine's interpretation of the sinful nature of humankind and its influence on politics serves as an example of a Christian worldview. This view is then compared and contrasted with other worldviews and resulting political systems, such as those of Plato, Rousseau, and Marx.

The Puritan philosophy of government is delineated in the lectures on American Political Thought, not only because of its significance during the colonial era, but so students will understand its later influences on the pro-gressive movement at the turn of the twentieth century and the resurgence of religious conservatism in the 1980s and 1990s. Presentations also highlight the paradox in the American ethos between control and freedom of thought, relate different biblical texts to those views, and illustrate ways both the abolitionist and civil rights movements were fueled by biblical thinkers.

The Introduction to Politics course relates the biblical tradition to the study of politics. Required texts include both Charles Colson's *Born Again* and Nic-colo Machiavelli's *The Prince*. Classroom presentations and student papers compare the amoral approach to politics as power relationships found in *The Prince* to Colson's personal and professional rejection of power politics in favor of a Christian life of love and service.

Course content is related to the biblical tradition in additional ways in other courses. In the American National Government course, the professor points out the paradox that secular textbook authors try to ignore religion as a factor in influencing political thought in America when, in fact, religious convictions are a major variable in public opinion and policy. The current textbook for this course was chosen because its author, Thomas Dye, is one of the few who acknowledge the powerful influences of theological views in public political opinion and policy making. Lectures and reading assignments in International Relations, American Foreign Policy, and Comparative Government address ways different religions affect various political systems, cultures, governments, and international relations. For example, students examine the impact of Christianity, Judaism, Islam, Western economics, and traditional societies on Middle Eastern affairs. They study biblical and Quranic texts that influence political policies, and learn about the conflict between the "MacWorld" of Western commercialism and the "Jihad" of Middle Eastern Islamic funda-mentalist adherents.

Nursing

Waynesburg College offers the bachelor of science in nursing (B.S.N.) degree. The program is fully approved by the Pennsylvania State Board of Nursing and is accredited by the National League for Nursing. A portion of the extensive course content required by the accrediting agency is located in a course entitled Nursing Care in the Community. This course blends nursing practice and public health practice. The objectives of the course include defining religious beliefs within the context of community nursing, discussion of the impact of culture on health behavior, and analysis of spiritual interventions. Students complete a "Culture and Religion" learning activity by writing a research paper in which they present a brief overview of the health-related beliefs of a religious group, relevant practices and rituals used to deal with health crises, possible communication barriers between nurse and patient, the effects of the beliefs and practices of the religion on the expressions of illness, an adherent's possible perception of health care professionals, and the potential impact of these factors on nursing care. Students are also encouraged to conduct an interview with an official representative of the faith. In this nursing course, the integration of faith and learning largely takes the form of worldview foundations, but occurs in several other ways as well.

The Parish/Congregational Nurse and Health Ministry Program at Waynesburg College is also a fully accredited program. The college and Mercy Hospital of Pittsburgh, Pennsylvania, jointly sponsor the program, which is accredited by the International Parish Nurse Resource Center. The parish nursing movement reclaims the historic roots of health and healing found in many religious traditions. The movement recognizes that the spiritual dimension is central to healing and wellness, believes that the personal spiritual formation of the nurse is essential to health care, and upholds such values as respect, dignity, compassion, mercy, justice, and well-being/wellness that are rooted in biblical tradition. Though courses in this program are not limited to reflection on the Christian tradition, the biblical tradition is a major consideration at every point, because a majority of the parish nursing students serve in Christian churches.

While many of the workshops in the accredited parish nursing programs apply previously utilized professional nursing skills to the parish context,[17] a significant number intentionally relate the content of the biblical tradition and the history of its interpretation to nursing in a parish context. Bibliography recommended by the accrediting agency includes well-known authors who reflect on the relation between the biblical materials and issues of health, healing, wholeness, spirituality, and congregational ministry.[18] The comprehensive nature of the parish nursing program, an extension of both theoretical and applied disciplines (theology and nursing), necessarily demands several forms of the integration of faith and learning.

Religion

Required General Education courses in biblical studies provide ample opportunities for students to relate the Judeo-Christian tradition to the full spectrum of the academic disciplines in a variety of ways. Obviously, course content deals intimately and in depth with the biblical materials. Students are held accountable for basic knowledge of the Scriptures and relate this knowledge of the Bible to their personal lives, contemporary societal issues, and the academic disciplines in several different ways.

The pedagogical rationale for student reflections on the biblical materials is the recognition that when course content is linked to personal concerns it is more likely to be remembered by students. According to the General Education curriculum objectives of the college, students are to "relate the Judeo-Christian tradition to contemporary issues [and] personal identity." Two different kinds of reflections, personal and contemporary issue reflections, allow the students to fulfill the objective. In course syllabi, students are instructed to write personal reflections that "tell a story" of their own personal lives that relates to a biblical text. For example, a student might write a personal story in a reflection about sibling conflict that relates to the story of Joseph in Genesis or the story of the prodigal's father in Luke. The instructions for the contemporary issue reflection require students to relate a biblical text to some issue or problem facing society (such as poverty, unemployment, violence, war) or a moral issue (such as capital punishment, abortion, homosexuality).

A second way in which students relate faith and learning in biblical studies and theology courses at Waynesburg is through service learning assignments. Students are required to complete five hours of community service for a nonprofit organization. They then must identify a biblical text that relates to the act of service. For example, students might relate Jesus' Sermon on the Plain in Luke 6 to service at the Good Neighbor's Lunch food ministry at St. Ann Roman Catholic Church in Waynesburg. Once a text is identified, students must locate scholarly print resources that comment on texts in ways that relate the text to the act of service. The service learning technique often has a dramatic transformative impact on students. They learn that the content of the Scripture relates to real-world problems that affect the persons they come to know through their service experience. This particular kind of experiential learning also helps meet larger institutional goals, such as acquiring a sense of civic and social responsibility, gaining exposure to cultural and socio-economic differences, and adopting a commitment to service and a foundation for lifelong learning that are consistent with the teachings of the biblical tradition. In addition, students are able to meet the second General Education curricular objective "to serve those in need and facilitate social justice." The use of this experiential teaching method in religion courses assists in proliferating service learning through the curriculum, reinforcing a larger "culture of service" at the college, which is also developed through the Bonner Scholarship Program[19] and the Service Leadership Office at Waynesburg College.[20]

A third learning activity required of all students in biblical studies courses is a "faith and learning paper." In this assignment, students must relate the theory, practice, or ethics of their academic majors to the content of the biblical studies courses. Students may approach this assignment in a variety of ways:

- They may locate scholarly print resources by writers who intentionally relate academic disciplines to the biblical tradition.
- They may locate biblical texts that relate to their academic major and then identify the works of scholars in the biblical fields or theology that comment on these texts in ways that relate to their respective disciplines.
- Students may locate "secular" authors who write on the theoretical, practical, and/or ethical dimensions of the various disciplines and relate those findings to biblical texts.

These assignments in the biblical studies and theology courses fit into the larger scheme for the institutional assessment of learning at Waynesburg. Students are advised to take biblical studies courses early in their college career. After they learn a basic method for relating the content of the Scriptures to their major programs in the biblical studies courses, they must then complete a "faith and learning" activity in an upper-level course in the major.

Conclusion

While some colleges may have endured a "dying of light"[21] by a disengagement from the church, these five examples show that "light is dawning" at Waynesburg College through the integration of faith and learning. Since this integration develops at the moment of a dawning of a new day of rapid institutional change, the future will demand of the college, as it journeys toward midday in this new day in its life as a Christian college, as William Hasker suggests, "the commitment [on behalf of] the college and its faculty to make the integration of learning with the Christian faith [a] part of the broader commitment to serve Christ in every aspect of [institutional] life."[22]

⧨⧨⧨⧨⧨

Waynesburg's explicit effort to express its church-relatedness through careful curricular integration of faith and learning stands in contrast to the emphasis at Rhodes College on being shaped by a meaningful and usable history of relationship to the Presbyterian Church (U.S.A.). Whether or not that history is appropriated by the faculty and continues to shape the identity of the institution may well define the nature of Rhodes's church-relatedness in the present and future.

RHODES COLLEGE: MORE THAN HISTORICAL

Stephen Haynes

Is Rhodes College's relationship with the Presbyterian Church (U.S.A.) best described as historical? Or is it dimensional? In the typology used among Presbyterians these days, most of the nearly seventy colleges and universities affiliated with the denomination fall into one of these two categories. "Dimensional" implies that in the institution's present embodiment one finds reflections of religious affiliation, while "historical" indicates that one must look into the institution's past for evidence of Presbyterian presence.

If this question were to be debated on the Rhodes campus, those who care about the college's relationship to the church would be reluctant to acknowledge that it has diminished to the point of "mere" historical affiliation. Various aspects of campus life would be invoked to qualify Rhodes as a dimensional school, even though most of these would be cocurricular programs with no organic connection to the college's academic program. Personally, I am skeptical of this desire to classify Rhodes as "dimensionally" Presbyterian; yet I am also hesitant to place us without qualification in the "historical" camp, since this seems to indicate that any meaningful Presbyterian identity can be kept safely in the irretrievable past.

In any case, Rhodes's "historical" ties to Presbyterianism reach back a long way, for the college has had an official connection of one sort or another with the Presbyterian Church since 1855. But are these ties enough to make us a church-related college in the present? And what, if anything, do they mean for the college's future? Perhaps more than we think. For the more I learn about the history of Rhodes College and the southern Presbyterian church, the more hopeful I am of a fruitful church affiliation in the future. This is because the college's religious history includes episodes and characters that illuminate the great social and religious questions of American history. In this respect the college's past constitutes usable history, history that is capable of inspiring us and guiding our reflections about what it means to be a liberal arts college in the Presbyterian tradition. A brief look at some of these episodes and characters will indicate the sort of inspiration and guidance I have in mind.

Civil War

Rhodes's southern roots are discernible throughout the institution's history, particularly in the antebellum period when southern nationalism pervaded the campus. In the 1850s, professor of mathematics William Forbes, an avid secessionist, organized a company of students for military drilling. When news came that Fort Sumter was under bombardment, Professor Forbes marched his students to the local fair grounds, "where they encamped until Tennessee withdrew from the Union, when Captain Forbes' company became the first in the county to answer the call of the Governor for troops."[23] All but two of the college's students (both from Kentucky) enlisted in the Confederate Army.[24] Expressing the college's Christian identity, campus representatives claimed theological sanction for the institution of slavery. In 1850, for instance, professor of moral and mental philosophy J. T. Hendrick opined that the existence of slavery indicated the special providence of God. "No truth is clearer to my mind," Hendrick wrote, "than that the hand of God is in all this matter, and that great and glorious results will follow from the existence of slavery in the United States."[25] With the commencement of hostilities, the college's buildings were turned over to the Confederate government and employed as a hospital. Then, following the Battle of Shiloh in 1862, the campus was occupied by Federal forces.

The college emerged from the Civil War a shadow of its former self, its buildings damaged and its professors and students scattered. However, despite the death of the Confederate cause, the southern character of the institution emerged stronger than ever. Since the1830s, Southerners had been aware that educating their youth "at home" should be a greater priority, but it was not until Reconstruction that Southerners, powerless to control much else about their lives, were motivated to take responsibility for determining how and where their children were educated. During this period, the antebellum ideal of building a regional Princeton in the old Southwest was revitalized by influential Presbyterian clergymen James A. Lyon and Benjamin M. Palmer.[26] Both had been vociferous advocates of "Bible slavery" up until 1865, and both were pivotal in the reorganization of the college as Southwestern Presbyterian University in 1873.

Palmer (1818–1902), pastor of New Orleans's First Presbyterian Church from 1855 to 1902 and a leading spokesman for secession in Louisiana, taught that preserving slavery was the South's divinely appointed mission. In the antebellum period, Palmer utilized the so-called "curse of Ham" in Genesis 9 to argue that Africans were doomed to perpetual servitude. After the war, he invoked similar biblical passages to sanction racial segregation. In 1861 Palmer was a founding father of the Presbyterian Church in the Confederate States, and during Reconstruction he became a leading apostle of the South's "Lost Cause." For the remainder of the nineteenth century, in fact, Palmer championed a variety of efforts to keep the South independent from Northern or radical Southern influence.[27]

Palmer is also known as the "the father of Southwestern" (the college's name between 1875 and 1984), a designation that honors Palmer's efforts in organizing Southwestern Presbyterian University as well as his responsibility for the institution's distinctive emphasis on study of the Bible.[28] As one "without whose aid the University could never have been established, nor would it have survived,"[29] Palmer was SPU's first choice to fill the office of Chancellor.[30] Though compelled by his New Orleans congregation to turn down the SPU chancellorship, Palmer became the most influential member of the board of directors during the 1870s and '80s.

Lyon (1818–82), who hailed from Columbus, Mississippi, was another founding father of the Presbyterian Church in the C.S.A. As moderator of the church's 1863 General Assembly, he defended slavery as "manifestly a Bible institution, and consistent with the highest type of piety and practical godliness." It is the special mission of the Southern people, Lyon proclaimed, "to take care of slavery, and to make it redound to the honor and glory of God, and the happiness of our fellow men, to correct its abuses, remove its evils, and bring it up to the Bible standard."[31] Throughout the late 1860s, Lyon and Palmer lobbied their fellow southern Presbyterians for the purpose of "establishing in the South a strong Presbyterian university."[32]

Two other Presbyterian clergy active in the establishment of the PCCSA became important figures in the development of Southwestern Presbyterian University. These were John W. Waddell, who was named SPU Chancellor in 1879,[33] and Joseph R. Wilson, the university's first professor of theology and a recognized leader "in the fight for Southern rights in Church and State affairs," at whose Augusta, Georgia, church the PCCSA had been born. Significantly, the SPU board's first two choices for the professorship in theology were Palmer and Robert L. Dabney, both unrepentant advocates of the Lost Cause.[34]

Thus, the men who organized and nurtured SPU in its formative decades were the very same men who in 1861 had parted ways with northern Old School Presbyterians to found the Presbyterian Church in the Confederate

States of America. Men such as Palmer, Lyon, Waddell, and Wilson were committed to SPU because it was an independent Southern institution designed to preserve the region's and the church's identity. Like other private religious colleges founded in Tennessee in the 1870s, SPU must be seen as a product of the Southern desire to ensure regional identity and independence during the period of Northern occupation.[35]

Civil Rights

In the century or so between the Civil War and the height of the Civil Rights Movement, the college underwent significant changes. It relocated from Clarksville, Tennessee, to Memphis in 1925 and changed names several times before becoming Rhodes College in 1984. More importantly, it took on a new character under a new sort of Presbyterian divine. Charles Diehl, who served as college president from 1917 to 1949, brought to the college a modernist vision that placed it in the service of the American nation. To create his Oxford on the banks of the Mississippi, Diehl hired eighteen Rhodes scholars to serve on the faculty. He consistently portrayed his institution as a "standard college of the liberal arts," by which he meant a seat of liberal learning infused by the spirit of Christianity. This pious liberal Protestant was internationalist, anti-isolationist, and ecumenist.[36] While these broad religious sentiments led him afoul of conservative Presbyterians for most of his career, they transformed Rhodes into the sort of place that attracted pious but progressive faculty and students.

Such students and faculty were much in evidence during the 1960s. According to articles in the student newspaper, campus consciousness of the civil rights movement began to emerge in the fall of 1962, when a group of Southwestern students traveled to nearby Oxford, Mississippi, to witness the spectacle surrounding James Meredith's attempt to enroll at Ole Miss. In the wake of the Meredith crisis, lines of controversy began to be drawn: President Peyton Rhodes—a protégé of Charles Diehl—counseled students against involvement in the region's troubles, while progressive student leaders condemned white resistance to integration. By the spring of 1963, Rhodes students were hosting formal discussions of the proposed Civil Rights Bill and were calling for the college to admit students regardless of race. That fall the student council invited James Meredith to speak on campus, openly repudiating the administration's judgment that Meredith was not of "sufficient intellectual calibre" to warrant such an invitation.[37] A year later, students welcomed controversial professor James Silver of Ole Miss, who was invited to lecture on Mississippi's "closed society."

The college was integrated peacefully in the fall of 1964, with the board of trustees and progressive students jockeying to take credit for the new policy. In 1967, after a black student was refused service at a local steakhouse, a group of activist faculty and students picketed the restaurant and eventually sent its owner into exile in Florida. In early 1968, when the Memphis Sanitation Workers' strike brought civic unrest a few blocks from campus, many students and faculty supported the workers' "I Am a Man" campaign, and several marched with Martin Luther King Jr. down Beale Street. Remarkably, a member of Rhodes's first integrated class organized "the Invaders," a militant group that pledged to defend black interests by any means necessary.

But the most interesting and far-reaching incident involving Rhodes students during these heady years of social change occurred in the spring of 1964. Influenced by attempts elsewhere in the South to integrate worship services at white churches, a group of students targeted Memphis's Second Presbyterian, one of the largest congregations in the southern Presbyterian church and a major source of support for the college. The campaign to integrate Second Presbyterian commenced on Sunday, March 10, 1964, when, under the leadership of the local Intercollegiate Chapter of the NAACP, a handful of students from Southwestern, Lemoyne-Owen College, and Memphis State University attempted to enter the church's sanctuary for morning worship. Because Second had a policy that prohibited racial mixing at church-sponsored events, the students were turned away.

They were undeterred, however, and returned to the church on at least eight subsequent Sundays. As the weekly drama at Second Church evolved, it featured between five and forty well-dressed college students seeking entry into the sanctuary; church officers linking arms to keep them out; the church's membership entering through a side door; the students remaining outside during the service to hold a prayer vigil; police making sure there were no disturbances; and curious onlookers and representatives of the media taking it all in.

Not surprisingly, the weekly spectacle attracted local and national notice. Attention was heightened because Second Church was among the largest Presbyterian congregations in the country, and because it was scheduled to host the 1965 meeting of the PCUS General Assembly. By early May, a presbytery in Virginia was requesting that the denomination pressure Second to reconsider its worship policy and, if it refused to do so, that the PCUS relocate the 1965 General Assembly. Meeting later that month, commissioners to the 1964 GA condemned Second's practice of admitting only white worshipers, proclaiming that for a century the denomination had precluded "any exclusion of persons from communing membership [and from participation in public worship] solely on the grounds of race or color."[38] Nevertheless, supporters of Second Church defeated a motion that would have moved the following year's General Assembly.

This small victory for Second Church was accompanied by the end of the academic year and the dispersion of the student agitators. Nevertheless, the controversy refused to die. By June, Memphis Presbytery had received communications from several synod and presbytery bodies urging it to bring Second Church into line with denominational policy. Meanwhile, the Synod of Tennessee instructed "the sessions of all churches within its jurisdiction to admit all persons desiring to attend divine services in any churches."[39] Still Second was defiant. On one hand, the church was determined to resist outside pressure. On the other hand, it insisted that the controversy should have no bearing on its contract to host the 1965 General Assembly.

Whether Second's defiance of church policy warranted relocation of the 1965 GA, and the proper method for deciding the question, were topics debated throughout the southern Presbyterian church during the summer and fall of 1964. When the fall of 1964 arrived and the student visitations did not immediately resume, Second Church's session became even more determined to resist change. To the committee of Memphis Presbytery assigned to mediate on the issue, they wrote: "The problems that [you] referred to no doubt were the demonstrators at our church but they have been gone for months, and we do not anticipate any further demonstrations."[40] In October, Second's session voted not to discuss "the race issue" until the following May. A church spokesman said, "I think we will do the right thing but we are not going to be pushed into something."[41]

No doubt one factor in Second's recalcitrance was its knowledge that any plot to relocate the 1965 General Assembly would have to be approved by the denomination's moderator, Felix Gear. Gear was a sixty-five-year-old theology professor at Columbia Theological Seminary, who was viewed as the sort of trusted moderate who would steer the denomination through the rough seas of social disruption. And as providence would have it, Gear had served as senior minister of Memphis Second from 1943 to 1947. Before joining the staff of Second Church, however, Gear had served for ten years as professor of Bible at Rhodes College. He had arrived in 1934, in the immediate aftermath of the Diehl affair, in which a group of local ministers accused the president and religion faculty of theological modernism. As one of Diehl's Bible professors during these years of attack from conservative Presbyterians, Gear had learned that the correct position on theological issues is not always the popular one. This experience no doubt prepared him for the abuse heaped on him during his year as moderator by conservative southern Presbyterians.[42]

Gear had been deeply impressed by Charles Diehl. On the occasion of Diehl's retirement, Gear publicly celebrated his legacy as one who "was willing to fight alone and against terrific odds," but could not lower his ideals. Significantly, Gear wrote, there was "no place in [Diehl's] nature for prejudice of race, class or section."[43] Gear stressed the Christian obligation for social justice long before the emergence of liberation theology.[44] And he spoke in favor of union with northern Presbyterians, not a popular cause in the 1960s, given the northern church's progressive stance on social issues.[45]

With specific regard to race, Gear emphasized that acceptance of Jesus Christ as Lord and Savior was the only condition of membership in the Presbyterian Church U.S. and that this "fundamental fact applies, therefore, to the matter of race." He reminded his fellow Presbyterians that since 1865 the southern Presbyterian church had "declared that exclusion on the basis of race or color of anyone from membership in the Church is unscriptural and therefore wrong."[46] To those who believed otherwise, he mailed a copy of the 1865 GA resolution that determined the church's stance on the issue.

Gear's courage during the Second Presbyterian controversy was matched by that of Peyton Rhodes, who succeeded Dr. Diehl as college president. When pressured to side with the interests of potential donors over those of his students, Rhodes was a model of principle. During the spring of 1964, Second Church sent a representative to meet with President Rhodes. According to witnesses, their conversation went something like this:

Disgruntled Churchman: This situation is deeply embarrassing to the church, and to those who support this good Presbyterian school. If you do not call off your students, this could prove very costly to the college.

President Rhodes: I understand very well what you are saying. I will communicate to the students the potential consequences of their actions, but I will not call them off. Furthermore, this college is not for sale.

Peyton Rhodes proved himself both a worthy successor to Charles Diehl and a model for Felix Gear, who a few months later would be faced with his own difficult decision regarding Second Church. In January 1965, having been informed by Second's clerk of session that the church would not alter its policy regarding segregation, Gear exercised his prerogative as moderator and unilaterally moved the upcoming General Assembly to the Montreat Conference Center in North Carolina.[47] Two months later, Second Church voted to revise its worship policy and seated a lone Negro man in its balcony. But its right to host the GA was not reinstated.

Conclusion

In the Second Presbyterian controversy a Rhodes administrator and a former Rhodes professor completed what a courageous group of Rhodes students had started, and dealt a crushing blow to a powerful congregation's attempt to maintain a segregated church. Nearly forty years later, in February 2002, a series of disturbing racial incidents shook the Rhodes College campus. Two black students had their cars vandalized, and several members of the Black Student Association received hate mail scrawled with the message "We don't want you here." For several weeks, the campus was in shock. These racist acts were repeatedly condemned by administrators, faculty, and students; there was a campuswide rally at which a group of student leaders read a petition demanding fundamental changes in the institution; classes were suspended for a "day of truth and reconciliation." Nowhere, however, in the process of institutional soul-searching that followed these incidents was the college's history or religious affiliation identified as a resource for responding to the crisis. The dean of the college, an active Presbyterian, noted that racial intolerance is incompatible with the college's academic mission; but neither he, the president, nor any other campus voice condemned the racial incidents as incompatible with the college's religious identity. Indeed, the college's response has revealed that Rhodes's religious history is not viewed as a resource for dealing with contemporary crises of meaning or identity.

It is not that members of the Rhodes community have interrogated our religious history and found it irrelevant to present concerns. Rather, the problem is one of ignorance—ignorance of the institution's legacy of racial progressivism during the 1960s, of the school's covenant obligation to "work to recruit racial ethnic persons at every level of the college's life," and of the Presbyterian Church U.S.A.'s strong antiracism stance. Thus, part of my vocation as a Presbyterian scholar-teacher (one who was ordained specifically to teach religion at the college) is to help administrators, faculty, and students to consider our religious identification as a resource rather than a burden.

As we have seen, Rhodes's religious tradition is rich and complicated, worthy of both repudiation and recovery. But if Rhodes's historic connection with the Presbyterian Church is to inform the present and future, the tradition must be better known. Stories such as those related here must be recounted as a way of passing on the tradition and of combating the misconceptions that are so common on the campuses of historically Presbyterian schools. These misconceptions are born of ignorance and nurtured by the college's failure to educate its faculty, administrators, or students about what Presbyterianism is or how it is embodied in institutions of higher education.

The problem is most worrisome with faculty, since they do more than any other group to define a college's ethos. At Presbyterian schools in the "historical" camp, faculty are not hired on the basis of their familiarity with the school's religious tradition, and life on campus does precious little to improve it. With professional socialization, in fact, ignorance gradually turns into alienation. Many faculty assume that religion is hopelessly oppressive, narrow, and sectarian, and thus believe that their own school's religious tradition is best relegated to an irrelevant past where it can do no harm. The way beyond these misconceptions is education, a process that begins with a rigorous and mandatory faculty orientation program that clarifies the religious tradition of the institution—warts and all—and makes it part of the shared history of those whom it employs. The tradition can be embraced or rejected, of course, but at least it becomes an item for discussion, a common story around which contemporary debates can turn. Thus, historic religious connections, if they are taken seriously, analyzed, and discussed, can be one method for making colleges and universities *more* than historically Presbyterian. These usable and living histories may even evolve into one dimension of the dimensional Presbyterian campus.

THE VOCATION OF TEACHING IN THE CHURCH-RELATED COLLEGE

Margaret Cowan

The diversity of Presbyterian institutions of higher education inevitably means that those who are called to teach in these colleges and universities will live out their vocation in different ways. Whether the focus is on critical reflection on all dimensions of life, including faith perspectives, on integrating Christian worldviews into all academic disciplines, or on reclaiming a past that can empower engagement in social change and church reform, Presbyterian colleges define their missions in relation to a rich tradition that can greatly enhance the sense of vocation of those who teach.

9

The Vocation of Teaching in Secular and Public Colleges and Universities

Iain S. Maclean and Cynthia Boyle

INTRODUCTION

James T. Burtchaell's exhaustive work on the historical relationship between American higher education and the church, *The Dying of the Light*, has been greeted with much approval and in turn has provoked much discussion about the future status and future prospects of church-related colleges and universities in the United States. As such, it is but the latest in a long line of jeremiads, such as those by George Marsden and Bradley Longfield, Mark Noll, and Douglas Sloan, that have chronicled the dramatic secularization of the denominational or church-related higher educational establishment.[1] What such accounts make clear is the impact of dramatic cultural and educational shifts on the whole higher educational establishment. What is somewhat obscured is that the light was not only in the church-related institutions of higher education. It has been and still is being reflected by (an increasing number of) faculty at state or nonreligious institutions. Most relevant to this chapter are the dramatic demographic shifts that have occurred in patterns of higher education since World War II. Church-related higher education establishments have been secularized during this period for a number of reasons, including but not limited to factors such as increasing cultural pluralism, the diminution of denominational rivalry, competition for students, and lack of denominational financial support. During the same period these same colleges experienced declining student enrollments, a matter of concern to the

130

colleges and the affiliated churches. Thus, for example, while a full 80 percent of undergraduates were taught in church-related colleges at the turn of the twentieth century, already by the end of the Second World War this percentage had halved to 40 percent.[2] By the year 2000 this percentage was under 10 percent.[3]

This study represents an initial attempt to address the numerous challenges presented by this dramatically altered higher education situation at the cusp of another millennium. Considerable research and theorizing has been devoted by denominational bodies to the situation (if not fate) of church-related schools and their faculties. Much work has been done by others on the growing state-funded institutions and their faculties, which now provide the bulk of the education for the majority of the American traditional or non-traditional student. Given these rather dramatic demographic shifts and thus changes in North American higher education, it should be clear that most faculty-student interactions where one or both participants are Presbyterian now occur in non–church-related institutions. This study, while noting the challenges presented, seeks to address those surrounding the understanding of the teaching vocation by those Presbyterian (or Reformed) professors teaching in state institutions of higher education. This has been attempted in two ways: both by outlining the present situation in terms of the realities of contemporary higher education, and by providing (with some commentary) the results of a preliminary survey taken among faculty at state institutions of higher education who self-consciously identify themselves as Presbyterian (or in the Reformed tradition).[4]

The contemporary higher education situation is marked by the rise and indeed dominance of the state-funded university or college system, which now educates the overwhelming majority of students. As educational costs rose in the second half of the twentieth century, more states established state universities with subsidized fees, drawing more and more students. By the '60s, only about a third of all colleges were private, with about half of that number being church-related, just over eight hundred in number.[5] Well under 10 percent of the total number of students enrolled now attend denominationally affiliated colleges or universities. Thus, as the number of church-related colleges shrank and the number of students attending the same dwindled, the number of state (by definition nonreligious) higher education institutions rose dramatically, with a corresponding increase in student numbers. As a result, only a relatively small percentage of the total number of students is enrolled, at the turn of the twenty-first century, in church-related colleges. The growth of higher education in the post–World War II period therefore was dramatic, and this is reflected in the increasing number of students in higher education, and in non–church-related institutions. Thus, from a total of about 597,000 students in

1919–20, enrollment in higher education institutions had risen to 1,500,000 in 1939–40, and to a high of 3.9 million (1.8 million in private and/or church-related, and 2.1 million in state institutions) in 1959–60. The statistical picture now begins to shift irrevocably in favor of state institutions. Thus, while the total number of enrollments had increased by the 1969–70 academic year to 7.8 million, the increase was to the state institutions' credit only. Enrollment in private and church-related institutions remained flat, at around the 1.9 million mark, increasing only slightly to just over 2 million over the next thirty years. Meanwhile, enrollment numbers continued their climb, to about 12 million in 1980. Enrollment increased by 16 percent between 1978 and 1988, and by 11 percent between 1988 and 1998, from 13.1 million to 14.5 million, and by 2001 to around 15 million.[6]

In addition, it should be noted that fully a third of this number represents students at two-year or community colleges. Community colleges also provide the education for 42 percent of all African American and 55 percent of all Hispanic students. The majority of these students were seeking training in the vocational, technical, and professional fields, in particular engineering, education, and business.[7] In addition, critical shifts in the demographics should be noted; during the decade of the '90s, while male enrollment increased by a few percent, that of females rose by 16 percent. Further, while the number of older (or "nontraditional")[8] students had been growing more rapidly than that of traditional-aged students, this growth is slowing.

Thus while the number of traditional-aged students increased by 8 percent during the same decade, that of nontraditional students increased by 7 percent. In short, according to the National Center for Education Statistics, a 24 percent rise in traditional-aged and a 9 percent rise in nontraditional-aged student enrollments are expected by the year 2010. By 1984 the number of women in graduate programs first exceeded that of men, and during the decade 1988 to 1998 the number of male graduate students increased by 16 percent, while that for women increased by an amazing 60 percent. The proportion of students who are minorities has likewise been increasing over the last twenty-five years. While 16 percent of students in 1976 were minorities, by 1997 this had climbed to 27 percent.[9] Much of this increase can be attributed to rising enrollment of Asian and Hispanic students, though African American enrollment has remained relatively consistent over the last decade at 11 percent.

CONTEMPORARY HIGHER EDUCATION

As the student numbers enrolled in institutions of higher education grew, so of course did the number of faculty. In fact, the number of faculty increased by about two-thirds in the years 1940 to 1960, from 147,000 to 244,000, and within the decade had doubled again to 509,000 in 1970.[10] The total number of full-time faculty at higher education institutions had climbed to 1.8 million by the end of the century.[11] This increase in the number of full-time faculty slowed during the 1980s, with the sharp increase in the number of part-time or adjunct, and non–tenure-track full-time faculty being employed (primarily or even exclusively as a cost-saving measure). These numbers support the idea that the majority of faculty-student interactions, in which one or both are Presbyterian, now occur primarily in such non–church-related or secular institutions.

Just as the numbers of students and faculty increased quantitatively over the last half century, shifts occurred in the demographics of the student body, and so did changes in the composition and self-perception of the faculty. The faculty has undergone, in the words of Martin J. Finkelstein and Jack H. Schuster, "a silent revolution."[12] This comprises dramatic alterations in the composition of faculty, their self-conception and perceived vocational tasks, and the long-term implications of these changes. As already noted, women now compose a majority of faculty, not so much in the traditional liberal arts, but rather in more career-oriented and professional fields. An even more radical shift has been the drop in tenure-track appointments among full-time educators. While such appointments were virtually unknown in the '60s, and four-fifths of full-time faculty held tenure as recently as 1992, by 1998 only two-thirds of all full-time hires were on tenure-track appointments. The long-term implications of this shift are not yet clear, but initial results of a study conducted by Roger J. Baldwin and Jay L. Chronister are suggestive. Their research draws on recent surveys that indicate that this new generation of non–tenure-track faculty are focused on the teaching task and devote much less time to the institution, far less to service and committee commitments (typically because ineligible, as not tenured), less time to research, and little if any time to informal interaction with students.[13] The implications of this are significant. As the number of non-tenured faculty grow, the tenured faculty are burdened with greater service and committee work, typically limited to such tenured faculty. The long-term implications of a two-tiered and unequal faculty body are not clear yet. An immediate effect already noted is that faculty morale suffers, with tenured faculty assuming an increasing load of administrative and committee assignments, while nontenured faculty, with little institutional loyalty, have less commitment to the institution and its students and are presumably seeking another (tenured) position elsewhere.

Interestingly, it was only in the recent past (and before the hiring of full-time nontenured faculty had assumed such proportions) that President Derek Bok's 1987 "Report to the Harvard Board of Overseers on American

Higher Education" noted that faculty now understand themselves not so much as teachers, but rather as specialists in their individual fields.[14] Such has been the effect of this specialization that doctoral candidates are now being produced who are not trained in teaching per se, and even less in undertaking the formation of student character or morality. This observation points to another issue, that this recent focus on specialization in one's field has largely become not only the criterion for an advanced degree, but also the criterion for advancement within academia. Such a focus has diminished the importance not only of pedagogy, but also that of service to the university (a community of scholars) and the wider civil and political society. State schools, surfing from one budget crisis to the next, with funding in competition with many other state-funded groups, soon begin to suffer from the effects of a loss of faculty morale. It is thus easier for faculty to narrow their involvement to "my own research" and withdraw from service activities or even commitment to students, because the research-service-teaching triad is not equilateral for academic advancement. The role of adjunct faculty may also undermine faculty morale, as well as the quality and continuity of teaching, because the greater advising and service now begin to burden the fewer and fewer full-time tenured faculty. This narrowing of the conception of the academic vocation has profound implications for understanding the vocation of the teacher.[15]

In addition, church research efforts and scholarly research have focused most of their attention on the church-related institutions, analyzing their history, strategies, faculties, and student bodies.[16] Further, any work that has been done on the sense of calling or vocation has tended to focus on those teaching in denominational seminaries, professional clergy, or those in church-related schools or teaching Christian studies, as is exemplified in the nonetheless outstanding study by Mark Schwehn.[17] Other significant works deal with the concept of vocation from a nonreligious perspective, such as David T. Hansen's *The Call to Teach* and numerous works by Wayne C. Booth.[18] As far as the authors of this chapter know, little or no work up to now has been done on the sense of vocation of those Presbyterian lay faculty who teach in non–church-related and/or state institutions. The authors, though, are aware that the issue of vocation has become a central focus of the Association of Presbyterian Colleges and Universities (APCU) and of the Lilly Foundation. The last-mentioned institution has funded numerous research projects on the whole subject of vocation, most of which are presently in progress. In addition, Presbyterian colleges such as Davidson, Rhodes, and Whitworth, and Catholic ones such as Villanova, presently are offering Lilly Endowment grants for faculty who wish to develop courses that explore and develop the theological, ethical, social, and institutional implications of vocation.

THE PRESENT CHALLENGE FOR THE CHURCH

Shortly after the Second World War the mainline Protestant denominations were acutely aware of the rapid changes in higher education, with the growth both of institutions and of student numbers. Bold denominational and ecumenical initiatives were set up. Of the latter, the Faculty Christian Fellowship, with its accompanying journals, *The Christian Scholar* and the *Faculty Forum*, spearheaded such efforts. However, as Douglas Sloan demonstrates in his revealing study *Faith and Knowledge*, these efforts had all collapsed by 1971, victims not so much of ecumenical disorder and loss of vision as of the radical contexts then enveloping American institutions of higher learning.[19] This was also the period, it should be noted, where the almost overwhelming secularization of most church-related colleges and universities occurred.[20]

Only in the last decade of the twentieth century has interest in church relations to higher education institutions revived. However, the context now is different from the post–World War period. There exists now no "Protestant Establishment," and there is little dominant consensus on matters of faith, religion, common goods, or morality. Scholars describe this lack of consensus or dominant worldview as a cultural paradigm shift from a modern to a postmodern perspective.[21] Not only has the paradigm of modernity with its enthronement of rationality been questioned, but its "undersides," or irrational consequences, have been exposed in the litany of injustices, inequalities, and discriminations that have marked the last century. The results of this are only now affecting both church and higher education institutions.

Reason is no doubt still critical, but the postmodern exposure of its diverse and often occluded interests has tarnished its reputation among professional educators and laity alike. Together with such Weberian disenchantment of the world has come a loss of a common worldview and purpose. Such loss of common goal and thus vision affects church, academy, and students. The latter, sensing rather than knowing the cultural doubts concerning modern rationality, seem to rely on emotive or utilitarian motives (or both) as justification for their actions and worldviews. Further, modernity then can be characterized by a particularly narrow conception of reason, what Max Weber would describe as a technical or instrumental rationality. This has reduced knowledge to empiricism, to quantifiable information only, and thus to an over-sharp dichotomy between scientific knowledge and faith, and indeed ethics. Value cannot be discerned from brute matter alone. Such a narrow conception of human reason has already been questioned by postmodernist critics, and, as numerous theologians have noted, offered openings for addressing the contemporary culture's lack of grounding for values. While scholars might wish to frown on earlier distinctions such as those made by Paul Tillich between "technical reason" and "ontological reason," perhaps the relational concept of holism can offer a broader conception.[22]

It must also be noted, in drawing distinctions between the past and the present, that the "mainline" churches have lost not only their social influence, but large percentages of their earlier membership, becoming, rather, more "sideline" in Wade Clark Roof and William McKinney's memorable phrase.[23] In addition, many of these same churches are beginning to experience the onset of a looming shortage of clergy. This points to a critical clergy vocational crisis as the clergy who trained in the 1960–70 period reach retirement age and fewer candidates are coming forward, and thus seminaries are not producing enough M.Div. candidates to meet the expected vacancies.[24]

So, unlike the situation at mid-century, the present is marked not only by a constriction of vocational task and uncertainty among professional educators, but also by a shortage of clergy and an uncertain, and as yet unclear, vision for the future. In such a situation, the resources of nonclerical church members can become critical for service and outreach. This recognition of the vocation or calling of all to serve not only the church, but the common good of society, has prompted the interest in the sense of vocation in recent years. Not only, as noted earlier, has the Lilly Endowment embarked on the funding of numerous projects around the concept and practice of vocation in higher education institutions, but organizations such as the APCU affiliated with the PC(USA) have initiated national conferences on the issue.[25]

THE REFORMED UNDERSTANDING OF VOCATION

Despite the emergence of a postmodernist worldview in the general culture and in academia, a reductionist, mechanistic, and empiricist view of knowledge still holds. This leads, as it has done in the past, to a dualistic conception of knowledge, which is either empirically verifiable fact or nonverifiable belief, legend, or myth. Of course, this also applies to questions of ethics and values. Hence the crisis of values in contemporary American society. If knowledge is so narrowly defined, from where do ethical norms come, and on what authority can they be accepted? Christians are left trying to deal with a two-tiered worldview: natural knowledge, and knowledge that comes from faith and revelation.

In a strikingly similar fashion, contemporary Christians seem to have accepted a dualistic—and pre-Reformation—conception of vocation. Thus it is assumed that pastors, religious professionals, and seminary professors all have a vocation or calling that is somehow higher or more "spiritual" than other, mundane callings, such as those involved in becoming community pharmacists, professionals, mechanics, or mathematics teachers at vocational technical schools. However, in sharp contrast with this primarily mediaeval view, the Reformers Martin Luther and John Calvin held that all work, whether in or beyond the church, is work that God has called all Christians, indeed all people, to perform. Calvin states quite clearly that all work is to be understood as involving a calling. He states that

> The Lord bids each one of us in all life's actions to look to his calling. . . . From this will arise also a singular consolation: that no task will be so sordid and base, provided you obey your calling in it, that it will not shine and be reckoned very precious in God's sight.[26]

This recognition of divine calling to perform all work has continued to be an essential feature of Reformed thought, and it is reiterated by the late Union Theological Seminary theologian John Leith, who has stated,

> Good works are covered by God's mercy; their flaws are forgiven. . . . Good works are not distinguished by their own nature. Christians do the same work as non-Christians. Good works in the Christian definition are distinguished by the faith, the disposition, and the commitment with which they are done. There are no distinctively Christian works apart from the faith that motivates and shapes them. . . . Good works are used by God to enhance human life and to accomplish his purposes.[27]

Christian educators at secular institutions can take heart that their work, whether teaching physics or music, religious studies, mathematics, or nursing, affects the essence of individual students who need the knowledge, skills, abilities, and values that an education comprises.

The Reformed tradition, drawing on the conviction that the God revealed by Scripture governs all of creation, and not just the "religious" parts, thus informs the fulfilled vocation of all teachers. God has granted to all, including academics, a vocation to continue the reordering of the world toward the common good. Further (and these points are no doubt amplified elsewhere in this volume), the Reformed emphasis on belief and practice, which the church Reformed is always reforming, requires continual education. Education is therefore a critical element of such ongoing reformation, not only of the church, but also of the academy, the wider society, and the world.

Nonetheless, the increasing fragmentation, both of our common societal norms and also of the professoriat, does put the vocation of the teacher in question. Given the polarization discerned in the faculty, and the division appearing in the traditional triad of research, teaching, and service, what precisely is the contemporary teacher's vocation? Is it primarily that of a researcher? a teacher? one who contributes through service to institution and the common life? Or is it to be found in some revised combination of these three? Certainly the stark dichotomy between research and teaching is overdrawn and should be avoided. After all, how can teaching be perfected if the teacher is not *au fait* with current research? Typically higher education training requires the first, while more and more institutions are now stressing the second and third. Yet what about the teacher's role in facilitating character formation, with the formation of ethical norms in the student in and through the content and the presentation of content matter? Surely the vocation of the teacher includes all these elements (of course modified by individual context), perhaps summed up in the metaphor of the cultivation of friendships, not only with colleagues, but with staff, and especially with students. This building of faculty relationships between peers and with students has often been undervalued, but its prominence in the survey undertaken for this project (on which see below) points to a great but unharnessed resource.

To return to the issues of faith and knowledge: The nature of the teaching task, the ascendancy of moral pluralism and even relativism within the teaching profession and the student body, the sharp separation of science from ethics and religion, and the ambiguous place of religion within academy and society are all factors that call for a redescribing, or perhaps reforming, of the (post)modern worldview(s).

As numerous contemporary philosophers, social theorists, and theologians have indicated, an alternative to the fragmentation, atomistic individualism, and *anomie* that seem to haunt Western societies must be sought in some relational understanding of life. This is often described as holism—in fact, an ancient concept that refers to a whole composed of many parts, or in its modern usage to a whole greater than the individual parts of which it is composed. The English term holism was coined and came into common English use as a consequence of its employment by South African philosopher and statesman Jan Christian Smuts in his work *Holism and Evolution* (1926).[28] Smuts developed this philosophical doctrine to express his conviction that the universe is understood as an evolutionary process that produces wholes of ever-increasing complexity and self-awareness. The constituent parts are such that their totality is greater than the sum of their individual parts. While this is, of course, a concept with an ancient genealogy stretching from the pre-Socratics through to Teilhard de Chardin, Smuts expressed through this term his remarkable synthesis of modern science with this concept. Not only is the concept of holism conceived of as a process of synthesis, but it is combined with a deep belief in personalism. For Smuts, personality was the highest level of development in an ever-developing universe. This included belief in the value of the individual, and in love as the force that brought humans together in associations.

Holism then represented a reaction against the mechanistic conceptions of science and the accompanying individualistic fragmentation that marked much of the modern philosophical and cultural *Weltanschauung* (worldview). Against such reductionism, holism understands all the elements of the human whole as continuous with each other, the world, and the whole universe. The part is, rather, a manifestation of a prior whole. The human personality is the center of self-determination, and evolution is the achievement of higher forms of self-determination, resulting in an inner cosmos where the part is more related to the whole than to the constituent parts. Such spirituality in turn gives purpose to the whole. This almost mystical perception enables the individual to strive to the whole through the struggles and negations of existence.

Holism, then, is a comprehensive worldview that produces order and coherence, not only among the sciences, but also in the realms of politics, aesthetics, and morals. It provides meaning for the parts and the whole as they mutually and reciprocally influence and modify each other. In this way holism introduces concepts of history and teleology into the scientific worldview. The political and social consequences of holism are the positing of the relational nature of all reality and thus the interdependence of all beings and matter.

Holism became a central organizing principle of both ecological and theological movements in the late twentieth century. These are ably synthesized and presented in the recent works by theologians, ecological and feminist ethicists, and certainly in those of the Reformed tradition with its concern for all of life. Such works stress the interrelatedness and complexity of all being. The holistic paradigm strives to overcome the polarities and dichotomies that have characterized modernity, and offers a context in which Christian educators in secular institutions can integrate their own research and course specializations.

REFORMED UNDERSTANDING OF TEACHING AND PEDAGOGY (FAITH AND REASON)

How does the Reformed tradition inform the teaching of the Presbyterian teacher? Primarily in the recognition that everything is subject to God's rule, and that humanity has been created with the ability to seek understanding of all the spheres of life. Humanity, through the ability to reason, is able to learn, and then to pass on that knowledge by teaching. However, all this in itself is subject to human imperfection, which is lessened by human cooperation as expressed through social institutions. Education is one of the primary institutions in this task.

The Reformed tradition is characterized by numerous emphases: the rule of God over all spheres of life; the importance of the role of the mind (while recognizing both its potential and imperfection); the proper role of both the experiential and the noetic in the Christian life; and the necessity (because of human finitude) of a collegial understanding of church governance, of the common life, and of the necessity for continual "reforming" in all these spheres. The most critical of these are considered in more detail.

Presbyterianism has always placed a high emphasis on the training and forming of the mind and character of all Christians. Thus wherever the Reformed tradition has emerged, it has sought to establish educational institutions for precisely those purposes. In fact, the early Calvinist reformers followed Calvin in his understanding that Christ's prophetic office implied the establishment of the office of a "teacher doctor" as a separate ministerial office from that of the pastor, as occurred in early Reformed Geneva.[29] Such education was not only "theological" in the professional sense of the term, but included all areas of human knowledge. Again, Calvin himself provided the example by his own education in Renaissance humanism, as well as in the most contemporary results of the theological sciences. It is often overlooked that Calvin's first published work was not in theology, but in classical philology, with a commentary on the Stoic Seneca's *De Clementia*.[30]

The church Reformed is always reforming. This principle applies not only to the ecclesiastical institution, but also to our understanding, to other social institutions, and to our perceptions of reality and knowledge. This challenges the Presbyterian teacher to comprehend not only the (changing) Reformed tradition, but also the (changing) context in which she or he exercises a vocation. This leads to the critical issue for the Presbyterian tradition of how the faith (revelation/theological tradition) and human reason or knowledge are related. The twentieth century witnessed a sharp sundering of these two elements of human being and knowing in the world, a division that has led many people (and popular culture in general) to assume that a sharp dichotomy exists between religion and reason. However, from the first chapter of Calvin's *Institutes*, it is clear that he affirms and reiterates the Augustinian emphasis on the role of reason in religious belief (an emphasis stressed more recently, as in the work of Edward Dowey, William Placher, Stacy Johnson, and others).[31] One critical implication of this position is that the believer can share with the non-believer a common reason and understanding of reality and our place therein. This understanding of common grace forms a basis for common striving for a better world and provides the ability to work to transform this world (an emphasis in the modern period of the Dutch tradition of Abraham Kuyper and others).[32]

Despite this commonality between all men and women, the Reformed recognition of the reality of sin means the recognition not only of human imperfection, but also of human reason itself. As all spheres of human being (including the church) are affected, continual reformulation of knowledge, institutional renewal, and pedagogical approaches are demanded. Thus, in spite of the reality of human finitude, the Reformed tradition recognizes the continual calling of God in our efforts, in all spheres of life, to contribute to the common (human and nonhuman) good and therefore, inter alia, to human flourishing. Thus, the Christian educator uses her mind and knowledge to the greater glory of God in whatever field she is called to exercise the teaching task.

SURVEY AND RESULTS

As an initial step to characterize Presbyterian educators at secular institutions, the authors drafted a survey (fig. 1). Even with a relatively small sample size, common themes and trends developed.[33] Other groups throughout the country are encouraged to adapt this survey for further research in this emerging area of interest.

Tentative Trends and Observations

Demographics were included in order to compile information for educators in all four categories (full-time, part-time, adjunct, and retired). While all four were represented in the responses, almost three-fourths of the responders were full-time faculty members. Half of the faculty were tenured, with the remaining indicating nontenure track or administration; 86 percent were members of PC(USA) congregations. Half of the faculty had been ordained, with years of service ranging from two to twelve years, and two-thirds attend church on or near the campus where they work. Half stated that their campus had a Presbyterian chaplain, but a fourth of the remaining faculty were unsure.

Surprisingly, almost a third of the faculty believed that their local church was not interested in what they are doing professionally, and did not call on them for their expertise. The majority who were utilized by local congregations listed teaching and leadership roles. Far fewer (less than 20 percent) had been called on for their expertise by presbytery, synod, or General Assembly. Forty percent of the faculty had been involved in campus outreach to students.

In response to the question "As a Christian educator, how are you perceived by your peers on campus?" one educator replied with "hope that my concern for students and my personal integrity are evident to my colleagues." Another stated that "I don't see myself as a Christian educator, but as an educator that is Christian." Most commonly faculty cited respect and trust, but

Figure 1. The Vocation of the Presbyterian Teacher

On Fulfilling One's Calling to Teach from a Reformed Perspective

1. Name (optional, but helpful for follow-up) _____
2. Institution _____
3. Faculty Status: Full-time ___ Part-time ___ Adjunct ___ Retired ___
4. Tenured _____ Nontenured _____
5. Are you a member of a local PC(USA) congregation? Yes ___ No ___
6. Are you an elder, deacon, or minister? _____ Please specify _____
7. Years of Service: Elder _____ Deacon _____ Minister _____
8. Is the church you attend located on or near the campus where you work?
   Yes ___ No ___
9. Does your campus have a Presbyterian chaplain? Yes ___ No ___
10. Does your campus have Presbyterian or Reformed student organizations?
    Yes ___ No ___
11. Is your local church interested in what you are doing professionally?
12. Are you called upon by your local church for your expertise? Yes ___ No ___
    If yes, how?
13. Has the church beyond your local congregation (Presbytery, Synod, General
    Assembly) called upon your expertise? Yes ___ No ___
    If yes, how?
14. Have you been resourced or utilized by the local congregation, Presbytery, Synod,
    etc., to assist in the church/chaplain's outreach on campus? Yes___ No___
    If yes, how?
15. Are you asked, or do you volunteer, to be part of the church's outreach on
    campus? Yes ___ No ___
    If yes, how?
16. As a Christian educator, how are you perceived by your peers on campus?
17. Has that changed in the last five years?
18. Do you have a sense of your calling to teach?
19. If called to teach, who or what was most influential in your call to teach?
20. Have you been active in church your whole career?
21. If not, what were the circumstances when you were not active?
22. How does your Christian faith and/or your call to teach influence:
    Research?
    Pedagogy?
    Academic freedom?
    Office hours?
    Participation in student organizations?
    Personal stewardship (time/talent, resources, self-care)?
    Advising/counseling?
    Respect for religious differences?

one said, "I am well received, but probably because of my overall nature and personality, rather than my religious beliefs."

The core question for this chapter reads "Do you have a sense of your calling to teach?" Almost three-fourths of the responders answered "Yes" or "Absolutely." People influential in their call to teach were: family members; elders and ministers; fellow Christians; and teachers and advisers. Other influences included poverty in childhood, personal desire to associate with young people, specific interests and abilities, and prayer. One Vietnam-era graduate recalled that "usually the role models were negative, so the sense of vocation was contrarian."

When asked "How does your Christian faith and/or your call to teach influence research, pedagogy, academic freedom, office hours, participation in student organizations, personal stewardship, advising/counseling, and respect for religious differences?" faculty provided interesting insights into their roles within secular institutions. Some additional points have emerged from the authors' research and reflection.

First, the majority of respondents understood themselves as role models for both colleagues and students, or as faculty counselor for student groups or for a local campus ministry. The opportunity for advising students was deemed critical. Another aspect of this was to serve as church "parents" for students by creating friendships and by inviting them to homes or to social events.

Second, faculty did not seem limited by First Amendment interpretations of their freedom to express their faith or talk about it. This question had been included in the survey because it seemed that there exists a common assumption that religious belief could be deleterious to a faculty member's promotion prospects. It was surprising to learn that this was almost a nonissue, though perhaps the survey instrument needs refining at this point. Further, the regions where the survey was administered are generally socially and religiously homogeneous, and this might account for the general acceptance of faculty with religious beliefs and practices. So there was no opposition from faculty colleagues, as it seemed a nonissue to many, though some indicated that their colleagues were surprised on learning that they attended church. They see teaching tasks as engaging students in subject matter so that the encounter might be transformative. Overwhelmingly they treat students with dignity and respect, listen to their views, and engage in argument.

CONCLUSION

These early responses to the survey suggest that there is need for more support from local churches, not only in supporting specific religious ministries to students, but also in affirming and utilizing faculty. These faculty offer their vocations for their specific skills and expertise, and also their avocations as Christian lay ministers who are in contact with many younger individuals at risk for becoming inactive in church, as had many of these faculty during their college careers. Overall, there is a failure to recognize the increasing numbers of Presbyterians studying at state schools, with the consequence that there are fewer and fewer of them studying at the more expensive denominationally affiliated and private schools. Is this failure related or connected to the present clergy vocations crisis in the Presbyterian Church (U.S.A.)?

The teacher's role involves recognizing his or her (and the students') own changing contexts, along with a willingness to include and address this in inter-action with traditions of the past. In many ways teaching is, if not a collegial (for the professor remains as the "authority" or "resource person"), then at least a communal and ongoing process. The teacher can then only live in hope and anticipation, as in most cases it may be years, perhaps, before the results of teaching will mature and bear results.

By placing a greater emphasis on the vocation of teaching in its many expressions and locations, the church affirms the holistic and Reformed con-viction that "the earth is the Lord's," and that all disciplines are critical in revealing not only the interconnectedness of all being, but also God's purposes for the world and the church. So greater attention needs to be given to the col-leges and universities that are not church-related, where today more Presby-terian faculty are exercising their calling to teach and more Presbyterian and Reformed students are exercising theirs.

10

Teaching and Learning
in Presbyterian Theological Education

INTRODUCTION

EDWARD C. (TED) ZARAGOSA

We've looked at teaching in church-related and secular colleges and universities, and the effects of demographic changes on Presbyterian Seminaries. Presbyterian educators are also called to teach in theological seminaries, which present their own distinctive challenges. This chapter will focus on three of those challenges: teaching women, teaching racial ethnic students, and teaching in an ecumenical setting. The preparation the teacher brings to the classroom includes not only research, publication, and competence in his or her chosen field, but often equally as obvious in a seminary context is his or her own sense of Christian identity. For Presbyterian educators, this sense of Christian identity is informed and shaped by a number of things, such as previous pastoral experience; knowledge of and appreciation for the Reformed tradition; a striving for faithfulness to the call to teach; demonstrating "faith seeking understanding," or a desire to know the truth; and accountability to the seminary's many "publics." Outside the seminary these publics include the academy and the larger church. Inside the seminary, the publics not to be ignored are the other resident faculty, the administration, the board of trustees, and ultimately the denominations represented by the student body.

Still, the focus remains squarely on the students—their expectations, needs, and requirements. Not to be forgotten, however, are the corollary educational demands of the denominations and the historic mission of the seminaries to educate "learned clergy," or scholar-pastors, as well as to train leaders for the varied ministries of the church. And because the students are the priority, each of the case studies below displays some common, if not pervasive, concerns. As pervasive as the increase in the number of female and racial ethnic students is the second-career student. While women and people of color have their own histories and perspectives that require close attention, second-career students may constitute the greatest challenge to more "traditional" seminary models of curriculum and community.

Whoever the student, three general challenges for tomorrow's Presbyterian seminary educators emerge from the three overlapping case studies presented in this chapter. The first regards the student's social world and includes concerns about adult learners, diversity, and "finding one's voice." The second reframes curricular issues around relevance and pastoral application on the one hand and use of technology on the other, in an academic world constrained by limited resources. And third, formation issues challenge us by asking lingering questions about sexism in ministry, racism in the church, pluralism, and the global context of the church.

Each of the authors speaks to more than one of these challenges directly out of personal experience as a Presbyterian seminary educator concerned with teaching women, teaching racial ethnic students, or teaching in an ecumenical setting. They are confident that the reader will find kindred spirits in these three case studies, as well as common challenges. We begin with teaching women.

FROM THE EXCEPTION TO THE NORM: WOMEN IN SEMINARIES AND MINISTRY

Cynthia M. Campbell

Women have been students in theological schools (or colleges with seminaries) since the late nineteenth century. Degrees in, and schools of, Christian education were created for women early in the twentieth century. It was not until the last two decades of the twentieth century that women entered master of divinity programs in significant numbers. Now, as the twenty-first century opens, women make up the majority (or close to it) of the student bodies of many Presbyterian seminaries. In the twentieth century, women students in theological schools went from a status of "special case or exception" to the "norm." The situation for women as faculty members and administrators lags behind and varies greatly from one seminary to another, but the trajectory is roughly the same. Having made the passage as student, as faculty member, and now as administrator, I offer this as a reflection on the experience of women in teaching and learning in Presbyterian theological education.

The Exception

When I entered seminary in 1970, it was the first year in the history of the Harvard Divinity School that women were provided residence in housing owned by the divinity school. Up until that time, the numbers of women students had been so small that women were required to live at Radcliffe or in the law school housing. There were eight or ten of us: Unitarian, Roman Catholic, Southern Baptist, Jewish, United Church of Christ, and Presbyterian. There was one woman on faculty, a junior professor in world religions. There were a number of women in doctoral programs, however, some of whom have gone on to become highly respected leaders in their academic fields.

The situation in Presbyterian seminaries was similar. Until the 1970s, women students could generally be counted on the fingers of one hand. They were "exceptions," and many (as a result) were exceptional students. Like women in other professional fields, as they sat in class with men, some of the male students tolerated (at best) or openly resisted (often on biblical grounds) their presence. Well into the 1970s, women were considered "problems" for candidate committees. ("What will you do when you get married and your husband is transferred? What will happen to your ministry then?" I was asked by my presbytery in 1971.)

Being an "exception" required strength, tenacity, and a certain stubbornness. The challenge was to "find one's own voice" in the midst of an intellectual and professional realm only newly opened to women. For some, the voice that was found was one of confrontation in theology, anthropology, and biblical interpretation dominated by men. For others, it was one of critique from within church and academy. In a variety of forms, "feminist studies" began to take shape across the disciplines of theological study, and "women's issues" became prominent in church and ministry.

A primary issue that emerged was inclusive language (removing the "masculine generic" when referring to persons, as well as challenging exclusively male language and imagery for God). Courses oriented toward women and "women's experience" were developed. This was followed by seemingly endless debates about whether women candidates were "qualified" as opposed to "qualifiable" for faculty positions.

When I began teaching at Austin Presbyterian Theological Seminary in 1981, I was, like many women at that time, the only woman on faculty. Many other women who began teaching during that time were the "first ever" or the "first in a long time" to be named to a faculty position. Women in administrative positions were generally found in student services or library positions.

Once again, the challenge was to find one's voice theologically as well as socially in a decidedly male-oriented faculty culture. Issues now taken for granted in theological education, such as the importance of social location for the reading of biblical texts and for theological reflection, were often seen as passing fads or deviations from traditional doctrine. The first time I taught a seminar in feminist theology, there was a serious debate about changing the word "feminist" to something like "contributions of women."

The list of "firsts" and "onlys" for women continued from the 1980s up to the beginning of the twenty-first century. Now, all the Presbyterian seminaries have significant numbers of women on faculty; many are tenured; a few hold named chairs. Three Presbyterian seminaries have or have had a woman as dean of faculty, and three seminaries are currently led by women presidents (Auburn, Columbia, and McCormick).

The Norm

Over the past twenty years, the number of women students has increased significantly in all Presbyterian seminaries. In a few seminaries, they are the majority, or at least the majority of Presbyterian candidates. While women students are no longer automatically the "brightest and best" in terms of academic and leadership potential, they continue by and large to be very bright, articulate, and deeply committed to church and ministry.

Between the early 1970s and the early 1980s, seminary student populations underwent another significant change, as older or "second career" students began enrolling in record numbers. Even now, the average age of students in most seminaries is in the high thirties or low forties. Women have accounted for a significant proportion of the second-career student population. Almost all of them have a similar story: they thought about ministry when they were younger, but the doors were (or appeared to be) closed; they had no role models; they wanted to raise their families first; they entered professions more accepting of women. The call to ministry could be deferred but it would not be denied, and so they came to seminary in their forties rather than their twenties.

Today, the women students represent a balance between "first" and "second" career. At McCormick, for example, an increasing number of women have begun seminary within a year or two of college. For the most part, their postgraduation years were spent in volunteer ministry with the Presbyterian Church or other not-for-profit agencies. Volunteer service was a mark of their college years. Church background is also strong. The second-career women have come from successful jobs in social work, teaching, law, and even law enforcement. They are drawn to ministry, not because their first profession did not work out, but because they could not incorporate their faith into their work or because they felt limited in how much they could do for people in a secular setting.

A similar shift has occurred for women in faculty positions. Women are found in all fields of academic study, and they are highly sought after in faculty searches. The growing edge is for women of color, who bring to their scholarship and teaching the diversity of cultural and ethnic backgrounds desired by seminaries as they attempt to respond to the challenge to expand the non-white membership of traditional denominations such as the PC(USA).

Impact on Teaching and Learning

As women in theological seminaries have gone from being exceptional cases (one or one of a very few) to a significant plurality if not majority of students and faculty, a number of changes have taken place. They may be described under two rubrics: what has been added to the curriculum and what is missing.

Although women in general and feminist scholars in particular are not the sole cause, women's studies have been a significant force in the ascendancy of the postmodernist approach to theological education. Beginning in the late 1960s and early 1970s, feminist scholars were among those who argued that the context of the reader or interpreter has a decisive impact on the meaning assigned to texts and on the interpretations made by both history and doctrine. What was once regarded as near heresy, namely, that the experience of the reader shapes the meaning of the Bible, is now taken for granted. At McCormick, for example, students are encouraged to understand the African Americans, Asians, and Hispanics, as well as Euro-Americans, looking at the well-off and socially powerful as well as at the poor and marginalized. Faculty are encouraged to review course syllabi so as to ensure that a variety of voices and perspectives are represented in required readings. As a result, students are exposed to a much greater variety of Christian experience and perspectives today than was the case thirty years ago.

Again, while women are not the sole cause, the presence of second-career women has led seminary faculty to take seriously the needs and opportunities that "adult learners" bring to the classroom. While recent college graduates are clearly adults, the term "adult learner" refers to those with ten or more years of professional life behind them when they enter seminary. Such learners require different approaches in teaching and learning (as indicated in Ted Zaragoza's companion article later in this chapter). It is important, among other things, to bring the prior experience of the learners into the classroom and into course requirements. Interest in theories of "multiple intelligences," while not developed or promoted exclusively by women, is certainly in line with ways in which women have traditionally operated.

One of the most significant changes I notice is that what were once "feminist issues" (specifically issues relating to women, gender studies, children, sexuality, alternative leadership styles) are now "mainstream" issues. Men are as likely as women to include such topics in courses and to make them the topics of research. The reading of a biblical text from the woman's point of view (e.g., the widow and the unjust judge or the woman at the well), taking seriously what can be known about the social, economic, and religious condition of women in the first century and analogies to human experience today—such a reading can be heard in sermons preached by men as readily as those preached by women.

That, however, leads to the question of what has been lost, and whether this is a problem or an achievement. With a very few exceptions (notably a D.Min. program at San Francisco Theological Seminary), there are no longer many programs designed specifically for women in ministry. At McCormick, we have programs in Hispanic ministry, African American ministry, and Korean American ministry; we do not have a program for "women in ministry." Women students have organized a support group and have meetings quarterly, but there are no staff or faculty members who are "responsible" for this activity.

On the one hand, issues and concerns of women are widely present in the seminary curriculum, just as women are visible in all aspects of seminary life. But on the other hand, it is worth asking whether some of what was accomplished in an earlier time has not been lost. McCormick (like most Presbyterian seminaries) has a policy on inclusive language (focusing primarily on language about persons). But given the ethnic and denominational diversity, language about God is much more varied. This leads one to ask whether the theological issue of language about God continues to be raised in the ways in which it should.

In the area of formation for ministry, questions should be raised. While there are significantly more women in ministry today than there were even twenty years ago, resistance to women has not disappeared. Sometimes this is voiced as fear that there will be "too many" women in leadership and that this will lead to the "feminization" (understood, of course, as a negative) of the ministry. Are seminaries preparing women for leadership in a church that still has resistance to them? How do we help prepare women so that they do not leave ministry after their first or second call? What are seminaries doing to mentor women to become pastors of multiple-staff congregations? Even though women are no longer a small minority group, are we as committed to meeting their needs in preparing for ministry as we should be?

Changes for Women

Women, as both students and faculty, are no longer the exception, but the norm. As a result, the church has available to it a wider range of leadership than at any time in history. But the challenge to theological education in preparing women as well as men for ministry remains. Numbers alone cannot guarantee that the "voices of people long silenced" will be able to be heard.

When the numbers of women admitted to seminary began to increase, theological schools had to make changes in the way things had always been done (such as changing housing policies). As with most changes, some have been easier than others. But as institutions representing the Reformed tradition, we accept as part of our vocation a continual reformation according to the Word of God, some of which (thanks to the gifts of women) we now read and hear in new ways.

⟨⟩⟨⟩⟨⟩⟨⟩⟨⟩

It is clear from President Campbell's experience as a student, faculty member, and administrator that the challenges to teaching women seminary students today include old issues as well as new realities. Her assessment that hard-won change in one part of the curriculum can diminish an equally valuable piece in another part is as insightful as it is troubling. The next case study addresses the challenge of teaching racial ethnic students, who not only experience racism in the world around them, but who also endure a church that does not speak out against that racism. This leads to questions about the nature of God.

A REFORMED THEOLOGICAL PERSPECTIVE AT JOHNSON C. SMITH THEOLOGICAL SEMINARY

David M. Wallace

History

Johnson C. Smith Theological Seminary is one of the ten theological institutions of the Presbyterian Church (U.S.A.). It was established on April 7, 1867, as a part of the Freedman's College of Charlotte, North Carolina. Classes were held in what was initially called the Old Colored Presbyterian Church; the name of the church has since been changed to First United

Presbyterian Church. Because of a significant gift of land from a major donor, the school was moved to the west side of Charlotte and renamed Biddle Memorial Institute.

In 1923, Mrs. Jane Berry Smith of Pittsburgh, Pennsylvania, generously endowed the institution and constructed several buildings on the seventy-five-acre campus in honor of her husband, Johnson C. Smith. In recognition of this gift, the board of trustees voted on March 1, 1923, to change the name of the institution to Johnson C. Smith University.

The seminary operated as a department of the university, graduating its first class of three in 1872. In 1969, the religion department moved from Charlotte, North Carolina, to Atlanta as Johnson C. Smith Theological Seminary. Through official action of the university board of trustees and the 182nd General Assembly of the Presbyterian Church (U.S.A.), the seminary became a constituent institution of the six Protestant seminaries known as Interdenominational Theological Center (ITC). This consortium of black seminaries is located in the Atlanta University Center, with the largest concentration in the country of African American institutions involved in the enterprise of higher education.

A Description of the Student Population

Students enrolled through Johnson C. Smith Theological Seminary to pursue degree programs at the ITC are affiliated with Reformed denominational bodies. The majority of the student body is comprised of African Americans who are members of the Presbyterian Church (U.S.A.). A small percentage come from other Reformed bodies, such as United Church of Christ and Disciples of Christ. The seminary's program also has a global dimension, enrolling Christian leaders from countries around the world. Churches in Africa have largely benefited from this emphasis. In Kenya, East Africa, alone, over thirty leaders have received degrees from the seminary. International students have also come from Ghana, Cameroon, Sudan, Ethiopia, South Africa, Congo, and Korea.

Students come to the seminary with a broad range of academic preparation and career backgrounds. Some have made significant career sacrifices to pursue degrees in ministry. For example, in the current student body there is a young man who quit his job with the Sarah Lee Corporation to enroll in the seminary to pursue the master of divinity degree. A number of students in this category come from other significant careers to pursue degrees in response to God's claim and call on their lives.

Challenges to Teaching at the Seminary

The challenge that is always a concern at our institution is how we teach—especially a course such as Reformed Theology—so that the class experience is relevant to the black Presbyterian experience. The central affirmation of the Reformed tradition is the sovereignty of God. This affirmation is expressed in the *Book of Order*, G-2.0500:

> In its confessions, the Presbyterian Church (U.S.A.) expresses the faith of the Reformed tradition. Central to this tradition is the affirmation of the majesty, holiness, and providence of God who creates, sustains, rules, and redeems the world in the freedom of sovereign righteousness and love.

In light of this affirmation, the questions and concerns that students constantly raise are: How could a sovereign God allow the sin of racism and oppression to affect and dehumanize the lives of countless numbers in the African American community? And why are African American Presbyterians still involved with a denomination that has not taken a significant leadership role in addressing the concerns and issues of marginalized people? There are many other concerns and issues that students bring to the classroom experience. However, "Race matters," to borrow from an expression used by Cornel West, and this is among the issues we try to address.

Since the student population is mainly persons in their second career, many have experienced racism firsthand, or have been affected by the anecdotal experiences of relatives and close acquaintances, not to mention the volumes of reading material on slavery and racism in America. If God is omnipotent, omnipresent, and omniscient as the church teaches and preaches, students want to know, where were God and the church during the era of some of the most heinous experiences of blacks in America? Consequently, a significant and cogent challenge at our institution is to answer the question: How do we teach and communicate the Reformed tradition in a relevant way so that it speaks to the implicit and explicit issues of racism and oppression in our world today?

A second challenge that we face in preparing leaders for Christian service is the diversity of the student body. When I was a seminary student almost thirty years ago, classes were comprised of men. The twenty-first-century theological seminary community is radically different. A significant percentage of our students are women. The majority of the students are second-career persons. There is an increase in racial diversity due to cross-registration from white institutions in our area, as well as a small increase in Asian American students. Consequently, there is more diversity in classrooms that ever before.

The challenge that is before us is to teach in this new reality, incorporating into the classroom experiences insights from both teachers and students that produce a learning experience that is dualistic and not so heavily monolithic, with the professor as chief "know it all" in the classroom.

The third challenge we face in forming and preparing leaders for Christian service at our institution is the need to prepare students for various and sundry vocational experiences, by stretching and being good stewards of the limited resources at our disposal. In the African American context, there has always been the need to be creative with limited resources. The creation of the Inter-denominational Theological Center is a perfect example of good stewardship at work. Each member institution agrees to use the same faculty and to purchase services from the umbrella institution (ITC), so that all provide the highest caliber of theological education to students in our respective denominations. Without ITC, these six schools would have disappeared from the landscape of graduate-level higher education years ago.

During the early years of the institution, the major focus was on producing preachers and Christian educators. We provided two degree programs for this purpose, the master of divinity and the master of arts in religious education. In today's world, in which the needs of God's people are affected by integration in the job market, new technology, and pressures from a constantly evolving environment, we have increased our degree offerings to remain relevant. New concentrations have been added in the master of divinity degree program. In addition, two new degree programs have been added to the curriculum, the master of divinity coupled with the master of public health, awarded in conjunction with the Morehouse School of Medicine, and the doctor of theology in pastoral care and counseling, which is provided in cooperation with the faculties from three Atlanta theological seminaries (ITC, Columbia, and Candler). These degree programs help us to address a number of multifaceted interests and needs within the student population.

The final challenge in forming and preparing leaders for Christian service is presented by the new age of technology and computerization. We can use "high tech" methods to ensure that we know God with our heads and that we have learned the theological concepts of Paul Tillich, Richard Niebuhr, and Dietrich Bonhoeffer. But we must also be concerned about coming together in community, providing opportunities for "high touch" to ensure that we know God with our hearts and souls. At our institution, we take seriously the issue of the Christian and African concept of creating the beloved community. Acts 2:43–47 talks about the early Christians sharing their goods and resources and worshiping and praising God together. The African concept of community is similar, but places greater emphasis on corporate sharing and the advancement of community and less emphasis on individualism. If we are not careful, the new age of technology and computers can be a threat to our sense of community.

These are four challenges that have an impact on theological education at our institution. They are not inclusive of all the challenges we face, but they are major concerns and would probably surface in most discussions. Now we turn to the Reformed perspective I use in teaching and forming leaders at Johnson C. Smith/ITC.

Reformed Perspective on Teaching and Forming Leaders for Christian Service

We face serious difficulty in asserting that one must teach only from a Reformed perspective, with specific doctrines in mind and without appreciating its catholicity. In our confessional heritage, there are doctrines that are foundational to our tradition, serving as guides and parameters to prevent us from being heretical in our teaching. We must keep this in mind as we approach both teaching and preaching. However, the sovereignty of God is an essential theme and emphasis of the Reformed tradition. This theme permeates all the other doctrines we embrace. Even the doctrine of predestination, which postulates the view that God has elected some to eternal salvation and others to eternal damnation, reflects God's awesome power and dominion. Ultimately, God will have God's way.

In teaching a course such as Reformed Theology, I seek to help students to understand how important it is to practice what we say we believe about our sovereign God. This has implications for the ways in which we seek to address all the challenges we face as Reformed theologians and teachers. Biblically, this view is expressed in the words of the Letter of James:

> But be doers of the word, and not merely hearers who deceive them-
> selves. For if any are hearers of the word and not doers, they are like
> those who look at themselves in a mirror; for they look at themselves
> and, on going away, immediately forget what they were like. But those
> who look into the perfect law, the law of liberty, and persevere, being
> not hearers who forget but doers who act—they will be blessed in their
> doing. (James 1:22–25)

Consequently, if we say that God is sovereign, we must help students to understand the practical applications of this tenet when addressing an issue such as racism. And how do we take this teaching about a sovereign God and address the issue of universal health care? There are large corporations and insurance companies that are opposed to the church's supporting a mandate of equal health care coverage for persons, regardless of income. The Confession of

1967 has practical implications for how a sovereign God was in Jesus Christ reconciling the world unto God's self. In other words, we cannot experience peace and true shalom communities, free from crime and social deterioration, unless all of God's people are healthy and whole.

Then again, when large businesses ignore federal guidelines regarding the problem of toxic waste, the church has a responsibility to say what it believes about this problem. It cannot stand by and be a spectator, developing biblical amnesia, while God's good creation is destroyed. The Bible says that God so loved the world, meaning that he loves everything he has created—plants, animals, air, streams, lakes, and oceans. He has given us the good earth over which to have dominion. This does not mean that it is ours to destroy or abuse; rather, God expects us to use these good gifts in a responsible fashion.

Thus, in my teaching I am concerned with making clear the practical applications of the Reformed tradition. I strongly believe that our theology is worthless and meaningless unless it can be practiced, so that it becomes a living theology.

Approaches to Teaching and Formation
That Help to Address the Challenges

There are several approaches to teaching and forming students that I have found helpful in addressing the challenges in our particular context. Foremost, we have been using a team-teaching approach to providing leadership for our Reformed Theology course. Dr. Mark Ellingsen and I have collaborated in teaching the course. Dr. Ellingsen, a white Lutheran minister who has devoted much of his doctoral work and subsequent publications to John Calvin, brings to the teaching/learning experience significant knowledge, research skills, and strong academic foundation for teaching in the area of church history. I bring to the classroom my many years of experience as an African American minister trained in the Reformed tradition, as well as insights and knowledge gained from reading broadly in Reformed theology.

The first half of the course focuses on the theoretical framework for Reformed Theology. The second half deals with applying the Reformed heritage to case studies and having students formulate their own theologies. These assignments are fulfilled in dialogue with the whole class, thereby nurturing our seminary's vision of the "beloved community." Since the Presbyterian Church (U.S.A.) is now in full communion with the Evangelical Lutheran Church in America, we schedule several classes with Lutheran students enrolled in the Lutheran Theology class to discuss how our theologies differ and agree. This gives our students familiarity with Lutheran doctrine, allowing them to be eligible to serve Lutheran congregations and, vice versa, allowing Lutherans to serve Presbyterian congregations.

The course is intentionally designed to address the questions of the relevancy of the Reformed confessional heritage for the African American experience. Students study classical Reformed theologians such as John Calvin and Karl Barth, along with black theologians such as St. Augustine, Francis Grimke, Gayraud Wilmore, Alan Boesak, and Delores Williams. Our point of departure is that the Reformed heritage is relevant for the black experience because it affirms the principle *ecclesia reformata, semper reformanda*, which means the church reformed, always reforming. The church recognizes problems within and without that are in need of resolution in order for it to become more diverse and inclusive, and more like the kingdom of God. Its goal is to become the beloved community that Jesus preached about and worked to establish, with all persons feeling that they are affirmed, included, and empowered. We demonstrate the commitment of black ministers and theologians to the tradition throughout the years, giving faithfully and unstintingly of their resources because they believe in its essential tenets, while simultaneously confronting and calling attention to those moments when they disagreed with the positions of the church that did not affirm the value and human worth of all people under God. There are concerns and problems with which African Americans continue to struggle. Nevertheless, we have faith and firmly believe that our sovereign God will ultimately resolve the problems. Our commitment must be to persevere in faith and love.

Last, we feel that a diverse student body enhances the classroom experience. The increase in gender, age, and ethnic representation brings different perspectives to the entire educational process. The institution's enrollment is predominantly African American; therefore, the need to teach courses primarily from this perspective and to address needs in the black community remains an important consideration. Because of the increase in the African American population in our county, this perspective on teaching will continue to be an important part of our mission well into the twenty-first century and beyond. The diversity of our community, however, lifts us into a broader context and helps to enrich and enlighten how we train and teach students to be Christian leaders in a pluralistic society. We live in a global context, and theological education must take this into consideration.

The holistic approach to theological education is further enhanced as we seek to address the financial, social, psychological, and spiritual needs of students. Financial considerations are important because many students come to seminary with large indebtedness and from small congregations that cannot afford to assist them in a significant financial way. Thus, students are given the maximum financial aid packages our small endowment will allow, so that they can focus on learning, not on paying bills.

Also, experiences are provided to help students to continue to develop socially and psychologically. We challenge all students to participate with organizations such as the Presbyterian Student Fellowship and the ITC Student Christian League. Within the Presbyterian fellowship, regular social activities are planned around meals and other activities, where leaders have an opportunity to discuss issues in ministry and to shape and mold the thinking of our students. Furthermore, students are aided with counseling and psychological needs through the ITC Counseling Center and through my office, as I also serve as dean of the seminary. I spend a good percentage of my time counseling, guiding, and directing students.

Finally, we are concerned about students' spiritual growth and development. It is not unusual at our institution to enter a class and experience a devotional period that precedes the assigned lesson. Beyond the classroom, students are encouraged to attend the inspiring ITC chapel services, to read the Bible, to use Reformed devotional literature, and to participate in worship life in a local congregation. All these activities taken together help us to mold and teach students more holistically in order to prepare them for Christian service in the life of the churches, communities, and agencies they will serve.

⋙⋙⋙⋙⋙

Dean Wallace has clearly outlined the multiple challenges inherent in teaching seminary students. Like President Campbell in the preceding study, he addresses a particular constituency, in this case study the African American seminary students. Even with their specific concerns regarding racism, as with the women students and their concern about sexism, it is clear that both Presbyterian seminary educators face similar challenges regarding the needs, expectations, and requirements of tomorrow's seminary students.

In the last case study, the special situation of the second-career student who is an adult learner will be addressed head-on, in the context of an ecumenical setting.

PRESBYTERIAN TEACHING AT A UNITED METHODIST SEMINARY

Edward C. (Ted) Zaragoza

In 1871, the Church of the United Brethren in Christ founded Union Biblical Seminary in Dayton, Ohio. The name of the school was changed to Bonebrake Theological Seminary in 1910 in honor of a generous donor. In 1923 the seminary established its current campus at the corner of Cornell and Catalpa Streets. The Church of the United Brethren in Christ and the Evangelical Church merged in 1946 to form the Evangelical United Brethren Church. With the union of these two denominations came the union of their two seminaries. The Evangelical School of Theology in Reading, Pennsylvania, merged with Bonebrake Theological Seminary in 1954 to form United Theological Seminary. With the merger, administrations, faculties, libraries, and financial services were consolidated in Dayton. Then, when the Evangelical United Brethren Church merged with The Methodist Church in 1968 to form The United Methodist Church, what was now United Theological Seminary became one of the thirteen United Methodist seminaries and the repository of the archives of the Evangelical United Brethren Church. In 1995 United began offering "in-context" courses in upstate New York and West Virginia. The seminary's mission statement reads: "United Theological Seminary prepares Christ-centered leaders for the church of the twenty-first century through experiences of faith in Jesus Christ, study in the biblical tradition, and the practice of ministry."

Today United Theological Seminary has a full-time faculty of fourteen, all of whom have Ph.D.'s. In addition to representing five denominations, eleven of the faculty are ordained clergy, with varying amounts of pastoral experience. The master's-level programs include the master of divinity (M.Div.), master of arts in religious communication (M.A.R.C.), master of arts in specialized ministries (M.A.S.M), and master of arts in theological studies (M.A.T.S.). At the doctoral level, United offers doctor of ministry (D.Min.) and doctor of missiology (D.Miss.) degrees.

Students

As United Theological Seminary is a seminary of the United Methodist Church, it should come as no surprise that 72 percent of its students at the master's level are affiliated with that denomination. Still, thirty-two other denominations are also represented in the student body. Clearly ecumenical in both its faculty and its students, United Theological Seminary maintains its denominational identity through its strong ties with the surrounding conferences, their local churches, and bishops. It does not tout a "Methodist" point of view in the classroom or the curriculum. The average student age in the master's-level programs is forty-three. Females represent 45 percent of the student body. And 72 percent of the students are white. Most of the students are second- and third-career, and come from geographically proximate areas. Their academic preparation is most often in technical or scientific fields rather than the classical liberal arts, and there have been an increasing number of admissions of students "on probation." While the minimum GPA may be lacking on admission, these students' letters of recommendation indicate real promise for ministry.

And, with the current shortage of ministers in the seminary's constituent conferences, churches are asking for educated clergy.

Challenges of the Adult Learner

The literature on adult learners describes how adults learn best: in short, adult learners learn best when the environment is safe and supportive, relevant to their experience here and now, self-directed, and speaks to their hearts as well as to their heads. With regard to the adult learner, I work very hard to make sure that my syllabi are clear about my expectations and the relevance of the course's contents and methods to the real, lived situation of students preparing to be pastors. The work is not condescending but takes seriously each student's background, competencies, thoughts, and feelings. I see myself as more of a "guide on the side" than a "sage on the stage." United's context asks these questions:

- At what level do non–religion majors need to be introduced to theological education, its content and methods?
- What kind of support does the development of writing skills require?
- What special needs do part-time students or commuter students bring?
- How does the faculty combat consumerism, anti-intellectualism, parochialism, and individualism inside the classroom?

All these questions are really addressed to adult learners, because adult learners characterize the overwhelming majority of students at United. For ease of discussion, however, I have broken up my comments into categories.

As noted above, most of the students at United are non–religion majors who do not have a background in the humanities. This means that the non–religion major comes with little or no philosophical background or conversations about theology beyond the congregational level. One student recently confessed that he came to seminary thinking that Christology was "the theology about people named Chris."

I focus on relevance and teach church history from the perspective of "these are living voices," part of the cloud of witnesses, people who tried to live out the life of faith, asking many of the same questions that are foundational for theological education, such as: Who is God? Jesus Christ? What are we doing here?

Students who are not recent college graduates find writing research papers a special challenge. The writing skills that they bring to seminary reflect the brief, to-the-point style of a reporter, instead of the leisurely narrative usually associated with classical training in the humanities. Initially it is often very upsetting to students that seminary professors now ask them to write in a foreign format. It takes students often well into their second semester before they feel comfortable with this new style of writing. Patience on the part of the student and encouragement from the faculty member help greatly. Short papers can help the adjustment, as do multiple opportunities for grading—for example, several short papers, not just one big one. And allowing students to tap into their gifts for visual media, music, and drama, by offering project alternatives to constantly writing papers, is welcomed and an effective learning tool. It is vital that teachers accept these students as valued adult learners and, in so doing, build mutual trust, so that a leisurely narrative style of writing can develop and thinking with theological categories can occur.

Many students are responsible for managing their time in ever more complex ways. A growing number of them are part-time and attend evening classes due to the demands of regular, full-time employment as well as family and weekend church responsibilities. (Our students are required to work part-time in a church or community agency for the first two years of the M.Div. program.) This part-time status results in more requests than formerly for evening and weekend classes. Most of the students are also commuters. Since they do not live on campus, adjustments to the course schedule, such as offering required courses in the evening or during the shorter summer session, are requested annually. Dorm rooms once reserved for full-time, on-campus students now serve as commuter rooms. Although we still offer the traditional Tuesday/Thursday schedule (with chapel services on both days), more and more classes are offered once a week, in three-hour blocks. This schedule allows students to shorten their time spent on campus after they have completed their first year of basic requirements. Although the traditional formation model of living, studying, and praying together may be minimized at United, the seminary achieves many of those goals through core group, a small-group gathering that continues for four consecutive semesters with the same students and faculty and field advisers.

I have experimented with United's first completely online course. This course enabled students literally not to come to campus. "Attending class" meant reading online materials, and "class discussion" meant posting answers and comments online during the week. I am planning additional online courses that will include several face-to-face meetings a semester, because so many of the students really missed the interaction of the physical classroom. So online teaching, for students in the "people business" of ministry and seminary education, will be more of a hybrid.

Some faculty bemoan all these requests for schedule changes as student "consumerism." This assessment is perhaps one of the byproducts of adult learners. They know that what they learn at seminary is only an introduction, and so the "delivery system" is not as crucial to their preparation as once thought. Gone are the days when the faculty and traditional curriculum are taken for granted as presenting the best form for seminary education. Students crave relevance and convenience in their pastoral preparation because of their busy lives and personal commitments. This is one reason why United is still offering off-campus courses in Buffalo, New York, and Buckhannon, West Virginia. Students can now earn an M.Div. degree in four years without uprooting their families. Their preparation is in the context where they live and where they will minister.

There remains an anti-intellectual strain in some of our students that can be found in the nation as well. This may be attributable to our national penchant for results instead of reflection, or the action orientation of our culture and its emphasis on experience over thought. Anti-intellectualism enjoys a long history in our culture. In students who have been local (licensed) pastors for a long time, this attitude appears in the form of "I already know everything I need to know to be a pastor, because I have done it." The style of the pastor they grew up with, and the King James Bible that filled the pews, are sufficient for their limited view of ministry. Experience and results are still more valued in the American psyche than the thoughtful reflection that provides no immediate return.

Other students come to United with such entrenched biases about Scripture and church practices that they often spend their first years proclaiming that they will take the foundational courses in Bible because they are required, while fully intending to ignore the content in the meantime. (Fortunately, this attitude does not last very long.) One way I deal with this is to ask students to articulate, on paper, just what it is that they believe, and not just what the book says, or what I said, for that matter. This is one of the most difficult assignments they tackle. I also "hang out" with students at common meal (the lunch served in the dining hall Tuesday through Thursday) and try to get to know them as people, to accept them where they are, and not try to break them or their faith down, but to get them to see that they can enhance it, deepen it, enrich it. Some students get quite upset when you suggest from a lectern that they change what they believe.

This anti-intellectualism has its corollary in parochialism. This narrow range of focus is typical of many new seminary students when it comes to theology and conceptions of ministry. Perhaps rooted in our nation's history of isolationism, this parochialism sometimes gets expressed as a student's not wanting to learn anything that is not instantly applicable to the traditions and practices of the student's particular parish setting. This position, which views only the present as vital and relevant, makes teaching church history especially difficult. Some change their minds when they understand that the past holds the present accountable for being the stuff out of which the future beloved community is built. Another way United addresses parochialism is through its intercultural immersion requirement. Each student is required to spend no less than two weeks living in a culture vastly different than his or her own. Many students report that this immersion is life-transforming.

There is also a persistent thread of individualism in many of our students. A student's experience becomes the way she or he adjudicates competing truth claims, and since it is "my" experience, it is not only valid, it is also indisputable. Another sign of this individualism is turning the experience of another into something the student needs to oppose or control. For example, when exposed to liberation theology, some students will refuse to hear the plight of the oppressed. Instead, they want to argue that the oppressed are really people who want to take their hard-earned money or jobs. These students are the same people who ask, "What would Jesus do?" I answer that question in this context by pointing to all the Scripture passages where Jesus based his response on need, not social status.

Conclusion

Meeting the challenges of adult learners is rewarding. Given the variety of people entering seminary, and the wealth of their life experience, the class discussions are rich and very fruitful. I suspect that these trends and their accompanying challenges will be with us for a long time to come, and that United is not unique.

SUMMARY

Most of what has been reported and discussed in this chapter will probably not be news to other Presbyterian seminary educators. That may be a comfort, or it may be a disappointment. In either case, those of us who teach and guide today's seminary students, and who look forward to greeting those of tomorrow each fall, can be pleased and hopeful that Presbyterian seminary educators are not only aware of the challenges, they are addressing them with whatever group pushes for change and in whatever setting they find themselves. And when the day is done, with all its vicissitudes, these educators can reflect on what a privilege and joy it is to be a part of educating and training the future clergy and leaders of the varied ministries of the church.

11

The Dawning of the Light

Duncan S. Ferguson

CALLED TO TEACH: THE PRESBYTERIAN
MISSION IN HIGHER EDUCATION

This volume begins with an introduction to the current situation in church-related higher education, and especially Presbyterian-related higher education. Dr. Weston argues that Presbyterian higher education has largely followed the course of American higher education and has become essentially secular in character. Using the imagery of fire and light, he says that the fire has all but gone out, the light is dim, and there are only embers of the original fire. He wonders if the embers can be fanned into a fire that might provide enough light to see into the future and create institutions that are more in keeping with the founding visions. It is a good question, and he invites us to begin the argument.

In Section 1, "The Calling to Teach: Foundations," the argument begins at the beginning, with the conviction that our call to teach is rooted in the Bible. Teaching is a vocation, a true calling from God, and we must find ways to be true to this vocation in our time and on into our future. Nearly all Christian traditions have understood that teaching (especially teaching within the church) is a divine calling and fundamental to the church's mission in the world. The Reformed tradition has been especially attuned to the mission of education and the calling of teachers to carry out this mission, not only in the service of the church but also in the service of the public good. From its beginning in the sixteenth century in Geneva, Reformed and Presbyterian Christians have attempted to be true to the "call to teach." Those following within this tradition found ways to be true to the vocation of teaching and founded educational institutions that served the church community and contributed to the common good.

Section 2, "The Context of Teaching: Engagement," picks up the flow of the argument with a description of the contemporary situation and how we are currently "living out" our vocation to teach in the range of educational institutions in our landscape. There is a description of the complex and diverse character of Presbyterian colleges and universities. There is an analysis of the challenge of teaching in these institutions, coupled with a case for teaching in these institutions from a centered and theological frame of reference. A similar argument is made for those who are called to teach in the theological institutions of the church.

Section 3, "Case Studies of Teaching: Application," describes the particular character of three different Presbyterian-related colleges. The case-studies section continues with a discussion of the challenge of bringing one's divine calling to teach into the secular or public college and university. Finally, there is a discussion of the challenge of being true to one's calling to teach in the theological institutions, given the diverse character of their students.

How should the argument conclude? There are some observations on which nearly all would agree, and which might serve as a basis for the continuing discussion.

- The divine call to teach is as clear and compelling as it ever was.
- The need for excellent teachers, true to their vocation, is urgent and universal.
- Our biblical, theological, and historical traditions guide and inform us in the execution of this mission.
- We teach in a world and society that are changing fundamentally and rapidly.
- The educational institutions of the church, and particularly within the Presbyterian context, are struggling in the attempt to find their identity and mission.
- It is profoundly challenging to be true to one's vocation and to teach in these institutions or the secular and public institutions of higher education.

So what do we do? Which way do we turn? Do we fan the flames of a dying ember? Yes. Do we give up on the church's mission in higher education? No. Do we continue to be faithful and try to find our way? Yes. What follows are only some premonitions.

BETWEEN THE TIMES: FROM DYING TO DAWNING

The church-related schools, colleges, universities, and seminaries are living between the times. This situation is especially true in the Presbyterian context, and it may be true in most other denominational contexts as well. *These institutions look back to a time when their church identity was clear and when there was genuine support from the church community*. But now that identity, with a few exceptions, is unclear, and there is little more than token support from the church. The educational institutions have been inclined to blame the church community, regardless of their denomination, for the separation between the church and the institutions that it founded. Often the argument gets around to the fact that the church bodies no longer provide sufficient financial support. The church community is inclined to blame the institutions for their drift toward secularism, or, in some cases, for moving toward the "Christian college" model that is rooted in an American version of conservative evangelicalism. Regardless of who is to blame and why, the end result is the same—the church and its educational institutions have drifted apart.

The catch phrase for this drift is the title of a very important book published in 1998, James Burtchaell's *The Dying of the Light: The Disengagement of Colleges and Universities from Their Christian Churches*.[1] In this volume, Burtchaell examines colleges and universities from several denominational traditions and sees the vast majority of them caught in the cultural shift to secularism. There is not much hope and great lament in this volume, and Dr. Burtchaell is persuaded that the light is dying. Others, such as George Marsden and Bradley Longfield in *The Secularization of the Academy*, make a similar case.[2] Neither of these volumes addresses the precollegiate institutions or theological institutions, but perhaps a similar case can be made. And it is a persuasive case; there has been a clear drift in the academy, and in the church-affiliated academy, toward secularism. The churches are right in "blaming" the educational institutions for drifting away from their roots. Most of these institutions will never fully regain their church identity, and those that stay related to a church body may do so for historical and financial reasons. The church, observing the secular character of the institutions, rightly asks why it should be supportive. In addition, few church bodies are willing to acknowledge that quality education is a divine end in itself, that God's name is often spelled with two O's, and generally view the institutions as of value to the church in an instrumental way, as these institutions provide spiritual nurture and direction for young people and cultivate the future leadership of the church. Besides, for most denominations, there are other mission priorities.

As the churches cease to be as supportive, then there is little incentive for the educational institutions to stay connected to the church. If there is limited money, only a handful of potential students, and only a few committed church persons to provide leadership within the church and as trustees, then the incentive is less and depends almost exclusively on the sense of Christian mission of the trustees and senior administrators of the educational institutions. There is the additional tension of blending the two cultures, that of the academy and that of the church. The culture of the academy has many dimensions, but one dimension that is central to the culture of the academy is inquiry. To be sure, the academy has its values and beliefs, even dogmas. But at its best the academy seeks answers and pursues knowledge. The academy transmits knowledge, but is suspicious of final answers. Even the very notion of truth, or Truth, is not popular in the academy. The culture of the church, on the other hand, is characterized as preserving and proclaiming the truth—Truth. Churches at their best are humble about their understanding of the truth, constantly engaged in refining their understanding of truth, and in awe before the majesty of the Truth. The church's culture is one of belief and commitment more than it is one of inquiry. The differences between the cultures often create reserve and even suspicion.

There is another trend, however, only partially documented and described, and one that I have observed in my years of association with church-related schools, colleges, universities, and theological institutions. *This trend may point to a new time, as yet unclear and undefined, but nevertheless beckoning the institutions.* At the core, this new trend is the desire of many of these institutions to have a clear and distinguishable identity. See, for example, *The Recovery of Spirit in Higher Education,* edited by Robert Rankin,[3] or Warren Bryan Martin, *The College of Character.*[4] If the decades of the '60s and the '70s were characterized by these institutions' making a clear movement away from the church (partially for tax purposes), the decades of the '80s and '90s were characterized by the desire to be distinctive—not that the drift toward secularity came to a halt. But to be just another school, college, university, or seminary was not enough in order to survive the stiff competition from all sides, and especially from the public sector. Private institutions had to have distinctive features and the "value added" dimension in their identity. There were many models to choose from for these institutions. For example, one was to become a truly outstanding institution, with the financial capability to offer the finest education and prestige reputation. Another was to become more creative and offer alternative educational programs that honored different learning styles. Still another was to seek new student markets, and especially the nontraditional adult market. There were many others.

In the mix was also a desire to return the institution to its heritage, although not with the goal of expressing the heritage in the way that it was expressed in an earlier time. For many, there was a sincere desire to recover the church connection and Christian roots, and most of the private institutions had these roots. This new movement was not characterized exclusively as looking backward, although there certainly was a review of the founding vision. But it was more characterized as looking forward to a new way of being church-affiliated, and certainly one that avoided the worst forms of church control and the violation of academic freedom, two great fears of the academy. The question became "What would a church-related educational institution look like in a 'post-Constantinian age' or a postmodern age?"[5]

If the Christian era has truly come to an end (we no longer live in the Roman Empire declared Christian by Constantine, nor its many successors through to the Christian West of the early twentieth century), and if there are doubts about the "Enlightenment project" (Is it possible to know in other ways than rational and empirical ways and to celebrate the life of the mind and the *life of the spirit?*), then are there implications for the identity and mission of the church-related educational institution? What should a church-related educational institution look like in this new, yet not fully defined, cultural era?

Although there were some who spoke in terms of a "return," the majority believed that it should not be a return to the kind of institution that was once clearly identified as a church-related institution, but a new expression of the founding principles. As we wrote in the October 20, 1994, edition of *Point of View*, about the Presbyterian-related institutions of an earlier time, "The institutions reflected the values of a homogeneous, educated section of society." They were characterized in the following way:

- Boards of trustees were elected by denominational bodies.
- Financial support was provided by denominational bodies, and in some cases the General Assembly assumed responsibility for the indebtedness of the institution.
- Attendance was required at chapel services.
- Courses in religion were required.
- Expectations were narrowly defined for student conduct.
- Creedal affirmations and/or church membership were required for faculty members.
- Recruitment and training for church vocations was emphasized.

A new era has come, and the tectonic plates that have held the "modern" world together have shifted. Those called to teach and lead educational institutions of the church must respond to the new realities of the culture and wider world, as I argued in chapter 6. There is the reality of secularism, as we have discussed. We live in a *global age*, one in which distances have shrunk and connections with peoples from all over the world are direct. The dramatic changes in the political realities of our time serve to underline the global character of our existence. What happens in the Middle East or in Kashmir has direct

implications for us. The economies of Asia, Europe, and America are inter-
twined. Nearly all countries are asking how to educate their young people so
that the country can stay competitive in the world market.

We are reminded daily that we live in a *multicultural* society, one that
requires us to learn how to live with those whose culture, language, customs,
beliefs, and values are different from our own. And these differences create
tensions and conflict. We live as well in an *ecologically threatened world*, one that
requires fundamental changes in our way of life. We ask with more intensity
than ever before, "What kind of world will our children inherit? Will they be
able to breathe freely, know the joy of a peaceful mountain lake, and appreciate the beauty and diversity of the animal kingdom?" In the past several
decades, the state of the world's environment has deteriorated. Air pollution
has increased in most cities, broad atmospheric changes such as ozone deple-
tion and buildup of greenhouse gases are alarming, and the world's farmers
have lost millions of tons of topsoil. Lakes and rivers have been turned into
industrial wastelands, and the world population has grown faster than our systems can accommodate. Is sustainable development possible in a world that
has distributed its wealth in such an inequitable way?

We live in a time of an *information explosion and technological advancement*, a
time when the increase of knowledge is exponential, and the access to it is challenging the fundamental ways education is being provided. College degrees
are available through interactive technology, and there is a trend away from
education rooted in values and community and toward utilizing technology to
both manage the information explosion and give access to it.

We have turned toward what has been called a bit imprecisely and vaguely
a *postmodern moment*, a time when so much of the culture and technology of
our political and intellectual geography are fading from view. The landscape
has changed. The modern *Zeitgeist* has been deconstructed, and there is little
in its place. For nearly two centuries, we have lived and been educated in
modernity, and the modern is a hard act to follow. How do we confront what
is to follow, an era for which as yet we have no name? Philosophers speak of
postfoundationalism or poststructuralism, the trend to call into question the
search, since Descartes, for a method that would provide indubitable truth
claims to serve as foundations for human knowledge and action. Postmodernism, rooted more in the arts and humanities, has come to represent a movement that celebrates the loss of unambiguous meaning. It is a time of major
paradigm shift, a time when the seismic activity has caused a profound intellectual tsunami. There has been a fundamental shift in our ways of knowing
and describing our deepest beliefs and the world around us. The old paradigm,
rooted in Western philosophy and exclusively rationalistic in character, is passing. A new paradigm, holistic and ecological, is emerging, and it is poignantly

relevant to those engaged in education as they seek and disseminate knowledge. This new paradigm has many elements. For example:

- It is a shift from focusing on the part to grasping the whole.
- It is a shift from understanding reality in terms of static structures to understanding reality in terms of dynamic processes.
- It is a shift from an objective pursuit of truth to an epistemology that incorporates personal and intuitive knowing.
- It is a shift from understanding knowledge in terms of building blocks to seeing reality as connected and an interdependent network.
- It is a shift from believing that we have absolute and final certainty to approximate understanding and an appreciation of complexity and mystery.

This paradigm—synthetic, nonlinear, holistic, and integrative—is not necessarily dominant in all situations, but is emerging, and is exerting a profound influence on our mode of thinking and being. It is certainly present in the world of higher education and will influence the way we pursue our vocation of teaching and lead our church-affiliated educational institutions. So we live between an earlier time when our calling and the institution's identity were less ambiguous and an emerging time as yet not fully understood. How do we set our course, living between the times?

TOWARD THE DISTINCTIVE INSTITUTION
WITH A CHURCH-RELATED DIMENSION

The report of the Presbyterian Church's Office of Higher Education to the General Assembly described three types of church-related colleges.[6] The report does not include an assessment of the precollegiate institutions or the theological institutions. The report underlines the diversity of the collegiate institutions, and then argues that they fall broadly within the categories of historical, dimensional, and pervasive. The historical institutions "reflect in their common life the values of the Reformed tradition. Founded by faithful Presbyterians, these institutions are guided by a founding vision that continues to influence the life of the institution. These institutions exist primarily to serve the public good. . . . These institutions endeavor to be nonsectarian and diverse." Pervasive institutions are also described. "These institutions view their educational mission as an expression of the Christian gospel. This point of view is expressed in the covenant with the church, and every effort is made to place Christian theology, traditions, and values at the center of the institution's common life." It is likely that both of these types of institutions will continue into the future, although some of the institutions falling into the category of historical may discontinue formal relationships with the church. Two have in the past decade: Occidental College and Lewis and Clark College. Both categories of institutions were judged acceptable by the General Assembly (1994), and as valid expressions of Presbyterian-related educational institutions. It has been possible for many who are called to teach to express their vocation in these institutions.

But the future for the majority of the Presbyterian-related educational institutions may be in the dimensional category, especially for those institutions who sincerely want to preserve their church heritage and see their church-related character as part of what gives them a distinctive identity and mission. The risk for those institutions in the category of historical is that they may be viewed as essentially secular in character, and the risk for those in the category of pervasive is that they may be viewed as sectarian in character. The category of dimensional offers a way of living between the times, nurturing the finest expression of the founding principles of the institutions, yet open to the new realities in our society and world. The 1994 report describes the dimensional institutions as those that intentionally cultivate church-relatedness, and give a high priority to this "dimension" in the common life of the institution. These institutions remain nonsectarian and diverse while sustaining a vital Christian community and providing opportunities "for spiritual nurture, worship, and service" (34).

These institutions certainly "measure up" to the definition of church-relatedness in the 1994 report. They intentionally cultivate "a cooperative and collaborative connection with the Presbyterian Church (U.S.A.)" and seek "to reflect Christian values and convictions" in their common life. Further, they have the essential qualities:

- These institutions share a common history with the church, sharing traditions, values, and guiding beliefs.
- They attempt to be faithful to the Reformed heritage by incorporating these traditions, values, and guiding beliefs into their day-to-day life.
- The "relationship is formalized by a covenant or written agreement that is mutual in character and is based upon trust and fidelity" (32–33).

Further, the historical goals, renewed and reformulated for the contemporary situation, are affirmed. With all institutions of learning, they are committed to teaching, research, and service. But they also stress those goals, shared by other traditions but basic to the Reformed traditions.

- They serve "the educational mission of the church by teaching the essentials of Christian faith and practice, nurturing the Christian life, and guiding students and the college community to faithful service and mission in the world."

- They serve "the public good by educating for responsible citizenship, for advocacy for a just and humane society, and for seeking a peaceful, global community" (33).

The vast majority of the dimensional institutions reflect the characteristics mentioned in the report as important in sustaining the church connection (35–36):

- They have a clear mission statement reflecting the commitment to provide an education rooted in the values of the Judeo-Christian faith as expressed in the Reformed tradition.
- They have a covenant with a church governing body spelling out the expectations and responsibilities in the relationship.
- They have a clear contemporary statement of desired outcomes for the graduates, reflecting the values of the heritage.
- They have a value-oriented curriculum and cocurricular program consistent with the institution's mission.
- They have a program that nurtures the spiritual life and gives guidance to students who are exploring their vocation.
- The community is inclusive and supportive, and expresses the ideals of love and justice.

The dimensional institutions, for the most part, are expressing their beliefs and commitments in the structures of their institutional life, as the 1994 report also proposes (36–37):

- The boards of trustees are monitoring the connection between the educational institution and the church, providing continuity.
- The presidents, with the assistance of many administrators, are developing and sustaining the church connection in regularly scheduled contacts and tangible programs.
- The dimensional institutions are making their facilities and human resources available to the church.
- The faculty are finding ways to introduce the issues of faith, the life of the spirit, and ethical values into the curriculum, always respectful of differences and carefully avoiding any trace of proselytizing.
- The interpretive literature of the dimensional institutions contains information about the connection with the church.
- Throughout the daily life of these institutions, there is a vital spiritual presence—in program, worship, celebration, ceremony, and symbol.

I stated in a 1998 article in *Point of View* that the challenge for the dimensional institution is to preserve the abiding principles and articulate and implement these principles in creative and constructive ways for the new world that is being born. The overarching design for those who are called to teach in and lead the institutions of the church should be "abiding principles—new strategies."[7] In this article, which appeared also in *Church and Society*,[8] I argued for ten abiding principles applied appropriately to our emerging new era. I want to focus on three.

1. The first principle is what I called then the integration of faith and learning, but which I would now prefer to call *the nurture of the life of the mind and the life of the spirit*. This principle is based on the conviction that mind and spirit are not fundamentally at odds, but are connected at the core of human existence and needing affirmation and cultivation in the educational process. It is the whole person that needs affirmation and education, not a part of the person. The whole educational program, grounded in the work of those called to teaching, but structured in the entire educational mission of the institution, must draw out and celebrate all aspects of the human experience. Only then will we have truly educated people able to say "yes" to life and assume all of life's responsibilities.

2. A second principle, which has been called traditionally and which I named in the earlier chapter as *freedom of inquiry*, is the *need for an openness to the new way of understanding the world and our place in the world*. Our educational institutions must not be places that prohibit inquiry or by their norms limit free exploration and expression. Rather, they need to be places that encourage the "grappling" with the new ways of perceiving the world around and in us, as hard, challenging, and even threatening as it may be. Deep down, we know that all human knowledge and especially "faith formations" are limited and approximate and need constant exploration, examination, and study. Free inquiry is necessary to protect against narrow orthodoxy, whether it has to do with faith or more broadly with our understanding the world we inhabit.

3. The third principle grows out of the need to educate and structure our curriculum around these new realities and understandings of the world. We need to see the world as it is, in all its beauty and in all its terror, not in the neat and tidy order of discipline descriptions in our college catalogs. Our education must be grounded in our understanding of the world as an organic whole, held together by systems, rhythms, and energies. Further, our problems are so staggering in size, so overwhelming in scope, so complex and multidimensional, a more *integrated and holistic approach to the curriculum and to teaching is necessary*. No isolated discipline or random fact, however well understood, can provide a solution to the problems of the exploited environment, world hunger, and international conflict and terrorism. Our approach to teaching and the building of the curriculum must acknowledge that the new heartbeat of the world is relationship and interdependence, not dominance and hierarchy.

CONCLUSION: THE EDUCATION GOALS
OF THE DIMENSIONAL INSTITUTION

We need not turn away from the classic goals of education: to teach, do research, and provide service. They remain, but in themselves they do not contain, or contain only in an embryonic way, the need for our teaching and our educational institutions to be more responsive to our new world. They do not provide a road map, or suggest a way of living between the times. We must add, then, to these three goals another set of goals, which in part restate these goals, but turn them in a more missional direction. Let me suggest three categories.

1. Nearly every academic institution, from the precollegiate through the professional school, would describe its educational mission as in some sense *informational* in character. In the traditional formulation of goals, it teaches and does research. The purpose of an educational institution is to impart information, to teach students, to discover and provide knowledge. Most would say that they want to provide comprehensive and up-to-date information and would urge faculty to be diligent in their research and in preparing their courses so that students are well served. There is of course a great variety of quality among the institutions in giving students this information. It depends so much on the nature of the faculty, the institution's resources, and the preparation of the students. It also depends on the stated aims of the institution. It may be that the precollegiate institution, the college or university, or the theological seminary is quite focused in its mission and prepares students for the next step, another educational level, a particular field or career. But for all institutions, the real issue is *quality* and how to ensure it. For those who sense their vocation to teach is from God and those responsible for the church-related educational institutions, there is a sense of mandate from God to enable students to learn about the marvelous creation in all of its many, beautiful, and complex forms in the best possible way.

2. Our mission in education in not only informational, but also *vocational*. Here I do not mean to use the term as it is often used in the United States, as training for a skilled job, as important as this may be. Rather, I use the term in the Christian sense of calling. We believe that every human being has a purpose in God's will for the world, that everyone is "tapped on the shoulder" by God and invited to participate in the building of a more just and humane social order. We are all gifted differently, and each has a different role to play. We have the special responsibility in our teaching and leading of our educational institutions to "stir up the gifts" of the students, to help them find their calling and develop the skills required to fulfill their calling. We also believe that

all students are gifted, and we have a responsibility to treat all who come to us as those created in the image of God. Through challenge, inspiration, and discipline, we help students find their way into the purposes of God for the world.

3. This naturally leads us to a third characteristic of our teaching in and leading of the educational institutions, namely to provide an education that is *transformational* in character. Not all teachers would see their role, nor educational institutions describe their purpose, as transformational, but those with a sense of God's call understand that they are in the "people making" business. In addition to providing information and helping students toward their careers, we also want students to become all that God intends for them to become. To say it another way, we do share with the church the responsibilities to redeem (that is, to set free) and to sanctify (to make holy) the students who come to us. We must be good stewards of their beautiful and precious lives. We set them free from ignorance, prejudice, and provincialism. We provide a life-giving and value-centered community that helps them see their life and talents as the gift of God to be used in a life of service. So we do more than provide information and knowledge, more than build skills for a successful career—we join God in transforming people into what God wants them to be.

The light is dawning.

The Vocation
of the Presbyterian Teacher

A Select Annotated Bibliography

ARLIN C. MIGLIAZZO

It is a daunting task to choose from among hundreds of published works about Presbyterians engaged in the enterprise of education those which would most appropriately complement the essays in this anthology. The direct literary lineage of exposition on the subject extends back at least as far as the Protestant Reformation, with numerous ancillary lines to Augustine, Jerome, Boethius, Cassiodorus, Bonaventura, Duns Scotus, Thomas Aquinas, and a multitude of similar luminaries. Given the constraints of space, I have been forced to make bibliographic decisions that others have every right to question. But my primary intent has been to select titles that place the essays in this volume in a broader and more comprehensive context. It is my hope that the brief annotations of each title will assist the reader in pursuing any of the many research directions that have comprised the literature on the vocation of the Presbyterian teacher over time and across cultures.

The interested layperson might well begin with any of a number of helpful surveys of the Presbyterian way of being Reformed that highlight, to some extent, teaching, learning, and the life of the mind. John H. Leith's *Introduction to the Reformed Tradition* (Atlanta: John Knox Press, 1977) is arguably the best place to begin as he provides a cogent analysis of all things Reformed and ties educational matters clearly to theological ones. *Presbyterian Heritage: Switzerland, Great Britain, America* (Atlanta: John Knox Press, 1965), by A. Mervyn Davies, links three great strands of Presbyterianism while giving each its proper due. More recent overviews of Presbyterianism include Randall

Balmer and John R. Fitzmier, *The Presbyterians* (Westport, Conn.: Praeger Publishers, 1994), and James H. Smylie, *A Brief History of the Presbyterians* (Louisville, Ky.: Geneva Press, 1996). *The Presbyterian Enterprise: Sources of American Presbyterian History*, ed. Maurice W. Armstong, Lefferts A. Loetscher, and Charles A. Anderson (Philadelphia: Westminster Press, 1956), provides a rich collection of primary source documents on the American Presbyterian experience. Leonard J. Trinterud, in *The Forming of An American Tradition: A Re-Examination of Colonial Presbyterianism* (Philadelphia: Westminster Press, 1949), surveys the colonial period, although from a somewhat dated, reverential point of view. Elwyn Allen Smith's *The Presbyterian Ministry in American Culture: A Study in Changing Concepts, 1700–1900* (Philadelphia: Westminster Press for the Presbyterian Historical Society, 1962) carries the story through the nineteenth century. The recent seven-volume series, *The Presbyterian Presence: The Twentieth Century Experience* (Louisville, Ky.: Westminster/John Knox Press, 1990–92), ed. Milton J. Coalter, John M. Mulder, and Louis B. Weeks, is the most comprehensive attempt to describe the American Presbyterian experience over the past century. Three of its volumes bear more directly on the Presbyterian way of educating and will be discussed individually below.

Although Zwingli, Bullinger, Calvin, Farel, and other Protestant Reformation thinkers had much in common with Luther, their theological and cultural disagreements with him remained deep and ultimately unbridgeable. One of the key rifts resulted from the Luther's perspective on the political state. Perhaps in part because Lutheran reform occurred under the watchful eye of German aristocrats, Luther's "two worlds" social analysis allowed the German aristocracy to pursue its cultural agenda with little involvement from the church. On the other hand, the degree of autonomy granted to many of the Swiss cantons by the sixteenth century provided the cultural context for a much closer relationship between the political and ecclesiastical realms. Reformed theologians promoted a vision of politics that made the state an instrument of God's justice, mercy, and judgment. It was only natural that education serve as the vehicle to implement this vision.

Had Zwingli lived another decade, Presbyterians might look back at Zurich rather than Geneva as the cradle of Presbyterian educational thought and practice, for he, probably as much as Calvin, believed in the Christian mission of the state and the efficacy of education in fulfilling that mission. In *Zwingli's Thought: New Perspectives*, vol. 25 in *Studies in the History of Christian Thought*, ed. Heiko A. Oberman (Leiden: E. J. Brill, 1981), Gottfried W. Locher surveys the sweep of Zwingli's contribution to the Reformation spirit on a variety of topics, including educational philosophy. His comparative analysis also traces the Zwinglian humanist strain in the Scottish Reformation.

Any analysis of the Presbyterian way of educating would not be complete without an examination of John Calvin's educational thought. While his *Institutes of the Christian Religion* contain relatively few comments that directly pertain to education, his extensive writing on human reason and personality leads invariably to some crucial assumptions regarding education. Calvin expanded on these assumptions in the *Articles Concerning the Government of the Church*. The reformer's humanist heritage as well as his commitment to high-caliber scholarship find ample discussion in *The Christian Scholar in the Age of the Reformation* (New York: Charles Scribner's Sons, 1956), by E. Harris Harbison. Leroy Nixon's *John Calvin's Teachings on Human Reason* (New York: Exposition Press, 1960) gathers germane passages from Calvin's corpus to provide a helpful context for understanding the reformer's view of education. "Part Two" is particularly instructive as it extrapolates from Calvin's theology his philosophy of education and orients the reformer's views to modern educational concerns.

If Calvin himself did not address the vocation of teaching nontheological subjects to any great extent, the next best place to turn for some understanding of his educational philosophy is the Genevan Academy he founded and nurtured into one of the premier educational institutions of sixteenth-century Europe. William Monter's *Calvin's Geneva* (New York: John Wiley & Sons, 1967) illuminates the wide sweep of Calvin's influence on the Swiss city and demonstrates the deep significance of the Academy, not just in the intellectual life of Geneva, but also as a bastion of learning which drew students from all over Europe. Monter's analysis has been updated in three important studies, all of which demonstrate the wide-ranging objectives and impact of the Genevan educational system. W. Fred Graham argues that Calvin exerted a modernizing influence rather than a revolutionary one with regard to educational matters, in *The Constructive Revolutionary: John Calvin and His Socio-Economic Impact* (Richmond: John Knox Press, 1971). In *Calvin, Geneva and the Reformation: A Study of Calvin as Social Reformer, Churchman, Pastor and Theologian* (Grand Rapids: Baker Book House, 1988), Ronald S. Wallace concentrates his narrative on the many facets of Calvin's comprehensive educational system that prepared students both for church ministry and for civil service. Included are sections relevant to Calvin's perspective on the liberal arts and the place of secular educational pursuits in the life of the Christian. Karin Maag's definitive monograph, *Seminary or University: The Genevan Academy and Reformed Higher Education, 1560–1620* (Aldershot, Hampshire, England: Ashgate Publishing, 1995), charts the history of the Academy's first sixty years of existence and concludes that during this formative period the institution struggled with an educational mission committed to both the training of Reformed clergy and service to a more vocationally diverse clientele.

As Reformed theology expanded beyond the Swiss cantons, so too did the proliferation of creeds and confessions that guided the growing family of Reformed communions. The confessions served as the foundation for the varying philosophies of education that emerged in the regions where Calvin's theology prevailed. The Scots Confession (1560), the Belgic Confession (1561), and the Westminster Confession of Faith (1647) speak most directly to matters spiritual, but, like the *Institutes*, yield nuggets of educational philosophy.[1] It is with the *Book of Discipline* (1560),[2] however, that a distinctly Presbyterian educational philosophy began to take shape. William Croft Dickinson's edition of *John Knox's History of the Reformation in Scotland*, 2 vols. (New York: Philosophical Library, 1950), contains both of the 1560 documents cited above authored by John Knox and his collaborators. Even a cursory reading of the *Book of Discipline* makes evident the tremendous importance of multi-level education in Scottish Presbyterianism. A brief section in *The Mind of John Knox*, by Richard G. Kyle (Lawrence, Kans.: Coronado Press, 1984), connects the Scottish reformer's educational thought in the *Book of Discipline* with other Knoxite sources that contain educational components, including his 1559 *Brief Exhortation to England*, his 1560 study on predestination, and his 1564 remarks at the General Assembly. "Knox's Social Awareness: The Problems of Poverty and Educational Reform," chap. 10 in Richard L. Greaves, *Theology and Revolution in the Scottish Reformation: Studies in the Thought of John Knox* (Grand Rapids: Christian University Press, 1980), analyzes Knox's sometimes ambiguous stance regarding the propriety of secular learning in his educational vision for Scotland.

The College of Glasgow took seriously the educational imperatives of the *Book of Discipline* and implemented them in the constitution of the college, *Nova Erectio*, which is discussed at length in J. D. Mackie's *The University of Glasgow, 1451–1951: A Short History* (Glasgow: Jackson, Son and Co., 1954). Although meant initially as the guiding document only for the college, *Nova Erectio* served with only minor alterations as the constitution of the University of Glasgow until 1858. The final chapter in Ian B. Cowan's *The Scottish Reformation: Church and Society in Sixteenth Century Scotland* (New York: St. Martin's Press, 1982) takes a somewhat broader view of the Presbyterian influence by examining the range of educational innovations sparked by the Scottish Reformation. Two important volumes from an earlier era that present a systematic and comprehensive overview of the legacy of Knox and his associates to Scottish education are *Scottish Education: School and University* (Cambridge: Cambridge University Press, 1913), by John Kerr, and *Rise and Progress of Scottish Education* (Edinburgh and London: Oliver & Boyd, 1927), by Alexander Morgan.

As the Kerr and Morgan studies make abundantly clear, in the centuries following the Scottish Reformation, Presbyterianism transformed the intellectual culture of the realm and infused Scotland's entire educational system, from primary schooling to universities, with a philosophy of education and an outlook on learning that would be of decisive import to Europe and America. But the eighteenth-century Enlightenment posed a great challenge to Scottish Presbyterianism, as it did to all religious persuasions in Europe. The Scottish resolution of this challenge marked a watershed in Presbyterianism as well as in the course of Scottish, and by extension American, educational theory and practice. For the struggle between two wings of Scottish Presbyterianism played out passionately in educational philosophy and foreshadowed the same tensions that would resurface again and again in North America.

The Scottish Moderates upheld reasoned civic engagement with Enlightenment ideals and aspirations that did not directly undermine the church. They emphasized the positive, civilizing role of Christianity and endeavored to join the best of secular thought with the best of Christian theology, and viewed themselves as post-Renaissance Christian humanists. In contrast, the Evangelicals (also called the Popular Party) were rather more suspicious of secular learning and became increasingly alarmed at the inroads Enlightenment thought seemed to be making in Scottish universities by the early 1730s. They debated Moderates on matters theological and educational, arguing for a more distinctly orthodox stance with regard to both. William Law Mathieson commits two chapters ("Ecclesiastical Politics," and "The Noontide of Modernism") in *The Awakening of Scotland, 1747–1797* (Glasgow: James Maclehose & Sons, 1910) to the intricacies of the debate. John R. McIntosh systematically presents the Evangelical case in *Church and Theology in Enlightenment Scotland: The Popular Party, 1740–1800* (East Lothian, Scotland: Tuckwell Press, 1998), while J. H. S. Burleigh's *A Church History of Scotland* (London: Oxford University Press, 1960, third impression, 1973) specifically focuses on the common ground shared by Evangelicals and Moderates concerning educational and ministerial issues. That this internecine struggle for the intellectual and spiritual soul of Scotland was conducted with less aplomb and reason than either the Moderates or the Evangelicals might like to admit becomes readily apparent in these studies.

The ultimate victory of the Moderates, though won at the cost of schism, resulted in the intellectual vitality of the Scottish Enlightenment and determined the course of Scottish education well into the nineteenth century. R. D. Anderson's opening essay, "Scottish Education before 1800," in his *Education and the Scottish People, 1750–1918* (Oxford: Clarendon Press, 1995), provides an enlightening but rather technical overview of the successes of the Scottish educational system just as the Moderates gained the upper hand. In showcasing the life and work of five of the most distinguished leaders of the Moderate party, Richard B. Sher's seminal study *Church and University in the Scottish*

Enlightenment: The Moderate Literati of Edinburgh (Princeton, N.J.: Princeton University Press, 1985) contextualizes their intellectual, theological, and social influence. In many ways, as Sher contends, Hugh Blair, William Robertson, Alexander Carlyle, John Home, and Adam Ferguson set the stage for the flowering of Scottish Common Sense Realism. It was this philosophical movement that not only shaped Scottish higher education, but also exerted significant power over the course of American intellectual life during the colonial and early national periods.

Archie Turnbull provides plenty of evidence for the integral relationship between Scottish and American intellectual currents, both educational and otherwise, in "Scotland and America, 1730–1790," in David Daiches, Peter Jones, and Jean Jones, eds., *The Scottish Enlightenment 1730–1790: A Hotbed of Genius* (Edinburgh: The Institute for Advanced Studies in the Humanities and The Saltire Society, 1996), 137–53. In *The Scottish Enlightenment and the American College Ideal* (New York: Teacher's College Press of Columbia University, 1971), Douglas Sloan argues that the deep association between Scottish and American intellectual currents can be traced via the extent and importance of the Presbyterian academy movement and in the lives and careers of representative American educators such as Francis Alison, John Witherspoon, Samuel Stanhope Smith, and Benjamin Rush. As if to add an exclamation point to Sloan's thesis, the entire first section of six essays in Richard B. Sher and Jeffrey R. Smitten, eds., *Scotland and America in the Age of the Enlightenment* (Edinburgh: Edinburgh University Press, 1990; published in the United States by Princeton University Press, 1990) is dedicated to the multifaceted influence of John Witherspoon. The volume also includes another essay by Andrew Hook, entitled "Philadelphia, Edinburgh and the Scottish Enlightenment," which connects the educational practice of an entire American city to Scottish precedent.

Gladys Bryson's *Man and Society: The Scottish Inquiry of the Eighteenth Century* (Princeton, N.J.: Princeton University Press, 1945) gives Witherspoon, and later James McCosh, presidents of Princeton, and Noah Porter, president of Yale, preeminent credit for spreading Scottish Common Sense inquiry to the American educational establishment.[3] George S. Pryde contends in *The Scottish Universities and the Colleges of Colonial America* (Glasgow, Scotland: Jackson, Son & Co., 1957) that while the Scottish philosophy did not have a decisive influence on all the colleges of early America, William and Mary, Penn, and, of course, Princeton took their raison d'être from it. *The Revolutionary College: American Presbyterian Higher Education, 1707–1837* (New York: New York University Press, 1976) by Howard Miller casts a somewhat wider educational net by examining the histories of seven colleges and academies established by American Presbyterians before 1800.

While some American advocates of Scottish Common Sense philosophy like Witherspoon attempted to temper its increasingly rationalistic bent after 1760, the unquestioned presuppositions of the movement committed its adherents to a reasonable religion that reflected the deepest aspirations and highest achievements of human culture. The preeminence of American Presbyterians in the eighteenth and early nineteenth centuries served to accentuate the presumed affinity between Presbyterian religious norms and the process of creating an American "civilization." In Scotland, the Moderates invited secular critics such as David Hume into polite and reasonable discourse over matters civic and political. But American Presbyterians, by virtue of their elite status and numbers, had the opportunity to assume a leadership role in the genesis of a new political entity that would embody both Christian ideals and Enlightenment rationalism. Dozens of academies and colleges founded by Presbyterians in the eighteenth and nineteenth centuries became the intellectual instruments of this grand union. P. C. Kemeny's *Princeton in the Nation's Service: Religious Ideals and Educational Practice, 1868–1928* (New York: Oxford University Press, 1998) can almost be viewed as archetypical vis-à-vis the attempt at synthesis. Kemeny carries the history of American Presbyterianism's premier educational institution into the second quarter of the twentieth century by documenting the challenges Princeton faced as a religious institution confronting a progressively more secularized academic culture.

The secularization process meant that the effort to forge a winsome synergy between revelatory faith and critical rational inquiry did not always result in the reasoned engagement envisioned by American Presbyterian intellectuals. Perhaps the most compelling recent historical study of church-related higher education, in America is George M. Marsden's *The Soul of the American University: From Protestant Establishment to Established Nonbelief* (New York: Oxford University Press, 1994). Marsden takes a rather pessimistic view of the trajectory of church-related higher education, as he documents a relentless movement away from a distinctly Christian educational framework to one that first became indifferent and then overtly hostile to any Christian influence. Since Presbyterians played such a crucial role in the educational history of the United States, his analysis pays close attention to the vicissitudes of the Presbyterian way of educating. Professor Marsden collaborated with Bradley J. Longfield to publish *The Secularization of the Academy* (New York: Oxford University Press, 1992), an anthology that really serves as a companion volume to *The Soul of the American University*. *The Secularization of the Academy* provides a variety of essays which all address the loss of Christian perspectives in academic life. The most recent contribution to this genre is James Tunstead Burtchaell, C.S.C., *The Dying of the Light: The Disengagement of Colleges and Universities from Their Christian Churches* (Grand Rapids: Wm. B. Eerdmans Publishing Co., 1998).[4]

While the "literature of decline" has many critics, what cannot be denied is that Presbyterians have had to reckon with significant tensions in their institutions of higher learning and the implications those tensions held for the future of Presbyterian higher education—especially since the 1950s. The 1961–62 Clarence Edward Macartney Lectures at Whitworth College delivered by Bernard Ramm were published the following year as *The Christian College in the Twentieth Century* (Grand Rapids: Wm. B. Eerdmans Publishing Co., 1963) and emphasize the necessity for church-related educational institutions to draw from many sources in the quest to remain vibrant. Ramm tracks the contributions of thinkers as diverse as Augustine, Philipp Melanchthon, John Henry Cardinal Newman, Abraham Kuyper, and Sir Walter Moberly to Christian educational theory and practice. Robert Rue Parsonage and his contributors present a number of different perspectives regarding the nature of the church-college connection in *Church Related Higher Education: Perceptions and Perspectives* (Valley Forge, Pa.: Judson Press, 1978). Former president of Austin College, John D. Moseley contributed a response essay for the book that underscores his understanding of the Presbyterian way of educating. The journal *Black Issues in Higher Education* dedicated an entire issue (December 31, 1992) to "Presbyterians and Black Higher Education."

Presbyterian institutions have served as case studies for monographs concerned with the future of church-related higher education for a number of years. The previously cited Parsonage study profiled two Presbyterian institutions—Davidson College and Whitworth College. Victor Stoltzfus compares the Presbyterian way of educating with Lutheran and Roman Catholic perspectives in *Church-Affiliated Higher Education: Exploratory Case Studies of Presbyterian, Roman Catholic and Wesleyan Colleges* (Goshen, Ind.: Pinchpenny Press, 1992). A few years later Richard T. Hughes and William B. Adrian chose Whitworth College as one of fourteen examples of successful church-related institutions in their book *Models for Christian Higher Education: Strategies for Success in the Twenty-first Century* (Grand Rapids: Wm. B. Eerdmans Publishing Co., 1997). Whitworth College is paired with Calvin College of the Christian Reformed Church as representatives of the Reformed tradition in contemporary American higher education. Burtchaell's *Dying of the Light* provides extensive analyses of both Davidson and Lafayette Colleges as representative of Presbyterian higher education, though from a somewhat less optimistic vantage point. For those interested in exploring the history of a particular Presbyterian college, most if not all of the denominational institutions have accessible monographs on the subject.

The multivolume study on twentieth-century Presbyterianism edited by Coalter, Mulder, and Weeks, cited earlier, provides important insights on educational themes in three of its volumes. *The Presbyterian Predicament: Six*

Perspectives (vol. 1, 1990), while not concerned specifically with education per se, does place Presbyterian educational dilemmas in a broader cultural context. The articles by Robert Wuthnow and Edward W. Farley are especially useful in this regard. *The Pluralistic Vision: Presbyterians and Mainstream Protestant Education and Leadership* (vol. 6, 1992) is particularly helpful in sorting out the course of the educational ministry of the church over the course of the twentieth century. The concluding monograph in the series, *The Re-Forming Tradition: Presbyterians and Mainstream Protestantism* (vol. 7, 1992), contains a number of essays of interest to those seeking further insight into the contemporary contexts of Presbyterian educational thought and practice.

The Presbyterian Church (U.S.A.) and its related agencies have contributed substantially to the national discourse on the nature and purpose of higher education over the past twenty years. The Task Force on the Church and Higher Education published "The Church's Mission in Higher Education," in the *Journal of Presbyterian History* 59, no. 3 (1981), highlighting the salient parameters of educational policy for the 1980s. In 1990, the Association of Presbyterian Colleges and Universities began disseminating the newsletter *A Point of View*, dedicated to addressing noteworthy (and sometimes controversial) issues pertinent to the Presbyterian family of colleges and universities. A year later, the Committee on Higher Education of the PC(USA) reviewed the church's calling in higher education and submitted the ensuing report to the 203rd General Assembly. It was adopted and published as *Loving God with Our Minds: The Mission of the Presbyterian Church (U.S.A.) in Higher Education within the Global Community* (Louisville, Ky.: Committee on Higher Education, 1991). *Loving God with Our Minds* surveys the church's ministry in higher education and sets an agenda for future directions. In 1993 *The Presbyterian Outlook* devoted an entire issue, vol. 175, no. 37 (October 25, 1993), to higher education. Articles by Gene Williams and Harry E. Smith complement "A Statement of the Association of Presbyterian Colleges and Universities," a profile of Agnes Scott College, meditations on Presbyterian campus ministry, and brief descriptions of the Presbyterian colleges and universities. *On Being Faithful: The Continuing Mission of the Presbyterian Church (U.S.A.) in Higher Education* (Louisville, Ky.: Higher Education Program Team, 1995) brings deliberative thinking on the topic into the late 1990s, when the higher educational concerns of the church were evident at General Assembly. The 210th General Assembly (1998) pursued the issue by asking the colleges and universities of the church to consider developing initiatives that would "creatively bring Christian faith and practice to bear on scholarship and teaching in the arts and sciences and professional education." Two years later the 212th General Assembly (2000) passed an amended overture from the presbytery of Transylvania, Kentucky, entitled "On Developing a Mission Strategy to Strengthen the Partnership between the

Church and Its Related Schools, Colleges, and Universities." The overture commits the church, especially through its middle governing bodies and the Association of Presbyterian Colleges and Universities, actively to encourage a "strong 'dimension' of the Presbyterian and Reformed faith within the common life" of its educational institutions, "especially in student learning and service." A progress report on the development of a strategy will be made to the 215th Assembly (2003). This present volume on the vocation of the Presbyterian teacher, as well as the formation of the Presbyterian Academy of Scholars and Teachers in 2000, are the most recent examples of the denomination's efforts to support its educational ministry.

In closing, I would like to mention a few titles that, while not distinctly speaking only to the Presbyterian educational experience, do contribute helpful comparative perspectives on church-related higher education. As a seminal legacy from the Scottish Enlightenment, Presbyterians have sought to engage American culture via their institutions of higher learning. The schools of the Christian Reformed Church and to some extent those of the Reformed Church in America, however, have endeavored to be agencies of cultural transformation. Of the many voices writing in this transformational vein, two of the more eloquent are James D. Bratt and Nicholas Wolterstorff. Bratt's "Reformed Tradition and the Mission of Reformed Colleges," unpublished paper presented at the Reformed University of North America (RUNA) Conference on March 11, 1993, in Grand Rapids, clearly lines out the transformational calling. His introductory essay in the Hughes and Adrian *Models* anthology entitled "What Can the Reformed Tradition Contribute to Christian Higher Education?" does an admirable job of comparing the cultural engagement more characteristic of Presbyterian institutions and the cultural transformationalism apparent more frequently at C.R.C. or R.C.A. colleges and universities. Of the many fine books by Wolterstorff, *Educating for Responsible Action* (Grand Rapids: CSI Publications and Wm. B. Eerdmans Publishing Co., 1980) and *Reason within the Bounds of Religion* (Grand Rapids: Wm. B. Eerdmans Publishing Co., 1984) are among his well-articulated reflections on the transformational nature of education. Ron Wells edited an incisive collection of essays written from this perspective, entitled *Keeping the Faith: Embracing the Tensions in Christian Higher Education* (Grand Rapids: Wm. B. Eerdmans Publishing Co., 1996). By using George Marsden's *The Outrageous Idea of Christian Scholarship* (New York: Oxford University Press, 1997) as something of a foil, Robert Sweetman distinguishes between two ways Reformed intellectuals have perceived their scholarly work. He argues in "Christian Scholarship: Two Reformed Perspectives," *Perspectives: A Journal of Reformed Thought*, vol. 16, no. 6 (June/July 2001): 14–19, that both approaches—integrationist and integralist—are Reformed and could play a significant role in presenting what he calls "the uniability of faith and scholarship." Reformed theologian Peter C. Hodgson is not as concerned with bringing together faith and scholarship as he is in articulating more deeply theological understanding of education itself. In *God's Wisdom: Toward a Theology of Education* (Louisville, Ky.: Westminster John Knox Press, 1999), he maintains that God's wisdom elicits a distinctive kind of wisdom in humans that contributes to vital human development.

Finally, three books would be of interest to those curious about possible directions for the future of church-related higher education, Presbyterian or otherwise. David S. Dockery and David P. Gushee brought together a diverse group, which included representatives of the Reformed family, for *The Future of Christian Higher Education* (Nashville: Broadman & Holman, 1999). The essayists range across the entire landscape of church-related higher education to imagine future needs and directions. In *The University through the Eyes of Faith* (Indianapolis: Light and Life Communications, 1998), Steve Moore and Tim Beuthin provide much the same type of anthology. In this case one essay is written by renowned Presbyterian minister Dr. Earl Palmer. Robert Wuthnow of Princeton University offers another. My own *Teaching As an Act of Faith: Theory and Practice in Church-Related Higher Education* (New York: Fordham University Press, forthcoming) brings together Anabaptist, Lutheran, Reformed, Roman Catholic, and Wesleyan scholar-teachers from a variety of liberal arts disciplines to reflect on the ways in which their theological traditions are translated into classroom practice before their students.

Notes

Chapter 1: The Dying Light and Glowing Embers of Presbyterian Higher Education

1. Ronald C. White Jr., "Presbyterian Campus Ministries: Competing Loyalties and Changing Visions," in Milton Coalter, John Mulder, and Louis Weeks, eds., *The Pluralistic Vision: Presbyterians and Mainstream Protestant Education and Leadership* (Louisville, Ky.: Westminster/John Knox Press, 1992), 126.
2. Higher Education Program Team, *On Being Faithful: The Continuing Mission of the Presbyterian Church (U.S.A.) in Higher Education* (Louisville, Ky.: Office of the General Assembly, 1995), 24.
3. "An Overture on Higher Education," 00–71, submitted by the Presbytery of Transylvania [Kentucky], enacted by the 212th General Assembly of the Presbyterian Church (U.S.A.), 2000.
4. See especially the work of George Marsden, cited in an earlier paragraph, for elaboration on this point.

Chapter 2: The Biblical Foundations of Presbyterian Education

1. Gilbert C. Meilaender, ed., *Working: Its Meaning and Its Limits* (Notre Dame, Ind.: University of Notre Dame Press, 2000), 12.
2. George Eldon Ladd, *A Theology of the New Testament* (Grand Rapids: Eerdmans, 1974).
3. Hosea 4:6. Taken from the *Holy Bible: New International Version*, ©1978 by the International Bible Society, used by permission of Zondervan Bible Publishers. All references in this chapter are to the New International Version unless otherwise noted.
4. George Eldon Ladd, *Presence of the Future: The Eschatology of Biblical Realism* (New York: Harper & Row, 1964; reprint, Grand Rapids: Eerdmans, 1974).
5. Anthony Hoekema recognizes that any "complete" understanding of the kingdom must address both the present realities and the future hope—the two are inseparable. Hoekema, *Bible and the Future*, rev. ed. (Grand Rapids: Eerdmans, 1982).
6. Darwin K. Glassford, "The Reformed Doctrine of the Kingdom of God as a Paradigm for Formulating and Evaluating Educational Programs" (Ph.D. diss., Marquette University, 1991), 42.
7. The Belgic Confession, Article 27. The Heidelberg Catechism, Question 31, in response to the question "Why is he called CHRIST, that is, the ANOINTED ONE?" declares that he is "our eternal King, governing us by his Word and Spirit, and defending and sustaining us in the redemption he has won for us."

And the Westminster Confession of Faith, *Book of Confessions* 6.043, reads "It pleased God, in his eternal purpose, to choose and ordain the Lord Jesus, his only begotten Son, to be the Mediator between God and man, the prophet, priest, and king; the head and Savior of his Church, the heir of all things, and judge of the world; unto whom he did, from all eternity, give a people to be his seed, and to be by him in time redeemed, called, justified, sanctified, and glorified." Philip Schaff, ed., "The Belgic Confession" in *The Creeds of Christendom: With a History and Critical Notes*, rev. by David S. Schaff, vol. 3, *The Evangelical and Protestant Creeds with Translations*, 383–436 (New York: Harper & Row, 1931; reprint, Grand Rapids: Baker, 1983). "The Heidelberg Catechism" is from *The Constitution of the Presbyterian Church (U.S.A.)*, Part I, *Book of Confessions* (Louisville, Ky.: Office of the General Assembly), 4.031. "The Westminster Confession of Faith," is from *Book of Confessions* 6.043.

8. Heb. 2:8.
9. 1 Cor. 15:25.
10. Hoekema, *Bible and the Future*, 44.
11. Charles Hodge, *Systematic Theology*, vol. 2 (Grand Rapids: Eerdmans, 1952). See also George Eldon Ladd, *The Gospel of the Kingdom: Popular Expositions on the Kingdom of God* (Grand Rapids: Eerdmans, 1959); idem, *Theology of the New Testament*.
12. Hoekema, *Bible and the Future*, 43.
13. Luke 20:21; John 18:36; 1:13, 16.
14. Hodge, *Systematic Theology*, vol. 2.
15. Hoekema, *Bible and the Future*.
16. Ladd, *Gospel of the Kingdom*, 67; idem, *Presence of the Future*.
17. Hoekema, *Bible and the Future*, 16.
18. In regard to the temporal blessings of the kingdom, it is important to maintain the distinction between the Age of Fulfillment and the Age to Come. Ladd, *Theology of the New Testament*.
19. Ladd, *Presence of the Future*, 169; idem, *Gospel of the Kingdom*.
20. Hoekema, *Bible and the Future*, 31.
21. Gen. 8:22; Jer. 3:3; 14:22; Job 36:27–33; Ps. 65:9–13; Ezek. 34:26–27; Joel 2:23; Matt. 6:25–34.
22. Gen. 15; 17; Exod. 3:14; Heb. 1:1–2; 2 Tim. 3:16–17; 1 Pet. 1:20–21.
23. The terms "preparation" and "equipping" are from the Greek word *katartismon*. W. F. Moulton and A. S. Geden, *A Concordance to the Greek New Testament According to the Texts of Wescott and Hort, Tischendorf and the English Revisers*, 5th ed., rev. by H. K. Moulton (Edinburgh: T. & T. Clark, 1978). This term will be translated "equipping" in the remainder of this chapter.
24. R. Schippers, "Right, Worthy," in *The New International Dictionary of New Testament Theology*, ed. Colin Brown, vol. 3 (Grand Rapids: Eerdmans, 1978), 350.
25. Schippers, 350; Walter Bauer, "*Katartismos*," in *A Greek English Lexicon of the New Testament and Other Greek Literature*, trans. William F. Ardnt, F. Gingrich, and Frederick Danker (Chicago: University of Chicago Press, 1979).
26. William Wilson, *New Wilson's Old Testament Word Studies* (Grand Rapids: Kregel, 1987).
27. See also Exod. 18:15–16; L. J. Wood, "*Zahar*," in *Theological Wordbook of the Old Testament*, vol. 1, ed. R. L. Harrison, Gleason A. Archer, and Bruce K. Waltke (Chicago: Moody Press, 1980), 237.
28. See also Exod. 4:12, 15; 1 Sam. 12:23; Ps. 27:11; 119:33; Francis Brown,

S. R. Driver, and Charles Briggs, *The New Brown-Driver-Briggs-Gesenius Hebrew and English Lexicon* (Peabody, Mass.: Hendrickson, 1979).

29. J. E. Hartley, "*Yara*," in *Theological Wordbook of the Old Testament*, vol. 1.
30. This same purpose is also evident in Matt. 5:19; Eph. 4:21; Col. 3:16; 2 Thess. 2:15; 1 Tim. 4:11; and Titus 1:11.
31. See Matt. 13:24; 1 Tim. 1:18; 2 Tim. 2:2; Bauer, "*Katartismos*."
32. This usage is found principally in Acts 11:4; 18:26; 28:22; Bauer, "*Katartismos*."
33. W. Bauer, "Disciple," in *New International Dictionary of New Testament Theology*, vol. 1, 491.
34. Robert Banks, *Reenvisioning Theological Education: Exploring a Missional Alternative to Current Models* (Grand Rapids: Eerdmans, 1999), 136.
35. Ibid., 174.
36. Ibid.
37. P. R. Gilchrist, "*Yasar*," in *Theological Wordbook of the Old Testament*, vol. 1, 386.
38. Brown, Driver, and Briggs, *New Brown-Driver-Griggs-Gesenius Hebrew and English Lexicon*, 407, 416.
39. Gilchrist, "*Yasar*," 387.
40. Ibid., 377.
41. Friedrich Buschel, "*elegxo*," in *Theological Dictionary of the New Testament*, ed. Gerhard Kittel, trans. and ed. Geoffery Bromiley, vol. 2 (Grand Rapids: Eerdmans, 1964), 473; quoted in Gilchrist, 377.
42. Bauer, "*Manthano*," in *Greek English Lexicon*.
43. D. Mueller, "Disciple," in *New International Dictionary of New Testament Theology*, vol. 1, 487.
44. L. Goldberg, "*Bin*," in *Theological Wordbook of the Old Testament*, vol. 1, 103; this usage is also found in Ps. 105:27.
45. Goldberg, "*Sakal*," in *Theological Wordbook of the Old Testament*, vol. 2, 877; the noun form, *sekel*, is used in a similar fashion in Prov. 1:3; 1 Chron. 28:19; and Dan. 9:22.
46. Bauer, *Greek English Lexicon*, 202.
47. "Sin is any want of conformity unto or transgression, of the law of God," Westminster Shorter Catechism, Question 14, cited in *The [Westminster] Confession of Faith of the Presbyterian Church in America Together with The [Westminster] Larger Catechism and The [Westminster] Shorter Catechism* (n.p.: Committee for Christian Education and Publications of the Presbyterian Church in America, 1983).
48. Janis Berkhof, *A Manual of Christian Doctrine* (Grand Rapids: Baker, 1933); Hodge, *Systematic Theology*, vol. 2; Robert Lewis Dabney, *Lectures in Systematic Theology*, 6th ed. (Richmond: Presbyterian Committee for Publications, 1927; reprint, Grand Rapids: Baker, 1985); *The Heidelberg Catechism*, Questions 7 and 8; *Belgic Confession*, Article 15; *The Canons of the Synod of Dort*, "Third and Fourth Heads of Doctrine," Articles 1–4, cited in Phillip Schaff, ed., *The Creeds of Christendom: With a History and Critical Notes*, rev. by David S. Schaff, vol. 3, *The Evangelical and Protestant Creeds with Translations*, 580–97 (New York: Harper & Row, 1931; reprint, Grand Rapids: Baker, 1983); *Westminster Confession of Faith*, Chapter 6.
49. James M. Boice, *God the Redeemer*, vol. 2 of *Foundations of the Christian Faith* (Downers Grove, Ill.: InterVarsity Press, 1978), 48.
50. Berkhof, *Manual of Christian Doctrine*.
51. J. Budziszewski, *The Revenge of Conscience: Politics and the Fall of Man* (Dallas: Spence, 1999).

Chapter 3: God, Creation, and Covenant

1. Wade Clark Roof and William McKinney, *American Mainline Religion: Its Changing Shape and Future* (New Brunswick, N.J.: Rutgers University Press, 1987), 34.
2. See Larry Rasmussen's *Moral Fragments and Moral Community: A Proposal for Church in Society* (Minneapolis: Augsburg Press, 1993), especially chap. 4, "Market and State as Moral Proxies," 61–76.
3. Robert Bellah, "Is There a Common American Culture?" *Journal of the American Academy of Religion* 66, no. 3 (Fall 1998): 622. See also Robert Bellah, Richard Madsen, William Sullivan, Ann Swidler, and Steven Tipton, *Habits of the Heart: Individualism and Commitment in American Life*, 2d ed. (Davis: University of California Press, 1996).
4. See Michael Walzer, *Thick and Thin: Moral Argument at Home and Abroad* (Notre Dame, Ind.: University of Notre Dame Press, 1994), esp. chap. 5, "The Divided Self," 85–104. See also idem, *Spheres of Justice: A Defense of Pluralism and Equality* (New York: Basic Books, 1983).
5. Robert Bellah, Richard Madsen, William Sullivan, Ann Swidler, and Steven Tipton, *The Good Society* (New York: Alfred A. Knopf, 1991), 155.
6. Robert Bellah, "Freedom, Coercion, and Authority," *Bulletin (Council of Societies for the Study of Religion)* 28, no. 2 (April 1999), 37.
7. Douglas Sloan, *Faith and Knowledge: Mainline Protestantism and American Higher Education* (Philadelphia: Westminster John Knox Press, 1994), ix.
8. See John Calvin, *Institutes of the Christian Religion* 1.2.1; Library of Christian Classics, ed. John T. McNeill, trans. Ford Lewis Battles (Philadelphia: Westminster Press, 1960). See also, Brian Gerrish, *Grace and Gratitude: The Eucharistic Theology of John Calvin* (Minneapolis: Fortress Press, 1993), 14–20.
9. Calvin, *Institutes*, 1.2.1.
10. Douglas Ottati, *Reforming Protestantism: Christian Commitment in Today's World* (Louisville, Ky.: Westminster John Knox Press, 1995), 119. See also Robert Hughes, *How Christian Faith Can Sustain the Life of the Mind* (Grand Rapids: Eerdmans, 2001), 67–76.
11. Ottati, *Reforming Protestantism*, 118.
12. Calvin, *Institutes*, 1.14.20.
13. H. Richard Niebuhr, *Radical Monotheism and Western Culture: With Supplementary Essays* (Harper & Row, 1960), 32.
14. See H. Richard Niebuhr, "The Idea of Covenant and American Democracy," *Church History* 23, no. 2 (June 1954), 134.
15. Max Stackhouse, "The Moral Meaning of Covenant," *The Annual of the Society of Christian Ethics*, 250. See also Daniel Elazar, *Covenant and Polity in Biblical Israel*, vol. 1 (New Brunswick, N.J.: Transaction Publishers, 1995), 86.
16. Gerrish, *Grace and Gratitude*, 43. See also Calvin's *Institutes*, 1.2.2 and 1.14.22.
17. See William Perkins, "A Treatise of the Vocations or Callings of Men," in *Working: Its Meaning and Its Limits*, ed. Gilbert Meilaender (Notre Dame, Ind.: University of Notre Dame Press, 2000), 108.
18. Ibid., 114.
19. Calvin, *Institutes* 3.7.5.
20. Ibid., 2.1.4–9.
21. Ibid., 2.1.5.
22. Ibid., 2.1.4.

23. Augustine, *The City of God*, trans. Henry Bettenson (Penguin Books, 1984), 868.
24. Perkins, "Treatise of the Vocations or Callings of Men," 109.
25. See Calvin's *Institutes*, 2.2.17, where Calvin discusses "common grace" or "general grace." He notes that human beings continue to possess significant gifts and abilities despite the destructive consequences of sin. This is due to God's graciousness alone. As Calvin writes: "If [God] had not spared us, our fall would have entailed the destruction of our whole nature."
26. See Calvin's *Institutes*, 3.2.6–8.
27. "The Confession of 1967," *The Constitution of the Presbyterian Church (U.S.A.):* Part I, *The Book of Confessions* (Office of the General Assembly, 1983), 9.44.
28. Michael Walzer, *The Revolution of the Saints: A Study in the Origins of Radical Politics* (Cambridge, Mass.: Harvard University Press, 1965).
29. Calvin, *Institutes*, 3.3.10
30. H. Richard Niebuhr, *The Meaning of Revelation* (New York: Collier Books, 1941), 139.
31. See, for example, Robert Bellah's "Freedom, Coercion, and Authority"; Robert Bellah et al., *The Good Society*.
32. Waldo Beach, "Christian Ethical Community as Norm," *Colleges and Commitments*, ed. Lloyd Averill and William Jellema (Philadelphia: Westminster Press, 1971), 169.
33. Calvin, *Institutes*, 2.2.15.
34. Richard T. Hughes, *How Christian Faith Can Sustain the Life of the Mind* (Grand Rapids: Eerdmans, 2001), 32–33.
35. The institution where I work, Davidson College, acknowledges this openness in its mission statement in the following way: "Davidson commits itself to a Christian tradition that recognizes God as the source of all truth, and finds in Jesus Christ the revelation of that God, a God bound by no church or creed. The loyalty of the college thus extends beyond the Christian community to the whole human community and necessarily includes the openness to and respect for the world's various religious traditions. Davidson is dedicated to the quest for truth and encourages teachers and students to explore the whole of reality, whether physical or spiritual, with an unlimited employment of their intellectual powers." Statement of Purpose, Davidson College (www2.davidson.edu/home/home_purpose.asp).
36. H. Richard Niebuhr, "Theology in the University," *Radical Monotheism and Western Culture*, 98.
37. Ibid.
38. Calvin's *Institutes*, 4.20.8.
39. H. Richard Niebuhr, "Theology in the University," 97–98.
40. Brian Gerrish, "Tradition in the Modern World: The Reformed Habit of Mind," in *Toward the Future of the Reformed Tradition*, ed. David Willis and Michael Welker (Grand Rapids: Eerdmans, 1999), 12–14.
41. Ibid., 13.
42. For a fine example of the tradition-based nature of the scientific enterprise and the way in which those traditions develop and change, see Thomas Kuhn, *The Structure of Scientific Revolutions*.
43. John Calvin, "*Defension contra Pighium*" (1543), in *Ioannis Cavini opera quae supersunct omnia*, ed. W. Baum, E. Cunitz, and E. Reuss, 59 vols. (Brunswick:

C. A. Schwetschke and Son, 1863–1900), 6:250. Quoted in Brian Gerrish, "Tradition in the Modern World," 15.

44. See James D. Bratt, "What Can the Reformed Tradition Contribute to Christian Higher Education?" *Models of Christian Higher Education: Strategies for Success in the Twenty-first Century*, ed. Richard T. Hughes and William B. Adrian (Grand Rapids: Eerdmans, 1997), 125–40.

45. For some of Calvin's harsh criticism of "empty speculation," see his *Institutes*, 1.14.4 and 1.5.9.

46. James Bratt notes that both Harvard and Princeton (products of Reformed Christianity—one Puritan, the other Presbyterian) were formed with this same mission, namely, to prepare leaders for church and society. See Bratt, "What Can the Reformed Tradition Contribute to Christian Higher Education?"

Chapter 4: The Reformed Understanding of Vocation in History

1. The choice of the British Isles is not arbitrary. Generally speaking, the heritage of colonial America was most heavily influenced by the settlement of emigrants from Great Britain, Scotland, and Ireland. See Winthrop S. Hudson and John Corrigan, *Religion in America*, 6th ed. (Upper Saddle River, N.J.: Prentice-Hall, 1998), 3, 38–39.

2. Quirinius Breen, *John Calvin: A Study in French Humanism*, 2d ed. (New York: Archon Books, 1968), 11.

3. Breen, *John Calvin*, 11.

4. Alexandre Ganoczy notes that in August of 1523, the month that Calvin arrived in Paris, an Augustinian monk had been burned alive in front of the entrance of Saint-Honoré. See *The Young Calvin*, trans. David Foxgrover and Wade Provo (Philadelphia: Westminster Press, 1987), 49.

5. Ibid., 57–61.

6. Breen, *John Calvin*, 15.

7. Erasmus, in his "Concerning the Eating of Fish."

8. Ganoczy, *Young Calvin*, 58.

9. Ibid., 59.

10. Thomas à Kempis, *The Imitation of Christ*, trans. Leo Sherley-Price (London: Penguin, 1952), 31.

11. Ganoczy, *Young Calvin*, 58.

12. Ibid., 60. It is worthwhile to note that although some of Calvin's likely curriculum can be reconstructed, we do not have a single contemporary shred of evidence on his religious development at the time. Was he rebellious? rigidly orthodox? We simply do not know—as Calvin has left us no material from which to conjecture. See Ganoczy, 60–63.

13. François Wendel, *Calvin: Origins and Development of His Religious Thought*, trans. Philip Mairet (Durham, N.C.: Labyrinth Press, 1987), 21.

14. Ibid., 22.

15. Breen, *John Calvin*, 46.

16. Ibid., 46–47.

17. Ganoczy, *Young Calvin*, 72.

18. For an interesting view into which of Luther's works Calvin might easily have been reading, see Francis Higman's "Les traductions françaises de Luther, 1524–1550," in *Lire et Découvrir: La circulation des idées au temps de la Réforme* (Geneva: Librairie Droz, 1998), 201–25.

19. For further reading on the education and early life of Calvin, see Bernard Cot-

tret's recent biography, *Calvin: A Biography*, trans. M. Wallace McDonald (Grand Rapids: Eerdmans, 2000), 12–70.

20. Wendel, *Calvin*, 36.

21. Not an unimportant question. In examining the commentary on Seneca, Émile Doumergue concluded that Calvin had become completely Augustinian, and noted, "Now Augustinianism is the contrary of humanism," *La jeunesse de Calvin*, 222. However, William Bouwsma has concluded the opposite: that not only is Augustinianism not contrary to humanism, but rather that certain strands of Augustinian thought are part of humanism. See his "The Two Faces of Humanism: Stoicism and Augustinianism in Renaissance Thought," in *Itinerarium Italicum: The Profile of the Italian Renaissance in the Mirror of its European Transformations*, ed. Heiko Oberman and Thomas A Brady Jr. (Leiden: E. J. Brill, 1975).

22. Calvin quotes *The City of God* 15 times. See Luchesius Smits, *Saint Augustin dans l'oeuvre de Jean Calvin* (Assen: Van Gorcum & Comp., 1957), vol. 1, 16ff.

23. Ganoczy, *Young Calvin*, 74.

24. Cottret, *Calvin: A Biography*, 56, states that "In 1530 Calvin's enthusiasm and vocation as a humanist still displayed no traits of the Reformer."

25. Ganoczy, *Young Calvin*, 76.

26. George Tavard, *The Starting Point of Calvin's Theology* (Grand Rapids: Eerdmans, 2000).

27. Lorna Jane Abray, *The People's Reformation: Magistrates, Clergy, and Commons in Strasbourg, 1500–1598* (Ithaca, N.Y.: Cornell University Press, 1985), 32.

28. Steven Ozment, *The Age of Reform 1250–1550: An Intellectual and Religious History of Late Medieval and Reformation Europe* (New Haven, Conn.: Yale University Press, 1980), 364.

29. John Calvin, "Subject Matter of the Present Work," in *Institutes of the Christian Religion*, trans. Ford Lewis Battles, ed. John T. McNeill, Library of Christian Classics (Philadelphia: Westminster Press, 1960), 6–7.

30. Calvin, *Institutes*, 7.

31. John Calvin, "Articles Concerning the Organization of the Church and of Worship at Geneva Proposed by the Ministers at the Council," in *Calvin: Theological Treatises*, ed. J. K. Reid (Philadelphia: Westminster Press, 1954), 54.

32. Ibid., 54–55.

33. Calvin, *Institutes*, 2.2.13.

34. For the best summary in English of the history of the Genevan Academy, see Karin Maag's *Seminary or University? The Genevan Academy and Reformed Higher Education, 1560–1620* (Aldershot, Hampshire [U.K.]: Ashgate Publishing, 1995), chaps. 1–3.

35. John Calvin, "Draft Ecclesiastical Ordinances, September and October 1541," in *Calvin: Theological Treatises*, 62.

36. Ibid., 63.

37. Calvin was adamant about this task of bringing the laity to the Scriptures. See my "*Ecclesia, Legenda atque Intelligenda Scriptura*: The Church as Discerning Community in Calvin's Hermeneutic," *Calvin Theological Journal* 36, no. 2 (2001): 270–89.

38. Maag, *Seminary or University?* 8–11. Maag notes that there was a general difference of opinion between the ministers of Geneva and the townspeople about the relative importance of the two branches. The ministers, motivated by concern for the training of ministers for the mission field, concentrated on the

upper *schola publica*. The townspeople felt "that the solid foundation of the *schola privata* was paramount for the city" (p. 11), and sometimes this lack of common purpose caused friction.

39. Maag outlines the occasional difficulty the Genevans had of securing qualified professors; ibid., 35–102.

40. Calvin himself, though trained as a lawyer, was against offering courses in law. He wrote to Caspar Olevianus on the subject of lawyers in 1562: "If you ever have to deal with jurists, you should know that almost everywhere these people are the opponents of Christ's ministers, because they do not believe that they can hold on to their status in places where ecclesiastical authority is firmly established." Ibid., 24.

41. See especially Maag's first chapter on this point.

42. For a further overview of the importance of humanism in Calvin's development, see Ford Lewis Battles's "Calvin's Humanistic Education," in *Interpreting John Calvin*, ed. Robert Benedetto (Grand Rapids: Baker Book House, 1996), 47–64.

43. In this regard, see Roland Frye, "Protestantism and Education: A Preliminary Study of the Early Centuries and Some Suggested Principles" (unpublished paper), 3–20. There is also pertinent background material in Christopher J. Lucas, *American Higher Education: A History* (New York: St. Martin's Press, 1996), 55–70; and John W. Kuykendall, "The Presbyterian Heritage and Higher Education," *Pacific Theological Review* 17:3 (Spring 1984): 57–67.

44. Frye, "Protestantism and Education," 9.

45. Ibid., 15.

46. Frederick Rudolph, *The American College and University* (New York: Knopf, 1962), 3.

47. One good source for the story of the academies in England is J. W. Ashley Smith, *The Birth of Modern Education: The Contribution of the Dissenting Academies, 1660–1800* (London: Independent, 1954). For a brief description of their Ulster counterparts, see Douglas Sloan, *The Scottish Enlightenment and the American College Ideal* (New York: Teachers College Press, Columbia University, 1971), 40, 64–65.

48. Ibid., 14–20.

49. Smith, *Birth of Modern Education*, 2.

50. Ibid., 237–52; 262–64.

51. Sloan, *Scottish Enlightenment*, 40.

52. Ibid., 14–23.

53. Ibid., 9ff.

54. Smith, *Birth of Modern Education*, 9.

55. The nine colonial institutions are Harvard (1636), William and Mary (1693), Yale (1701), College of New Jersey [Princeton] (1746), King's [Columbia] (1754), Philadelphia [University of Pennsylvania] (1755), Rhode Island [Brown] (1765), Queen's [Rutgers] (1766), and Dartmouth (1769). See Donald G. Tewksbury, *The Founding of American Colleges and Universities before the Civil War: With Particular Reference to the Religions Influences Bearing upon the College Movement* (New York: Columbia University, 1932), 32–33; and for narrative description, Rudolph, *American College and University*, 3–11.

56. This is the opening sentence of Thomas Jefferson Wertenbaker's superb history of Princeton, which was originally published at the bicentennial of the college, then recently reissued as the university celebrated its 250th anniversary.

Thomas J. Wertenbaker, *Princeton 1746–1896*, with a new preface by John M. Murrin (Princeton, N.J.: Princeton University, 1996), 3.
57. Howard Miller, *The Revolutionary College: American Presbyterian Higher Education 1707–1837* (New York: New York University Press, 1976), 102.
58. For a full narrative of the controversy, see Leonard J. Trinterud, *The Forming of an American Tradition: A Re-examination of Colonial Presbyterianism* (Philadelphia: Westminster Press, 1949), 38–143.
59. Trinterud expresses the opinion that the founding of the Log College was "the most important event in colonial Presbyterianism." Ibid., 63. It is frequently noted, though, that the Log College seems to have lacked the humanistic breadth of the English and Ulster academies, and that the course of study is better described as an "apprenticeship" for ministry. See, inter alia, John Murrin's comment in the preface to Wertenbaker, *Princeton*, xvii.
60. Trinterud, *Forming an American Tradition*, 82. See also the listing of American academies in Sloan, *Scottish Enlightenment*, 281–84.
61. See the sermon by Gilbert Tennent, *The Danger of an Unconverted Ministry*, for the classic statement of this point of view; see H. Shelton Smith, Robert T. Handy, and Lefferts A. Loetscher, *American Christianity: An Historical Interpretation with Representative Documents*, vol. 1 (New York: Charles Scribner's Sons, 1960), 321–28.
62. Lucas, *American Higher Education*, 106.
63. Murrin, in Wertenbaker, *Princeton*, xviii.
64. With respect to this latter point, it is important to note that both Harvard and Yale were controlled by leaders who were unfriendly to the revival. Indeed, several of the founders of the College of New Jersey were Yale alumni, offended by their alma mater's treatment of David Brainerd, a young advocate of the revival who was denied his degree by Yale College. See Trinterud, *Forming of an American Tradition*, 123–24.
65. Quoted in Miller, *Revolutionary College*, 67.
66. Ashbel Green, quoted in Mark A. Noll, *Princeton and the Republic, 1768–1822: The Search for a Christian Enlightenment in the Era of Samuel Stanhope Smith* (Princeton, N.J.: Princeton University Press, 1989), 29.
67. At the time of Witherspoon's appointment, the Old Side had offered its own candidate, Francis Alison of the College of Philadelphia, but the New Side majority on the Princeton board stole a march on their opponents by taking action to call Witherspoon before hearing the Old Side deputation. See Wertenbaker, *Princeton*, 48–49.
68. Ibid., 19.
69. Ibid., 55.
70. Sloan, *Scottish Enlightenment*, 110.
71. Ibid., 117.
72. Miller, *Revolutionary College*, 183.
73. Mark Noll, *Princeton and the Republic, 1768–1822: The Search for a Christian Enlightenment in the Era of Samuel Stanhope Smith* (Princeton, N.J.: Princeton University Press, 1989), 36–40.
74. Ibid., 292.
75. Contemporaries perceived him to be formidable, but aloof. The story was told that his clergyman brother, John Blair Smith (sometime president of Union College), had once confronted him with the statement, "Brother Sam, you don't preach Jesus Christ and Him crucified, but Sam Smith and him dignified."

Sloan, *Scottish Enlightenment,* 167. Stanhope Smith left the Princeton presidency under significant pressure to do so in 1812.
76. Noll, *Princeton and the Republic,* 9.
77. Ibid., 6.
78. Sloan, *Scottish Enlightenment,* 144.
79. Richard Hofstadter and Wilson Smith, *American Higher Education: A Documentary History,* vol. 1 (Chicago: University of Chicago Press, 1961), 275–91. This statement is made in the introductory paragraph, p. 275.
80. Rudolph, *American College and University,* 53.

Chapter 5: The American Presbyterian College

1. John Dillenberger, ed., *John Calvin: Selections from His Writings,* with introduction by Dillenberger (Garden City, N.Y.: Doubleday & Co., 1971), 234.
2. W. Fred Graham, *The Constructive Revolutionary: John Calvin and His Socio-Economic Impact* (East Lansing: Michigan State University Press, 1987, reissue of Atlanta: John Knox Press, 1971), 145ff.
3. James Mackinnon, *Calvin and the Reformation* (New York: Russell & Russell, 1962), 173–75.
4. C. Harve Geiger, *The Program of Higher Education of the Presbyterian Church in the United States of America: An Historical Analysis of Its Growth in the United States* (Cedar Rapids, Iowa: Laurance Press, 1940), 37.
5. Douglas Sloan, *The Scottish Enlightenment and the American College Ideal* (New York: Teachers College Press, Columbia University, 1971), 52.
6. Donald G. Tewksbury, *The Founding of American Colleges and Universities before the Civil War: With Particular Reference to the Religious Influences Bearing upon the College Movement* (New York: Bureau of Publications, Teachers College, Columbia University, 1932), 91ff.
7. Ernest Trice Thompson, "The Presbyterian Mark: An Educated Leadership," in Dewitt C. Reddick, ed., *Church and Campus: Presbyterians Look to the Future from Their Historic Role in Christian Higher Education* (Richmond: John Knox Press, 1956), 97.
8. National Opinion Research Center, General Social Survey, 1983.
9. Bradley J. Longfield and George M. Marsden, "Presbyterian Colleges in Twentieth Century America," in Milton J. Coalter, John M. Mulder, and Louis B. Weeks, eds., *The Pluralistic Vision: Presbyterians and Mainstream Protestant Education and Leadership* (Louisville, Ky.: Westminster/John Knox Press, 1992), 100.
10. Second Annual Report of the Board of Christian Education, *Minutes of the General Assembly (1925) of the Presbyterian Church in the U.S.A.,* Part II, 7–8, quoted in Longfield and Marsden, 114–15.
11. Longfield and Marsden, "Presbyterian Colleges," 109ff.
12. George Marsden, *The Soul of the American University: From Protestant Establishment to Established Nonbelief* (New York: Oxford University Press, 1994).
13. Jon H. Roberts and James Turner, *The Sacred and the Secular University* (Princeton, N.J.: Princeton University Press, 2000).
14. Longfield and Marsden, "Presbyterian Colleges," 118.
15. Executive Committee of Christian Education and Ministerial Relief, Henry Sweets, director, *Our Presbyterian Educational Institutions* (Louisville, Ky.: Presbyterian Church in the United States, 1914), 7.
16. Task Force on the Church and Higher Education, United Presbyterian Church (U.S.A.), "The Church's Mission in Higher Education: A Report and

Recommendations," United Presbyterian Church U.S.A. 193rd General Assembly (1981) (New York: Education in Leadership Development [Division], Program Agency), 7.

17. Association of Presbyterian Colleges and Universities, *A Ministry of Nurture: The Spiritual Life at Educational Institutions Affiliated with the Presbyterian Church (U.S.A.)* (Louisville, Ky.: Association of Presbyterian Colleges and Universities, 1998), 13.
18. William Weston conducted this survey and made a report to the Association of Presbyterian Colleges and Universities meeting in March 2000. This section quotes significantly from that report.
19. David Solomon, "What Baylor and Notre Dame Can Learn from Each Other," *New Oxford Review*, vol. 62, no. 10 (December 1995): 8–18.
20. See, for example, William Weston, "Centre and Religious Life: A Survey of Selected Alumni Classes," Centre College, March 2000.

Chapter 6: Teaching in the Collegiate Institutions of the Church

1. George Dennis O'Brien, *All the Essential Half-Truths about Higher Education* (Chicago: University of Chicago Press, 1998), 15.
2. George M. Marsden and Bradley J. Longfield, *The Secularization of the Academy* (New York: Oxford University Press, 1992), 80.
3. Samuel P. Huntington, *The Clash of Civilizations and the Remaking of World Order* (New York: Touchstone, 1996), 208.
4. Merrimon Cuninggim, *Uneasy Partners: The College and the Church* (Nashville: Abingdon Press, 1994), 82.
5. George M. Marsden, *The Soul of the American University: From Protestant Establishment to Established Nonbelief* (New York: Oxford University Press, 1994), 265; James Tunstead Burtchaell, *The Dying of the Light: The Disengagement of Colleges and Universities from Their Christian Churches* (Grand Rapids: Eerdmans, 1998), 823.
6. General Assembly Council, Presbyterian Church (U.S.A.), memo regarding mission prioritization, 2001.
7. *The Constitution of the Presbyterian Church (U.S.A.)*, Part II, *Book of Order* (Louisville, Ky.: Office of the General Assembly, 2000), G-1.0304.
8. "Brief Statement of Faith," *The Constitution of the Presbyterian Church (U.S.A.)*, 1990. Part I, *Book of Confessions* (Louisville, Ky: Office of the General Assembly, 1990).
9. Pierre Teilhard de Chardin, *The Phenomenon of Man* (London: Collins, 1959), 31.
10. Sharon Parks, *The Critical Years: Young Adults and the Search for Meaning, Faith, and Commitment* (San Francisco: HarperSanFrancisco, 1991).
11. Søren Kierkegaard, *Purity of Heart Is to Will One Thing* (New York: Harper & Brothers, 1938).
12. Robert Rankin, ed., *The Recovery of Spirit in Higher Education* (New York: Seabury Press, 1980).
13. Robert Benne, *Quality with Soul: How Six Premier Colleges and Universities Kept Faith with Their Religious Traditions* (Grand Rapids: Eerdmans, 2001).
14. Parker J. Palmer, *The Courage to Teach: Exploring the Inner Landscape of a Teacher's Life* (San Francisco: Jossey-Bass, 1998), 10.
15. Kenneth E. Eble, *The Craft of Teaching* (San Francisco: Jossey-Bass, 1976). Joseph Lowman, *Mastering the Technique of Teaching* (San Francisco: Jossey-Bass,

1984). Wilbert J. McKeachie, *Teaching Tips: A Guidebook for the Beginning College Teacher* (Lexington, Mass.: D. C. Heath & Co., 1986).

16. Palmer, *Courage to Teach*, 35.
17. Warren Bryan Martin, *College of Character* (San Francisco: Jossey-Bass, 1982).
18. Edward Farley, *The Fragility of Knowledge: Theological Education in the Church and the University* (Philadelphia: Fortress Press, 1988).
19. Sallie McFague, *Models of God: Theology for an Ecological Nuclear Age* (Philadelphia: Fortress Press, 1987).
20. Nina Cobb, ed., *The Future of Education: Perspectives on National Standards in America* (New York: The College Board, 1994). Alexander W. Astin, *Assessment for Excellence: The Philosophy & Practice of Assessment and Evaluation in Higher Education* (New York: American Council on Education, Macmillan, 1991).

Chapter 7: Teaching in the Theological Schools of the Church

1. Milton J. Coalter, John M. Mulder, Louis B. Weeks, eds., *The Pluralistic Vision: Presbyterians and Mainstream Protestant Education and Leadership* (Louisville, Ky.: Westminster/John Knox Press, 1992); Presbyterian Church (U.S.A.), Special Committee to Study Theological Institutions, a report approved by the 205th General Assembly (1993), Presbyterian Church (U.S.A.) (Louisville, Ky.: Presbyterian Church [U.S.A.], 1993); Anthony Ruger, "The Big Picture: Strategic Choices for Theological Schools," *Auburn Studies*, no. 7 (New York: Auburn Theological Seminary, 2000); Leon Pacala, *The Role of ATS in Theological Education, 1980–1990*, ATS Publications (Atlanta: Scholars Press, 1998); Barbara G. Wheeler, "Is There a Problem? Theological Students and Religious Leadership for the Future," *Auburn Studies*, no. 8 (New York: Auburn Theological Seminary, 2001); *Towards Viable Theological Education: Ecumenical Imperative, Catalyst of Renewal* (Geneva: WCC Publications, c. 1997).

Chapter 8: The Vocation of Teaching in the Church-Related College

1. Carolyn L. Blair and Arda S. Walker, *By Faith Endowed* (Maryville, Tenn.: Maryville College Press, 1994), 2–3.
2. Samuel Tyndale Wilson, *Isaac Anderson Founder and First President of Maryville College: A Memorial* (Maryville, Tenn.: Maryville College, 1932), 41.
3. Blair and Walker, *By Faith Endowed*, 4–5.
4. Wilson, *Isaac Anderson*, 61
5. Blair and Walker, *By Faith Endowed*, 6.
6. Samuel Tyndale Wilson, *A Century of Maryville College* (Maryville, Tenn.: Maryville College, 1935), 62.
7. Blair and Walker, *By Faith Endowed*, 182.
8. Ibid., 282.
9. "Preparing Thinking Christians for the Twenty-first Century," Report of the Faith and Learning Committee to President Gerald Gibson, December 2000, 5–6.
10. Maryville College, "Statement of Purpose."
11. Maryville College, *Faculty Handbook*.
12. Martha Hess, story told to Planning and Budget Advisory Committee, Maryville College, Maryville, Tenn., March 28, 2000.
13. Robert Bonham, Faculty Forum Discussion, Maryville College, Maryville, Tenn., April 6, 2000.

14. Dr. Kisner expresses gratitude to colleagues who assisted in the research and editing of this section of the chapter: Professors Mark Perry (Communication), Richard Leipold (Computer Science), Richard Waddel (Political Science), Melany Chrash (Nursing), J. Bradley Gambill (English), and Richard L. Noftzger, Vice President for Institutional Planning, Research, and Technology.

15. William Hasker, "Faith-Learning Integration: An Overview," *Christian Scholars Review* 21:3 (March 1992): 231–48.

16. Examples of texts supplied by the professor are Exod. 20; Num. 13:17; Prov. 3:21–22; Eccl. 1; Isa. 59:14; Matt. 24:14; Acts 17:16; 1 Cor. 1:9; 12:12; and 1 John 1:3–4.

17. Such course titles include Assessment: Individual, Family, Congregation; Accountability and Documentation; Legal Considerations; Grant Writing; and several courses regarding the functions of the parish nurse: Personal Health Counselor, Developer of Support Groups, Health Educator, Health Promotion and Maintenance, Referral Agent, Health Advocate, and Coordinator of Volunteers.

18. Ammerman, *Studying Congregations: A New Handbook*; Arnold, *Called by Christ to Heal*; Bakken and Hofeller, *Healing and Transformation: Into the Image and Likeness of God*; Bonhoeffer, *Life Together*; Broyles, *Journaling: A Spiritual Journey*; Brueggemann, *The Prophetic Imagination*; Carnes and Craig, *Sacred Circles: A Guide to Creating Your Own Women's Spirituality Group*; Dawn, *Keeping the Sabbath Wholly: Ceasing, Resting, Embracing, Feasting*; Fowler, *Stages of Faith*; Greenleaf, *Servant Leadership: A Journey into the Nature of Legitimate Power and Greatness*; Kelsey, *Healing and Christianity: A Classic Study*; Klug, *Soul Weavings: A Gathering of Women's Prayers*; Kubler-Ross, *On Death and Dying*; Lapsley, *Salvation and Health: The Interlocking Processes of Life*; Marty, *Healthy People 2000: A Role for America's Religious Communities*; Matthews, *The Faith Factor: Proof of the Healing Power of Prayer*; McNutt, *Healing and the Power to Heal*; Nouwen, *The Wounded Healer*; Nuechterlein and Hahn, *The Male-Female Church Staff: Celebrating the Gifts, Confronting the Challenges*; Oswald, *Clergy Self-Care*; Palmer, *Let Your Life Speak*; Ramshaw, *Ritual and Pastoral Care*; Rupp, *Praying Our Goodbyes*; Sanford, *Healing and Wholeness*; Shelly and Miller, *Called to Care: A Christian Theology of Nursing*; Steinke, *Healthy Congregations: A Systems Approach*; Thompson, *Soul Feast*; Vanier, *Community and Growth*; and Wilkinson, *The Bible and Healing: A Medical and Theological Commentary*.

19. The Corella and Bertram F. Bonner Foundation, Inc., a national philanthropic organization based in Princeton, New Jersey, supports this program. Waynesburg Bonner Scholarships are annual awards of $1,950–$3,050, renewable for four consecutive years, based on the fulfillment of program requirements. Bonner Scholars are expected to participate in community service for an average of ten hours per week during the academic year, participate in a service program each summer for six to eight weeks, and participate in the enrichment and orientation activities of the program.

20. This office administrates the Bonner Scholars program and the service learning General Education curricular requirement, and assists the placing of students at various service sites to fulfill course requirements and for various campus organizations.

21. James Tunstead Burtchaell, *The Dying of the Light: The Disengagement of Colleges and Universities from Their Christian Churches* (Grand Rapids: Eerdmans, 1998).

22. William Hasker, "Faith-Learning Integration: An Overview."

23. Waller R. Cooper, *Southwestern at Memphis, 1848–1948* (Richmond, Va.: John Knox Press, 1949), 26.

24. Ibid., 22.

25. *Union and Slavery: A Thanksgiving Sermon, Delivered in the Presbyterian Church, Clarksville, Tennessee, November 28th, 1850, by J. T. Hendrick, Pastor* (Clarksville, Tenn.: C. O. Faxon, 1851), 11.

26. The idea of a great southern Presbyterian university had been afoot in the 1850s. The idea was broached with new urgency by James Lyon at the first General Assembly of the Presbyterian Church of the Confederate States of America in 1861, but the realities of war intervened. At the 1868 Assembly many of the presbyteries gave a lukewarm response to the idea, and the matter was indefinitely postponed. Nevertheless, in response to an eloquent plea from Lyon, a committee recommended that a convention on education be held before the next Assembly to consider "a Southern institution common to the whole body." In 1869 Lyon pushed the issue by publishing an article in which he called for the church to make a unified effort to reassert itself in the field of higher education. See "The General Assembly of 1870," *Southern Presbyterian Review* (July 1870): 411–58, especially pp. 427–30.

27. See Stephen R. Haynes, *Noah's Curse: The American Biblical Justification for Slavery* (New York: Oxford University Press, 2002).

28. According to the *SPU Bulletin*, it was Palmer (along with J. B. Shearer) "who conceived the idea of putting the Bible in the curriculum of the institution, and requiring from every student a knowledge of its truths and precepts," *SPU Bulletin*, December 1921: 6.

29. Cooper, *Southwestern at Memphis*, 76. Since the 1850s Palmer had been advocating for the church to take a larger role in providing for higher education (ibid., 61). Palmer was among the synodical delegates sent to hammer out a plan for the new school. The Plan of Union arrived at was largely his work, as were the bylaws of the new Southwestern Presbyterian University. Not surprisingly, when the election of a chancellor was proposed, Palmer was elected unanimously (ibid., 492).

30. He was forced by his congregation, however, to turn down the chancellorship. On hearing his plans to leave New Orleans, "the whole city came down upon [him], together with the congregation" (ibid., 61). Palmer took several months' leave to work as SPU's financial agent, and from 1875 until his death in 1902 Palmer was the dominant personality on the board of directors.

31. James A. Lyon, "Slavery, and the Duties Growing out of the Relation," *Southern Presbyterian Review* (July 1863): 1–37; quotations, p. 16. On Lyon's view of slavery and his zeal for reforming the institution, see Ernest Trice Thompson, *Presbyterians in the South*, Vol. 2: *1861–1890* (Richmond: John Knox Press, 1973), 55–58, 61–62, 67–69, 195. Thompson describes Lyon as "liberal-minded," and "opposed to secession, critical of the political forces in his state, and yet loyal to the Confederacy."

32. Cooper, *Southwestern at Memphis*, 48.

33. Cooper, *Southwestern at Memphis*, 67.

34. Dabney authored one of the first defenses of the South's cause to appear after the war. It included a detailed consideration of the biblical evidence for the rectitude of slavery. See *A Defence of Virginia, and through Her, of the South, in Recent and Pending Contests against the Sectional Party* (New York: Negro Universities Press, 1969 [1867]).

35. See J. Treadwell Davis, "The Presbyterians and the Sectional Conflict," *Southern Quarterly* 8: 2 (January 1970): 117–34; esp. p. 130; and Daniel Stowell, "Educating Confederate Christians," in *Rebuilding Zion: The Religious Reconstruction of the South 1863–1877* (New York: Oxford University Press, 1998).

36. Diehl's progressivism was evident in many ways. In the late 1920s, while on a committee charged with exploring his church's position on divorce, Diehl stood alone in arguing for a broadening of the grounds on which it should be granted. Recurrent themes in his sermons were the shibboleths of liberal Protestantism: "the Fatherhood of God, and the Brotherhood of Man, the infinite value of the human soul and personality, and love as the law and life of the universe" (sermon as retiring Moderator of the PCUS, May 1942, in the Burrow Library Archives, Rhodes College). Diehl's 1945 baccalaureate sermon was on Micah 6:8, and its charge "to do justice, and to love kindness, and to walk humbly with your God" (Felix Gear, "Dr Diehl: His Service in the Church," 13; Presbyterian Church [U.S.A.] Department of History, Montreat, N.C.).

37. *Sou'wester*, November 22, 1963.

38. "Memphis, Second" (editorial), *Presbyterian Outlook* (May 18, 1964): 8.

39. Minutes of Memphis Presbytery, Called Meeting, June 15, 1964; Minutes of Memphis Presbytery, Winter Stated Meeting, January 26, 1965. Presbyterian Church (U.S.A.) Department of History, Montreat, N.C.

40. Letter of October 4, 1964, cited in Minutes of Memphis Presbytery, Winter Stated Meeting, January 1965.

41. Letter to Gear from L. Nelson Bell, October 10, 1964. Felix Gear Papers, Montreat.

42. Letter from Louise R. Goddard of Lakeland, Florida, July 1, 1964. Felix Gear Papers, Montreat. At some point during the year, Gear composed a "Race Relations" form letter which read, in part: "I am sorry that you do not agree with the actions of the General Assembly on these matters, but I would respectfully point out to you that . . . the Presbyterian Church has never officially sanctioned segregated churches. . . . Further, at no time has the General Assembly of the Presbyterian Church in the U.S. ever upheld the exclusion of a Negro from a church court or from membership on the ground of color or race. . . . Because we have accepted the policy of segregation for so many years, we have come to think that the Presbyterian Church is actually a segregated church constitutionally—this has never been true."

43. Though Diehl was twenty-five years older than Gear, the men's biographies show many parallels. Like Diehl, Gear was a West Virginian who received ministerial training at Princeton. Both men pastored Presbyterian churches in Mississippi before arriving at Southwestern in their thirties. In 1941 Diehl preceded Gear by being elected Moderator of the Presbyterian Church U.S.

44. In a sermon from the Second Presbyterian pulpit that was broadcast on CBS's *Church of the Air* in 1946, Gear characterized true religion as "the kind that loosens the unjust bonds of men and women, that relieves the oppressed, feeds the hungry, clothes the naked, shelters the homeless and reaches out in brotherly understanding and association to all of your unfortunate fellow-countrymen" ("Lifting the Burden of Religion," unpublished sermon in Gear papers, Montreat, N.C.). In this sermon, preached just a year after Diehl's baccalaureate sermon on Micah 6, Gear refers to the same passage (see ibid., 2).

45. In an important symbolic gesture, Gear made a series of joint appearances with his counterpart in the northern church, African American layman Edler G.

Hawkins. Together they issued "A Call for National Unity" on January 4, 1965, which is interesting for the insight it provides on Gear's thinking just before his fateful decision in the Second Presbyterian affair. This document called American Christians to "manifest the unity we have in Jesus Christ" and acknowledged that "often we have failed to serve as 'agents of reconciliation' within families, within congregations, and among our several churches."

46. Ibid., 3.

47. In the annual report he filed at the end of his term as Moderator, Gear wrote that "when God shakes things in our world the hardest thing we have to face is the fact that God is doing the shaking and that it is always a sifting process at work in our midst." Felix B. Gear, "Progress in a Time of Tension," *Presbyterian Outlook* (April 26, 1965), 5. Gear explicitly addressed the Second Presbyterian controversy this way: "All of us, I am sure, have become acquainted through the press, radio, television, and other channels of communication, with the situation that developed in our church during the past year concerning the meeting place of the General Assembly. I wish merely to state here that after nine months of waiting, hoping and praying, and working for a solution to this impasse, the only appropriate way to resolve it appeared to be to change the meeting place of the General Assembly to Montreat. Under the circumstances I think it was probably more difficult for me to make this decision than it would have been for almost any other person who might have been serving as moderator. This decision was made because it was my firm conviction that it was the best thing to do for all concerned and more nearly in accord with the divine will in the light of conditions existing at that time" (ibid.).

Chapter 9: The Vocation of Teaching in Secular and Public Colleges and Universities

1. James T. Burtchaell, *The Dying of the Light: The Disengagement of Colleges and Universities from Their Christian Churches* (Grand Rapids: Eerdmans, 1998); Mark Noll, *The Scandal of the Evangelical Mind* (Grand Rapids: Eerdmans, 1994); George Marsden, *The Soul of the American University: From Protestant Establishment to Established Nonbelief* (New York: Oxford University Press, 1994); George Marsden and Bradley Longfield, *The Secularization of American Higher Education* (New York: Oxford University Press, 1992); and Douglas Sloan, *Faith and Knowledge: Mainline Protestantism and American Higher Education* (Louisville, Ky.: Westminster John Knox Press, 1994).

2. Clarence P. Shedd, *Religion in the State University* (New Haven, Conn.: Hazen Foundation, 1947), 5.

3. *Digest of Education Statistics, 2000*, chap. 3, "Post-Secondary Education," 2.

4. The survey isolated faculty specifically identified as members of surrounding Presbyterian [PC(USA)] congregations. However some respondents indicated they were worshipers in those congregations, though not members. Or else they belonged to another Reformed body such as the PCA. While this survey attempted to limit its subjects to PC(USA) member faculty, later surveys can certainly be widened to include other Reformed traditions.

5. Manning M. Patillo and Donald M. Mackenzie, *Church-Sponsored Higher Education in the United States* (Washington, D.C.: American Council on Education, 1966), 177.

6. Statistics are from *Digest of Education Statistics, 2000*, chap. 3, "Post-Secondary Education." See also *Fact Book on Higher Education*. Statistics on higher educa-

tion up to midcentury are drawn from Lawrence E. Cremin, *American Education: The Metropolitan Experience, 1876–1980* (New York: Harper & Row, 1988), 248ff.

7. *Digest of Education Statistics, 2000*, chap. 3, "Post-Secondary Education," 1.
8. A "nontraditional" student is defined by the National Center for Education Statistics as any student over the age of twenty-five.
9. *Digest of Education Statistics, 2000*, chap. 3, "Post-Secondary Education," 2.
10. Figures from Seymour M. Lipset and Everett C. Ladd, "The Divided Professoriate," *Change* 3, no. 3 (May/June, 1971): 54–60, quoted in Sloan, *Faith and Knowledge*, 180–81.
11. *Digest of Education Statistics, 2000*, chap. 3, "Post-Secondary Education," 3.
12. Martin J. Finkelstein and Jack H. Schuster, "Assessing the Silent Revolution: How Changing Demographics Are Reshaping the Academic Profession," in *AAHE Bulletin* (October 2001): 3–7.
13. Roger J. Baldwin and Jay L. Chronister, *Teaching without Tenure: Policies and Practices for a New Era* (Johns Hopkins University Press, 2001).
14. Derek Bok, "Report to the Harvard Board of Overseers," extracts from, published in "Opinion Section" of the *Chronicle of Higher Education* 34 (April 27, 1988): B 4.
15. A trend, of course, resisted by many, from both religious and nonreligious perspectives alike. Note the rousing collection of essays in Wayne C. Booth's *The Vocation of a Teacher: Rhetorical Occasions 1967–1988* (Chicago: University of Chicago Press, 1988).
16. As for example in the works herein cited by James Burtchaell, Mark Schwehn, and Douglas Sloan. In addition should be noted the numerous histories of church-related colleges such as those by Mark Noll and George Marsden, as well as Merrimon Cuninggim's *Uneasy Partners: The College and the Church* (Nashville: Abingdon Press, 1994).
17. Mark Schwehn, *Exiles from Eden: Religion and the Academic Vocation in America* (New York: Oxford University Press, 1993).
18. David T. Hansen, *The Call to Teach*, with a Foreword by Larry C. Cuban (New York: Teachers College Press, Columbia University, 1995), and (among others) Wayne C. Booth, *The Vocation of a Teacher*.
19. Sloan, *Faith and Knowledge*, particularly chap. 6.
20. Burchtaell, *Dying of the Light*. See the Preface and chap. 2, "The Presbyterians."
21. See the descriptions offered by William Placher, in his *Unapologetic Theology: A Christian Voice in a Pluralistic Conversation* (Louisville, Ky.: Westminster/John Knox Press, 1989), chaps. 1, 2, 6, and *The Domestication of Transcendence* (Louisville, Ky.: Westminster John Knox Press, 1996), chaps. 7–10.
22. Paul Tillich, *Systematic Theology*, vol. 1 (Chicago: University of Chicago Press, 1951), 71–81.
23. Wade Clark Roof and William McKinney, *American Mainline Religion: Its Changing Shape and Future* (New Brunswick, N.J.: Rutgers University Press, 1987), for discussion of this shift in denominational influence.
24. For the Presbyterian situation, see, for example, Marcia Myers, "Where Have All the Pastors Gone?" pp. 8–10 and, indeed, the whole issue of *Presbyterian Outlook*, vol. 182, no. 30 (September 20, 1999).
25. For instance, the APCU "Consultation on the Vocation of the Presbyterian Teacher: Thirty Who Are Called to Teach," held in Louisville, Kentucky, August 11–13, 2000.

26. John Calvin, *The Institutes of the Christian Religion*, 2 vols. Edited by John T. McNeill and translated by Ford Lewis Battles (Philadelphia: The Westminster Press, 1960).

27. John H. Leith, *Basic Christian Doctrine* (Louisville, Ky.: Westminster/John Knox Press, 1993), 199.

28. Jan Christian Smuts, *Holism and Evolution* (New York: Macmillan Co., 1926), and "The Theory of Holism," Lecture XIV, in *Greater South Africa: Plans for a Better World: The Speeches of General, The Right Honorable J. C. Smuts* (Johannesburg: The Truth Legion, 1940).

29. See, on this point, J. L. Ainslie, *The Doctrines of Ministerial Order in the Reformed Churches of the Sixteenth and Seventeenth Centuries* (Edinburgh: T. & T. Clark, 1940), 91ff.; and the whole of Robert W. Henderson, *The Teaching Office in the Reformed Tradition: A History of the Doctoral Ministry* (Philadelphia: Westminster Press, 1962).

30. The modern critical edition was edited by Ford L. Battles and Andre Malan Hugo, *Calvin's Commentary on Seneca's de Clementia* (Leiden: E. J. Brill, 1967).

31. Edward Dowey Jr., *The Knowledge of God in Calvin's Theology* (New York: Columbia University Press, 1952); William Placher, *The Domestication of Transcendence* (Louisville, Ky.: Westminster John Knox Press, 1996); Stacy Johnson, *The Mystery of God* (Louisville, Ky.: Westminster John Knox, 1995).

32. Abraham Kuyper, *De Gemeene Gratie*, 3 vols. (Leiden: D. Donner, 1902–05).

33. The survey was distributed in September 2001, primarily in three regions: Southwest Virginia, Maryland, and the region covered by the Synod of the Trinity. The coauthors wish to express their thanks to the Rev. Dr. Sue Lowcock Harris, coordinator of Higher Education Ministries of the Synod of the Trinity, for both contributing to the construction of and distributing the survey questionnaire. In Southwest Virginia, individual congregations were contacted and asked to provide names of members who were faculty or administrative personnel in local state institutions of higher education.

Chapter 11: The Dawning of the Light

1. James T. Burtchaell, *The Dying of the Light: The Disengagement of Colleges and Universities from Their Christian Churches* (Grand Rapids: Eerdman's, 1998).

2. George Marsden and Bradley J. Longfield, *The Secularization of the Academy* (New York: Oxford University Press, 1992).

3. Robert Rankin, ed., *The Recovery of Spirit in Higher Education* (New York: Seabury Press, 1980).

4. Warren Bryan Martin, *The College of Character* (San Francisco: Jossey-Bass, 1982).

5. Douglas John Hall, *Thinking the Faith* (Minneapolis: Fortress Press, 1989), 20.

6. Office of Higher Education, "On Being Faithful: The Continuing Mission of the Presbyterian Church (U.S.A.) in Higher Education" (Louisville, Ky.: Office of the General Assembly, Presbyterian Church [U.S.A.], 1995), 33ff.

7. Duncan S. Ferguson, "The Church's Mission in Higher Education: Abiding Principles," *Point of View* 9, no. 2 (Fall 1998): 1–3.

The Vocation of the Presbyterian Teacher:
A Select Annotated Bibliography

1. The Heidelberg Catechism (1563) and the Westminster Shorter Catechism (1647) were generally accepted by the entire family of Reformed communions.

It is, however, important to note that in the United States both the Christian Reformed Church and the Reformed Church in America look to the Belgic Confession, while the major Presbyterian groups adopted the Westminster Confession. The similarities between the two confessions are legion, but it is entirely possible that the educational divergence between institutions founded by the C.R.C. and R.C.A., on the one hand, and the Presbyterians, on the other, began, at least in part, with this confessional differentiation, further ameliorated by the cultural contexts in which the confessions were lived out. See Leroy Nixon, *John Calvin's Teachings on Human Reason* (New York: Exposition Press, 1960), x, 137–41.

2. This document is often called the *First Book of Discipline* (or *Policy*) so as not to confuse it with the document Andrew Melville and a General Assembly committee wrote in 1577 as a constitution for the church called the *Second Book of Discipline* or the *Book of Policy*.

3. James McCosh's intellectual indebtedness to the Scottish Moderates was partially repaid by the 1875 publication of *The Scottish Philosophy: Biographical, Expository, Critical, from Hutcheson to Hamilton*. McCosh's entry for John Witherspoon sums up his perspective on Witherspoon's influence. The title is "American Philosophy—John Witherspoon."

4. For a recent alternative interpretation, see Jon H. Roberts and James Turner, *The Sacred and the Secular University* (Princeton, N.J.: Princeton University Press, 2000).

References

Abray, Lorna Jane. *The People's Reformation: Magistrates, Clergy, and Commons in Strasbourg, 1500–1598*. Ithaca: Cornell University Press, 1985.

Ainslie, J. L. *The Doctrines of Ministerial Order in the Reformed Churches of the Sixteenth and Seventeenth Centuries*. Edinburgh: T. & T. Clark, 1940.

Anderson, R. D. *Education and the Scottish People, 1750–1918*. Oxford: Clarendon Press, 1995.

Armstrong, Maurice W., Lefferts A. Loetscher, and Charles A. Anderson, eds. *The Presbyterian Enterprise: Sources of American Presbyterian History*. Philadelphia: Westminster Press, 1956.

Association of Presbyterian Colleges and Universities. *A Ministry of Nurture: The Spiritual Life at Educational Institutions Affiliated with the Presbyterian Church (U.S.A.)*. Louisville, Ky.: Association of Presbyterian Colleges and Universities, 1998.

Augustine. *The City of God*. Translated by Henry Bettenson. Penguin Books, 1984.

Baldwin, Roger G., and Jay L. Chronister. *Teaching without Tenure: Policies and Practices for a New Era*. Baltimore: Johns Hopkins University Press, 2001.

Balmer, Randall, and John R. Fitzmier. *The Presbyterians*. Westport, Conn.: Praeger Publishers, 1994.

Banks, Robert. *Reenvisioning Theological Education: Exploring a Missional Alternative*. Grand Rapids: Wm. B. Eerdmans Publishing Co., 1999.

Battles, Ford Lewis. "Calvin's Humanistic Education." In *Interpreting John Calvin*, edited by Robert Benedetto. Grand Rapids: Baker Book House, 1996.

Battles, Ford Lewis, and Andre Malan Hugo, eds. *Calvin's Commentary on Seneca's De Clementia*. Leiden: E. J. Brill, 1967.

Bauer, Walter. *A Greek English Lexicon of the New Testament and Other Greek Literature*. Translated by William F. Ardnt, F. Gingrich, and Frederick Danker. Chicago: University of Chicago Press, 1979.

Beach, Waldo. "Christian Ethical Community as Norm." In *Colleges and Commitments*, edited by Lloyd Averill and William Jellema. Philadelphia: Westminster Press, 1971.

Bellah, Robert. "Freedom, Coercion, and Authority." *Bulletin (Council of Societies for the Study of Religion)* 28, no. 2 (April 1999).

———. "Is There a Common American Culture?" *Journal of the American Academy of Religion* 66, no. 3 (Fall 1998): 622.

Bellah, Robert, Richard Madsen, William Sullivan, Ann Swidler, and Steven Tipton. *The Good Society*. New York: Alfred A. Knopf, 1991.

———. *Habits of the Heart: Individualism and Commitment in American Life*. 2d ed. Davis: University of California Press, 1996.

Berkhof, Louis. *A Manual of Christian Doctrine*. Grand Rapids: Baker Book House, 1933.
Blair, Carolyn L., and Arda S. Walker. *By Faith Endowed*. Maryville, Tenn.: Maryville College Press, 1994.
Boice, James M. *Foundations of the Christian Faith*. Downers Grove, Ill.: Inter-Varsity Press, 1986.
———. *God the Redeemer.* Downers Grove, Ill.: Inter-Varsity Press, 1978.
Bok, Derek. "Report to the Harvard Board of Overseers." *The Chronicle of Higher Education* 34 (April 27, 1988): B 4.
Booth, Wayne C. *The Vocation of a Teacher: Rhetorical Occasions 1967–1988*. Chicago: University of Chicago Press, 1988.
Bouwsma, William. "The Two Faces of Humanism: Stoicism and Augustinianism in Renaissance Thought." In Itinerarium Italicum: *The Profile of the Italian Renaissance in the Mirror of Its European Transformations*. Edited by Heiko Oberman and Thomas A. Brady Jr. Leiden: E. J. Brill, 1975.
Bratt, James D. "Reformed Tradition and the Mission of Reformed Colleges." Presented at the Reformed University of North America Conference, Grand Rapids, 1993. Unpublished.
———. "What Can the Reformed Tradition Contribute to Christian Higher Education?" *Models of Christian Higher Education: Strategies for Success in the Twenty-first Century*, edited by Richard T. Hughes and William B. Adrian. Grand Rapids: Wm. B. Eerdmans Publishing Co., 1997.
Breen, Quirinus. *John Calvin: A Study in French Humanism*. 2d ed. New York: Archon Books, 1968.
Brown, Colin, ed. *The New International Dictionary of New Testament Theology*. Grand Rapids: Wm. B. Eerdmans Publishing Co., 1978.
Brown, Francis, S. R. Driver, and Charles Briggs. *The New Brown-Driver-Briggs-Gesenius Hebrew and English Lexicon*. Peabody, Mass.: Hendrickson Pubs., 1979.
Bryson, Gladys. *Man and Society: The Scottish Inquiry of the Eighteenth Century*. Princeton, N.J.: Princeton University Press, 1945.
Budziszewski, J. *The Revenge of Conscience: Politics and the Fall of Man*. Dallas: Spence, 1999.
Burleigh, J. H. S. *A Church History of Scotland*. London: Oxford University Press, 1960.
Burtchaell, James Tunstead. *The Dying of the Light: The Disengagement of Colleges and Universities from Their Christian Churches*. Grand Rapids: Wm. B. Eerdmans Publishing Co., 1998.
Calvin, John. *Articles Concerning the Organization of the Church and of Worship at Geneva Proposed by the Ministers at the Council*, in *Calvin: Theological Treatises*. Philadelphia: Westminster Press, 1954.
———. "Defension contra Pighium." In *Ioannis Calvini opera quae supersunct omnia*, edited by W. Baum, E. Cunitz, and E. Reuss. Braunschweig, Germany: C. A. Schwetschke and Son, 1863–1900.
———. "Draft Ecclesiastical Ordinances, September and October 1541." In *Calvin: Theological Treatises*, edited by J. K. Reid. Philadelphia: Westminster Press, 1954.
———. *The Institutes of the Christian Religion*. Edited by John T. McNeill. Translated by Ford Lewis Battles. Philadelphia: Westminster Press, 1960.
Coalter, Milton J., John M. Mulder, and Louis B. Weeks, eds. *The Pluralistic Vision: Presbyterians and Mainstream Protestant Education and Leadership*. Louisville, Ky.: Westminster/John Knox Press, 1992.
———. *The Presbyterian Presence: The Twentieth Century Experience*. Louisville: Westminster/John Knox Press, 1990–92.

Coleman, John. *The Task of the Christian in the University*. Geneva: World Student Christian Federation, 1947.

Committee for Christian Education and Publications. *The Westminster Confession of Faith of the Presbyterian Church in America Together with The [Westminster] Larger Catechism and The [Westminster] Shorter Catechism*. N.p.: Presbyterian Church in America, 1983.

Committee on Higher Education. "Loving God with Our Minds: The Mission of the Presbyterian Church (U.S.A.) in Higher Education within the Global Community." Adopted by the 203rd General Assembly. Louisville, Ky.: Office of the General Assembly, Presbyterian Church (U.S.A.), 1991.

The Constitution of the Presbyterian Church (U.S.A.). Part I, *Book of Confessions*. Louisville, Ky.: Office of the General Assembly, Presbyterian Church (U.S.A.), 1983.

Cottret, Bernard. *Calvin: A Biography*. Translated by M. Wallace McDonald. Grand Rapids: Wm. B. Eerdmans Publishing Co., 2000.

Cowan, Ian B. *The Scottish Reformation: Church and Society in Sixteenth Century Scotland*. New York: St. Martin's Press, 1982.

Cremin, Lawrence E. *American Education: The Metropolitan Experience, 1876–1980*. New York: Harper & Row, 1988.

Cuninggim, Merrimon. *Uneasy Partners: The College and the Church*. Nashville: Abingdon Press, 1994.

Davies, Mervyn. *Presbyterian Heritage: Switzerland, Great Britain, America*. Atlanta: John Knox Press, 1965.

Dabney, Robert Lewis. *A Defense of Virginia, and Through Her, of the South, in Recent and Pending Contests against the Sectional Party*. New York: Negro Universities Press, 1969.

———. *Lectures in Systematic Theology*. 6th ed. Richmond: Presbyterian Committee for Publications, 1927; reprint, Grand Rapids: Baker Book House, 1985.

Davis, J. Treadwell. "The Presbyterians and the Sectional Conflict." *Southern Quarterly* 8, no. 2 (January 1970): 117–34.

Dillenberger, John, ed. *John Calvin: Selections from His Writings*. Garden City, N.Y.: Doubleday & Co., Anchor Books, 1971.

Dockery, David S., and David P. Gushee, eds. *The Future of Christian Higher Education*. Nashville: Broadman & Holman, 1999.

Dowey, Edward A., Jr. "*Ecclesia, Legenda atque Intelligenda Scriptura*: The Church as Discerning Community in Calvin's Hermeneutic." *Calvin Theological Journal* 36, no. 2 (2001): 270–289.

———. *The Knowledge of God in Calvin's Theology*. New York: Columbia University Press, 1952.

Elazar, Daniel. *Covenant and Polity in Biblical Israel*. New Brunswick, N.J.: Transaction Publishers, 1995.

Fairchild, Hoxie N., ed. *Religious Perspectives in College Teaching*. New York: Ronald Press Co., 1952.

Ferguson, Duncan S. "The Church's Mission in Higher Education: Abiding Principles." *Point of View* 9, no. 2 (Fall 1998): 1–3. And *Church and Society* 88, no. 3 (January/February 1998).

Finkelstein, Martin J., and Jack H. Schuster. "Assessing the Silent Revolution: How Changing Demographics Are Reshaping the Academic Profession." *AAHE Bulletin* (October 2001): 3–7.

Frye, Roland. "Protestantism and Education: A Preliminary Study of the Early Centuries and Some Suggested Principles." (Unpublished paper, n.d.).

Ganoczy, Alexandre. *The Young Calvin*. Translated by David Foxgrover and Wade Provo. Philadelphia: Westminster Press, 1987.

Gear, Felix B. "Progress in a Time of Tension." *Presbyterian Outlook* (April 26, 1965): 5.

Geiger, C. Harve. *The Program of Higher Education of the Presbyterian Church in the United States of America: An Historical Analysis of Its Growth in the United States*. Cedar Rapids, Iowa: Laurance Press, 1940.

Gerrish, B. A. *Grace and Gratitude: The Eucharistic Theology of John Calvin*. Minneapolis: Fortress Press, 1993.

Gerrish, Brian. "Tradition in the Modern World: The Reformed Habit of Mind." In *Toward the Future of the Reformed Tradition*, edited by David Willis and Michael Welker. Grand Rapids: Wm. B. Eerdmans Publishing Co., 1999.

Glassford, Darwin K. "The Reformed Doctrine of the Kingdom of God as a Paradigm for Formulating and Evaluating Educational Programs." Ph.D. diss., Marquette University, 1991.

Graham, W. Fred. *The Constructive Revolutionary: John Calvin and His Socio-Economic Impact*. East Lansing: Michigan State University Press, 1987.

Greaves, Richard L. "Knox's Social Awareness: The Problems of Poverty and Educational Reform." In *Theology and Revolution in the Scottish Reformation: Studies in the Thought of John Knox*. Grand Rapids: Christian University Press, 1980.

Habison, E. Harris. *The Christian Scholar in the Age of the Reformation*. New York: Charles Scribner's Sons, 1956.

Hall, Douglas John. *Thinking the Faith*. Minneapolis: Fortress Press, 1989.

Hansen, David T. *The Call to Teach*. New York: Teachers College Press, Columbia University, 1995.

Harris, R. L., Gleason L. Archer, and Bruce K. Waltke. *Theological Wordbook of the Old Testament*. Chicago: Moody Press, 1980.

Hasker, William. "Faith-Learning Integration: An Overview." *Christian Scholars Review* 21, no. 3 (March 1992): 231–48.

Haynes, Stephen R. *Noah's Curse: The American Biblical Justification for Slavery*. New York: Oxford University Press, 2002.

Henderson, Robert W. *The Teaching Office in the Reformed Tradition: A History of the Doctoral Ministry*. Philadelphia: Westminster Press, 1962.

Hendrick, J. T. *Union and Slavery: A Thanksgiving Sermon*. Delivered in the Presbyterian Church, Clarksville, Tenn., November 28, 1850. Clarksville: C. O. Faxon, 1851.

Higher Education Program Team. *On Being Faithful: The Continuing Mission of the Presbyterian Church (U.S.A.) in Higher Education*. Report to the General Assembly. Louisville, Ky.: Office of the General Assembly, Presbyterian Church (U.S.A.), 1995.

Higman, Francis. "Les traductions françaises de Luther, 1524–1550." In *Lire et Découvrir: La circulation des idées au temp de la Réforme*. Geneva: Librairie Droz, 1998.

Hodge, Charles. *Systematic Theology*. Grand Rapids: Wm. B. Eerdmans Publishing Co., n.d.

Hodgson, Peter C. *God's Wisdom: Toward a Theology of Education*. Louisville, Ky.: Westminster John Knox Press, 1999.

Hoekema, Anthony. *Bible and the Future*. Grand Rapids: Wm. B. Eerdmans Publishing Co., 1982.

Hofstadter, Richard, and Wilson Smith. *American Higher Education: A Documentary History*. Chicago: University of Chicago Press, 1961.

Hudson, Winthrop S., and John Corrigan. *Religion in America*. 6th ed. Upper Saddle River, N.J.: Prentice-Hall, 1998.

Hughes, Richard T. *How Christian Faith Can Sustain the Life of the Mind*. Grand Rapids: Wm. B. Eerdmans Publishing Co., 2001.

Hughes, Richard T., and William B. Adrian, eds. *Models for Christian Higher Education: Strategies for Success in the Twenty-first Century*. Grand Rapids: Wm. B. Eerdmans Publishing Co., 1997.

The International Bible Society. *Holy Bible: New International Version*. Zondervan Bible Publishers, 1978.

Johnson, Stacy. *The Mystery of God*. Louisville, Ky.: Westminster John Knox, 1995.

Kemeny, P. C. *Princeton in the Nation's Service: Religious Ideals and Educational Practice, 1868–1928*. New York: Oxford University Press, 1998.

Kerr, John. *Scottish Education: School and University*. Cambridge: Cambridge University Press, 1913.

Kittel, Gerhard, ed. *Theological Dictionary of the New Testament*. Translated by Geoffrey Bromiley. Grand Rapids: Wm. B. Eerdmans Publishing Co., 1964.

Knox, John. *"Book of Discipline."* In *John Knox's History of the Reformation in Scotland*, edited by William Croft Dickinson. New York: Philosophical Library, 1950.

———. *"Scottish Confession of Faith."* In *John Knox's History of the Reformation in Scotland*, edited by William Croft Dickinson. New York: Philosophical Library, 1950.

Kuykendall, John W. "The Presbyterian Heritage and Higher Education." *Pacific Theological Review* 17, no. 3 (Spring 1984): 57–67.

Kuyper, Abraham. *De Gemeene Gratie*. 3 vols. Leiden: D. Donner, 1902–1905.

Kyle, Richard G. *The Mind of John Knox*. Lawrence, Kans.: Coronado Press, 1984.

Ladd, George Eldon. *The Gospel of the Kingdom: Popular Expositions on the Kingdom of God*. Grand Rapids: Wm. B. Eerdmans Publishing Co., 1959.

———. *Presence of the Future: The Eschatology of Biblical Realism*. New York: Harper & Row, 1964; reprint, Grand Rapids: Wm. B. Eerdmans Publishing Co., 1974.

———. *A Theology of the New Testament*. Grand Rapids: Wm. B. Eerdmans Publishing Co., 1974.

Lefevre, Perry D. *The Christian Teacher: His Faith and His Responsibilities in Higher Education*. Nashville: Abingdon Press, 1958.

Leith, John H. *Introduction to the Reformed Tradition*. Atlanta: John Knox Press, 1977.

Lipset, Seymour, and Everett C. Ladd. "The Divided Professoriate." *Change* 3, no. 3 (May/June 1971): 54–60.

Longfield, Bradley J., and George M. Marsden. "Presbyterian Colleges in Twentieth Century America." In *The Pluralistic Vision: Presbyterians and Mainstream Protestant Education and Leadership*, edited by Milton J. Coalter, John M. Mulder, and Louis B. Weeks. Louisville, Ky.: Westminster/John Knox Press, 1992.

Lucas, Christopher J. *American Higher Education: A History*. New York: St. Martin's Press, 1996.

Lyon, James A. "The General Assembly of 1870." *Southern Presbyterian Review*, July 1870.

———. "Slavery, and the Duties Growing out of the Relation." *Southern Presbyterian Review*, July 1863: 1–37.

Maag, Karin. *Seminary or University? The Genevan Academy and Reformed Higher Education, 1560–1620*. Aldershot, Hampshire, U.K.: Ashgate Publishing, 1995.

Mackie, J. D. *The University of Glasgow, 1451–1951: A Short History*. Glasgow, Scotland: Jackson, Son & Co., 1954.

Mackinnon, James. *Calvin and the Reformation*. New York: Russell & Russell, 1962.

Marsden, George. *The Outrageous Idea of Christian Scholarship*. New York: Oxford University Press, 1997.

————. *The Soul of the American University: From Protestant Establishment to Established Nonbelief.* New York: Oxford University Press, 1994.

Marsden, George, and Bradley J. Longfield. *The Secularization of the Academy.* New York: Oxford University Press, 1992.

Martin, Warren Bryan. *The College of Character.* San Francisco: Jossey-Bass, 1982.

Mathieson, William Law. *The Awakening of Scotland, 1747–1797.* Glasgow, Scotland: James Maclehose & Sons, 1910.

McIntosh, John R. *Church and Theology in Enlightenment Scotland: The Popular Party, 1740–1800.* East Lothian, Scotland: Tuckwell Press, 1998.

Meilaender, Gilbert. *Friendship: A Study in Theological Ethics.* Notre Dame, Ind.: University of Notre Dame Press, 1981.

————, ed. *Working: Its Meaning and Its Limits.* Notre Dame, Ind.: University of Notre Dame Press, 2000.

Migliazzo, Arlin. *Teaching as an Act of Faith: Theory and Practice in Church-Related Higher Education.* New York: Fordham University Press, forthcoming.

Miller, Howard. *The Revolutionary College: American Presbyterian Higher Education, 1707–1837.* New York: New York University Press, 1976.

Moberly, Sir Walter. *The Crisis in the University.* London: SCM Press, 1949.

Monter, William. *Calvin's Geneva.* New York: John Wiley & Sons, 1967.

Moore, Steve, and Tim Beuthin, eds. *The University through the Eyes of Faith.* Indianapolis: Light and Life Communications, 1998.

Morgan, Alexander. *Rise and Progress of Scottish Education.* Edinburgh and London: Oliver & Boyd, 1927.

Moulton, W. F., and A. S. Geden, *A Concordance to the Greek New Testament according to the Texts of Wescott and Hort, Tischendorf and the English Revisers.* 5th ed., rev. by H. K. Moulton. Edinburgh: T.&T. Clark, 1978.

Myers, Marcia. "Where Have All the Pastors Gone?" *Presbyterian Outlook* 182, no. 30 (1999): 8–9.

Niebuhr, H. Richard. "The Idea of Covenant and American Democracy." *Church History* 23, no. 2 (June 1954).

————. *The Meaning of Revelation.* New York: Collier Books, 1941.

————. *Radical Monotheism and Western Culture: With Supplementary Essays.* New York: Harper & Row, 1960.

————. "Theology in the University." *Radical Monotheism and Western Culture, With Supplementary Essays.* New York: Harper & Row, 1960.

Nixon, Leroy. *John Calvin's Teachings on Human Reason.* New York: Exposition Press, 1960.

Noll, Mark A. *Princeton and the Republic, 1768–1822: The Search for a Christian Enlightenment in the Era of Samuel Stanhope Smith.* Princeton, N.J.: Princeton University Press, 1989.

————. *The Scandal of the Evangelical Mind.* Grand Rapids: Wm. B. Eerdmans Publishing Co., 1994.

Ottati, Douglas. *Reforming Protestantism: Christian Commitment in Today's World.* Louisville, Ky.: Westminster John Knox Press, 1995.

Ozment, Steven. *The Age of Reform 1250–1550: An Intellectual and Religious History of Late Medieval and Reformation Europe.* New Haven, Conn.: Yale University Press, 1980.

Pacala, Leon. *The Role of ATS in Theological Education, 1980–1990.* ATS Publications. Atlanta: Scholars Press, 1998.

Parsonage, Robert Rue, ed. *Church Related Higher Education: Perceptions and Perspectives.* Valley Forge, Pa.: Judson Press, 1978.

Patillo, Manning M., and Donald M. Mackenzie. *Church-Sponsored Higher Education in the United States.* Washington, D.C.: American Council on Education, 1966.

Perkins, William. "A Treatise of the Vocations or Callings of Men." In *Working: Its Meaning and Its Limits*, edited by Gilbert Meilaender. Notre Dame, Ind.: University of Notre Dame Press, 2000.

Placher, William. *The Domestication of Transcendence*. Louisville, Ky.: Westminster John Knox Press, 1996).

———. *Unapologetic Theology: A Christian Voice in a Pluralistic Conversation*. Louisville, Ky.: Westminster/John Knox Press, 1989.

———. *A Vulnerable God*: Louisville, Ky.: Westminster John Knox Press, 1999.

Plantinga, Cornelius Jr. *Engaging God's Word: A Reformed Vision of Faith, Learning, and Living*. Grand Rapids: Wm. B. Eerdmans Publishing Co., 2002.

Presbyterian Church in the U.S.A. Executive Committee of Christian Education and Ministerial Relief. *Our Presbyterian Educational Institutions*. Louisville, Ky.: Presbyterian Church in the United States, 1914.

Pryde, George S. *The Scottish Universities and the Colleges of Colonial America*. Glasgow, Scotland: Jackson, Son & Co., 1957.

Ramm, Bernard. *The Christian College in the Twentieth Century*. Grand Rapids: Wm. B. Eerdmans Publishing Co., 1963.

Rankin, Robert, ed. *The Recovery of Spirit in Higher Education*. New York: Seabury Press, 1980.

Rasmussen, Larry. *Moral Fragments and Moral Community: A Proposal for Church in Society*. Minneapolis: Augsburg Press, 1993.

Roberts, Jon H., and James Turner. *The Sacred and the Secular University*. Princeton: Princeton University Press, 2000.

Roof, Wade Clark, and William McKinney. *American Mainline Religion: Its Changing Shape and Future*. New Brunswick, N.J.: Rutgers University Press, 1987.

Rudolph, Frederick. *The American College and University: A History*. New York: Knopf, 1962.

Ruger, Anthony. "The Big Picture: Strategic Choices for Theological Schools." *Auburn Studies*, no. 7. New York: Auburn Theological Seminary, 2000.

Schaff, Phillip, ed. *The Creeds of Christendom: With a History and Critical Notes*. Rev. by David S. Schaff, vol. 3, *The Evangelical and Protestant Creeds with Translations*. New York: Harper & Brothers, 1931; reprint, Grand Rapids: Baker Book House, 1983.

Schwehn, Mark R. *Exiles from Eden: Religion and the Academic Vocation in America*. New York: Oxford University Press, 1993.

"Second Annual Report of the Board of Christian Education." *Minutes of the General Assembly (1925) of the Presbyterian Church U.S.*, Part II.

Shedd, Clarence P. *Religion in the State University*. New Haven, Conn.: Hazen Foundation, 1947.

Sher, Richard B. *Church and University in the Scottish Enlightenment: The Moderate Literati of Edinburgh*. Princeton, N.J.: Princeton University Press, 1985.

Sher, Richard B., and Jeffrey R. Smitten, eds. *Scotland and America in the Age of the Enlightenment*. Edinburgh: Edinburgh University Press, 1990.

Sloan, Douglas. *Faith and Knowledge: Mainline Protestantism and American Higher Education*. Louisville, Ky.: Westminster John Knox Press, 1994.

———. *The Scottish Enlightenment and the American College Ideal*. New York: Teachers College Press, Columbia University, 1971.

Smith, Elwyn Allen. The Presbyterian Ministry in American Culture: A Study in Changing Concepts, 1700–1900. Philadelphia: Westminster Press, 1962.

Smith, H. Shelton, Robert T. Handy, and Lefferts A. Loetscher. *American Christianity:*

An Historical Interpretation with Representative Documents. New York: Charles Scribner's Sons, 1960.

Smith, J. W. Ashley. *The Birth of Modern Education: The Contribution of the Dissenting Academies, 1660–1800.* London: Independent, 1954.

Smits, Luchesius. *Saint Augustin dans l'oeuvre de Jean Calvin.* Assen, Netherlands: Van Gorcum & Comp., 1957.

Smuts, Jan C. *Holism and Evolution.* New York: Macmillan Co., 1926.

———. "The Theory of Holism" in *Greater South Africa: Plans for a Better World: The Speeches of General, the Right Honorable J. C. Smuts.* Johannesburg, South Africa: The Truth Legion, 1940.

Smylie, James H. *A Brief History of the Presbyterians.* Louisville, Ky.: Geneva Press, 1996.

Solomon, David. "What Baylor and Notre Dame Can Learn from Each Other." *New Oxford Review* 62, no. 10 (December 1995): 8–18.

Special Committee to Study Theological Institutions. "A Report Approved by the 205th General Assembly (1993)." Louisville, Ky.: Office of the General Assembly of the Presbyterian Church (U.S.A.), 1993.

Stackhouse, Max. "The Moral Meaning of Covenant." *The Annual of the Society of Christian Ethics.*

Stoltzfus, Victor. *Church-Affiliated Higher Education: Exploratory Case Studies of Presbyterian, Roman Catholic and Wesleyan Colleges.* Goshen, Ind.: Pinchpenny Press, 1992.

Stowell, Daniel. "Educating Confederate Christians." In *Rebuilding Zion: The Religious Reconstruction of the South 1863–1877.* New York: Oxford University Press, 1998.

Sweetman, Robert. "Christian Scholarship: Two Reformed Perspectives." *Perspectives: A Journal of Reformed Thought* 16, no. 6 (June/July 2001): 14–19.

Task Force on the Church and Higher Education, United Presbyterian Church U.S.A. "The Church's Mission in Higher Education: A Report and Recommendations." *Journal of Presbyterian History* 59, no. 3 (1981).

———. "Presbyterians and Black Higher Education." *Black Issues in Higher Education* (December 31, 1992).

Tavard, George. *The Starting Point of Calvin's Theology.* Grand Rapids: Wm. B. Eerdmans Publishing Co., 2000.

Tewksbury, Donald G. *The Founding of American Colleges and Universities before the Civil War: With Particular Reference to the Religious Influences Bearing upon the College Movement.* New York: Teacher's College, Columbia University, 1932.

Thomas à Kempis. *The Imitation of Christ.* Translated by Leo Sherley-Price. London: Penguin Books, 1952.

Thompson, Ernest Trice. "The Presbyterian Mark: An Educated Leadership." In *Church and Campus: Presbyterians Look to the Future from Their Historic Role in Christian Higher Education,* edited by Dewitt C. Reddick. Richmond: John Knox Press, 1956.

———. *Presbyterians in the South.* Vol. 2, *1861–1890.* Richmond: John Knox Press, 1973.

Trinterud, Leonard J. *The Forming of an American Tradition: A Re-examination of Colonial Presbyterianism.* Philadelphia: Westminster Press, 1949.

Turnbull, Archie. "Scotland and America, 1730–1790." In *The Scottish Enlightenment 1730–1790: A Hotbed of Genius,* edited by David Daiches, Peter Jones, and Jean Jones. Edinburgh: The Institute for Advanced Studies in the Humanities and the Saltire Society, 1996.

Turner, James, and Jon Roberts. *The Sacred and the Secular University.* Princeton, N.J.: Princeton University Press, 2000.

Towards Viable Theological Education: Ecumenical Imperative, Catalyst of Renewal. Geneva: WCC Publications, 1997.

Wallace, Ronald S. *Calvin, Geneva and the Reformation: A Study of Calvin as Social Reformer, Churchman, Pastor and Theologian.* Grand Rapids: Baker Book House, 1988.

Walzer, Michael. *The Revolution of the Saints: A Study in the Origins of Radical Politics.* Cambridge, Mass.: Harvard University Press, 1965.

———. *Spheres of Justice: A Defense of Pluralism and Equality.* New York: Basic Books, 1983.

———. *Thick and Thin: Moral Argument at Home and Abroad.* Notre Dame, Ind.: University of Notre Dame Press, 1994.

Weber, Max. "Science as a Vocation." In *From Max Weber: Essays in Sociology,* edited by H. H. Gerth and C. Wright Mills. New York: Oxford University Press, 1977.

Wells, Ron, ed. *Keeping the Faith: Embracing the Tensions in Christian Higher Education.* Grand Rapids: Wm. B. Eerdmans Publishing Co., 1996.

Wendel, François. *Calvin: Origins and Development of His Religious Thought.* Translated by Philip Mairet. Durham, N.C.: Labyrinth Press, 1987.

Wertenbaker, Thomas J. *Princeton 1746–1896.* Princeton, N.J.: Princeton University, 1996.

Weston, William. "Centre and Religious Life: A Survey of Selected Alumni Classes." Centre College, March, 2000.

Wheeler, Barbara G. "Is There a Problem? Theological Students and Religious Leadership for the Future." *Auburn Studies,* no. 8. New York: Auburn Theological Seminary, 2001.

White, Ronald C., Jr. "Presbyterian Campus Ministries: Competing Loyalties and Changing Visions." In *The Pluralistic Vision: Presbyterianism and Mainstream Protestant Education and Leadership,* edited by Milton Coalter, John Mulder, and Louis Weeks. Louisville, Ky.: Westminster/John Knox Press, 1992.

Wilson, Samuel Tyndale. *A Century of Maryville College.* Maryville, Tenn.: Maryville College, 1935.

———. *Isaac Anderson, Founder and First President of Maryville College: A Memorial.* Maryville, Tenn.: Maryville College, 1932.

Wilson, William. *New Wilson's Old Testament Word Studies.* Grand Rapids: Kregel Publications, 1987.

Wolterstorff, Nicholas. *Educating for Responsible Action.* Grand Rapids: CSI Publications and Wm. B. Eerdmans Publishing Co., 1980.

———. *Reason within the Bounds of Religion.* 2d ed. Grand Rapids: Wm. B. Eerdmans Publishing Co., 1984.

Index of Scripture References

Index of Subjects and Names